T0360486

Experiencing Innovation in Asia

Cases in
Business Model
Development

Experiencing Innovation in Asia

Cases in Business Model Development

editors

ESSEC
BUSINESS SCHOOL

with

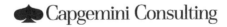
Capgemini Consulting

World Scientific

NEW JERSEY • LONDON • SINGAPORE • BEIJING • SHANGHAI • HONG KONG • TAIPEI • CHENNAI

Published by

World Scientific Publishing Co. Pte. Ltd.

5 Toh Tuck Link, Singapore 596224

USA office: 27 Warren Street, Suite 401-402, Hackensack, NJ 07601

UK office: 57 Shelton Street, Covent Garden, London WC2H 9HE

British Library Cataloguing-in-Publication Data
A catalogue record for this book is available from the British Library.

EXPERIENCING INNOVATION IN ASIA
Cases in Business Model Development

Copyright © 2015 by World Scientific Publishing Co. Pte. Ltd.

All rights reserved. This book, or parts thereof, may not be reproduced in any form or by any means, electronic or mechanical, including photocopying, recording or any information storage and retrieval system now known or to be invented, without written permission from the publisher.

For photocopying of material in this volume, please pay a copying fee through the Copyright Clearance Center, Inc., 222 Rosewood Drive, Danvers, MA 01923, USA. In this case permission to photocopy is not required from the publisher.

ISBN 978-981-4689-14-4

In-house Editor: Sandhya Venkatesh

Typeset by Stallion Press
Email: enquiries@stallionpress.com

Printed in Singapore

Introduction

Innovation transforms nations, economies and companies. It is what gives the world life-changing technologies, life-saving drugs and life-enhancing products. It can make or break businesses, create or dash fortunes and turn an ordinary person into a visionary. You need only wander through a bookstore or carry out a quick Internet search to realise that innovation is a preoccupation of governments, academics, and business leaders around the globe.

Yet, for such a well-known and much-discussed concept, innovation can seem hard to pin down and still more difficult to achieve. For students of business, it may appear a lofty goal: The path to fame and fortune beaten by a few renowned entrepreneurs and inventors. In reality, innovation can be small-scale, far-reaching, or anywhere in between. But however it manifests, it is something that is crucial to the survival of our species.

Defining Innovation

Before we embark on our own exploration of innovation, let us first define its meaning. The word derives from the Latin verb *novare*, meaning to make new, change or alter. It first came into usage in the English language in the 16th century and by the 19th century, at the height of the Industrial Revolution not surprisingly, it began to be used more widely.[1]

In recent years, innovation has continued to be associated with technological breakthroughs: The transformative power of the personal computer, the World Wide Web, or three-dimensional printing, for example. However, innovations in areas such as services, marketing and logistics have also had a huge impact on the business world. Walmart prevailed by transforming the supply chain process; FedEx's success stemmed from the novel way it

---

[1] Godin, B. (2015). *Innovation Contested: The Idea of Innovation Over the Centuries.* New York: Routledge.

handled logistics; and Dell created a hugely profitable new business model by selling computers directly to customers.

In this book, we focus on innovation in business models — from large multinational companies to small social enterprises — and how those innovations take root in the real world. Business model innovation involves rethinking or reinventing elements of how a business operates to deliver value in a new way. Apple is a classic example of how a company can transform by not only creating an innovative new product (the iPod) but by creating a distribution model (iTunes) that ensures consumers have an ongoing relationship with the company beyond the original hardware purchase.

In the chapters that follow, we will look specifically at the developing economies of Asia. Does business model innovation look the same in Asia as in the Western world? If there are differences, what can we learn from them? In attempting to answer these important questions, we present in this book a series of original cases, each one concerning a single company or organisation. We explore the challenges and opportunities they face in trying to find innovative solutions that will secure the survival and success of their business.

It is becoming increasingly clear that Asia is at the centre of the world's shifting innovation landscape. Asian countries are catching up with and even overtaking Western nations in spending on research and development[2]; and in terms of patent filings, China has already eclipsed the US and Europe.[3] We are witnessing the emergence of new innovation giants from China, such as consumer electronics company Haier, and Tencent, the corporation behind the wildly successful WeChat software application.

Thanks to 'frugal innovation', we are seeing new ideas and products emerge from the so-called bottom of the pyramid. In India, most notably, scarcity of resources has engendered ingenuity, creating a crop of products and services that are pared down in their complexity so as to be affordable to those previously priced out. In the same vein, 'reverse innovation' is bringing new low-cost products from developing markets to mature markets.

---

[2]OECD Main Science and Technology Indicators database (http://www.oecd.org/science/inno/msti.htm).
[3]World Intellectual Property Indicators Report 2014.

Introducing the Asian Strategy Project

In 2009, ESSEC Business School, in collaboration with global consulting firm Capgemini Consulting, launched the Asian Strategy Project, a unique initiative grounded in the idea of learning-by-doing. For three months students enrolled in ESSEC's Master of Science in Management programme explore a topic identified by a company based in Asia. They are given the opportunity to develop their understanding of a new business model in an emerging market by working on real strategic issues that the company is facing.

At the beginning of each project, students undergo intensive training on consulting skills, supervised by a manager from Capgemini Consulting. This training is followed by a management consulting assignment whereby the group of students is embedded in the company. Under the supervision of an ESSEC professor and coaches from Capgemini Consulting, students collaborate with managers at the partner company to develop strategic recommendations. They also co-write cases with their professors focusing on the innovative dimension of the business models they observe.

What makes these cases valuable is that they capture first-hand the experiences of students who, alongside their professors and supervisors, analysed, strategised and advised on a wide range of projects in Asia. The finished cases are used as teaching materials by ESSEC professors and this book gathers a representative selection, creating a repository of knowledge for business students, teachers and professionals who wish to learn more about innovative business models in Asia.

Business Cases in an Asian Context

The cases contained in this book represent the first five years of the Asian Strategy Project. Given the rapid pace of development in Asia, much has changed during that time. Companies have risen and fallen; the political and economic landscape has evolved; and the interest in and understanding of the continent's emerging economies has expanded. Thus the cases offer an insight into the recent past, as well as a way to grasp many of the issues faced by managers and entrepreneurs in Asia today.

Through them, we track the process of business model innovation, beginning with an analysis of the organisation's existing structure and the context in which it resides. The next stage involves recognising an issue or opportunity that needs to be addressed; then we follow company leaders as they wrestle with dilemmas and uncertainties before evaluating strategies and finally finding a path towards a solution. As you will see there are many questions along the way and the answers are not always obvious. But for students of business there is great value in seeing innovation in action, in learning by doing.

We, in our roles at ESSEC Business School and at Capgemini Consulting, are of the opinion that there is a great deal of value in learning business by doing business. We believe experiencing innovation is not always about witnessing the application of vast research and development budgets or the creation of cutting-edge technology products. In Asia, it is often about finding pragmatic business models that work in the context of fast-paced change, while having the courage to adapt them as required. In the face of ongoing globalisation and as developing nations try to transform into knowledge-based economies, nimbleness and innovation often go hand-in-hand, something that is evident in the cases contained in this book.

Exploring Innovation through Five Themes

We have divided the book into five sections, each of which explores a theme that is pertinent to Asia's developing economies. In the first section, on sustainable development, we witness the challenges of bringing to market new services that meet key requirements for the population: Water, education and energy. The cases provide an insight into the intersection of the public and private sectors and how this can be harnessed to provide essential services to citizens. As well as revealing the many problems that must be surmounted, they also challenge assumptions many in the West have about India's and China's development.

How does Asia approach innovation in media and technology? That is the theme of our second section. In particular, China is often accused of being imitative rather than innovative in its approach to new technologies, but the cases of Yek Mobile and StarryMedia provide a rather more nuanced view, as we see how high-tech entrepreneurs manoeuver in China's complex political and regulatory environment. In another case, we witness a gutsy Singaporean company trying to break into the Middle East and North Africa gaming market. And with Priya Entertainments, we are reminded that 'old' media still has an important role to play in people's lives.

In the third section, we look at how two global brands respond to local challenges. In the case of Capgemini, the company was dealing with an issue that will resonate with many multinationals operating in Asia: Hiring and retaining talented people. Renault, on the other hand, faced the challenge of leveraging its considerable brand value and marketing expertise to make its products more relevant to consumers in India and China.

In the fourth section, we gain insight into how two social enterprises navigate the grey area that lies between the not-for-profit and for-profit sectors. Can they achieve their social goals by implementing strategies from business?

Finally, in the fifth section, we encounter the challenges faced by a small business in an emerging economy. We see how an entrepreneur puts non-financial assets, such as tradition, local knowledge and relationships, to work to create an innovative business model.

A Commitment to Asian Business

This book is a demonstration of the joint commitment of ESSEC and Capgemini Consulting to work together to create a unique experience for students; one that combines academic and practical skills while harnessing our complementary knowledge and capabilities as part of Asia's business ecosystem. Exposing students to real-life challenges that require innovative thinking provides them with the skills they will need to operate in this unpredictable world. Through these experiences, they develop the creative and multicultural mindset required for a new generation of leaders and entrepreneurs. The Asian Strategy Project is about promoting a culture of innovation inside our respective organisations as well as in the wider sense, among the companies with whom we interact.

None of these valuable learning experiences would have been possible without the participation of a diverse and fascinating group of companies. Their managers and employees were true partners in the consulting process, giving students unprecedented access to critical business information and collaborating with them both as clients and as mentors.

Innovation is at the heart of the world's most successful economies and it is what is putting Asia's developing nations on a path toward greater prosperity. Ground-breaking work is happening here in big companies, small businesses, non-governmental organisations and, most of all, through human beings working together to make things better. We believe whole-heartedly that the entire world will benefit from the new sources of innovation that Asia is providing. We hope reading this book will help you think about all the different forms innovation can take and perhaps inspire you to innovate a little yourself.

Now let us allow the cases to speak for themselves.

Hervé Mathe,
Innovation and Services Chair,
Professor of Management,
ESSEC Business School

André-Benoit De Jaegere,
Vice President of Innovation,
Capgemini Consulting
February 2015

Acknowledgements

These cases would not have been possible without the hard work and commitment of ESSEC students, professors, the Capgemini Consulting coaches who lent their time and expertise, and the companies that welcomed us into their workplaces.

Please note that the cases contained in this book are not illustrations of good or bad management. They were written expressly for the purpose of discussion and learning.

For further information about the cases or to request teaching notes, email essecasia@essec.edu.

The authors wish to thank the following students for their contributions:

Chapter 1: Veolia Water India

Alice Chasseriaud, Charles-Henry Babin de Lignac, Simon Hupont, Frédéric Jousset, and Hoa Nguyen.

Chapter 2: Naandi Foundation

Juliette Bouchart, Caroline Conti, Marine Robert, Raphaëlle Sébag, and Nathalie Steege.

Chapter 3: PlaNet Finance China

Marie Camille Cornel, Aurélie Derché, and Quentin Dumouilla.

Chapter 4: Yek Mobile

Vincent Boche, Kevin Guieu, Clément Janicot, and Vincent Vainunska.

Chapter 5: StarryMedia

Ana Aliyari, Alexandre Basbous, Sylvain Désille, Laëtitia de Larturière, and Marie Leport.

Chapter 6: Mozat

William Zoric, Julien Guery, Alexandre Guichard, Larbi Chraibi, and Côme de Las Cases.

Chapter 7: Priya Entertainments

Alexandre Juvin, Pierre Labat, Claire Pinot de Villechenon, and Lila Sumino.

Chapter 8: Capgemini India

Students: Marilia Bossard, Aurélien Boyer, Alizée Brière, and Meryem El Alami.

Chapter 9: Renault India

Gatti Etienne, Lenhardt Jerome, and Sfez Isabelle.

Chapter 10: Renault China

Margaux Tiberghien, Pierre-Antoine Brun, and Charles Decock.

Chapter 11: PlaNet Finance

Antoine Cuénin, Gregoire Delamare, Valentin Lecouteux, and Suzanne Mercereau.

Chapter 12: Pour un Sourire d'Enfant

Nicolas Prévotel, Balthazar Raguin, and Shahan Sheikholslami.

Chapter 13: Weavers Studio

Lamia Berrahma, Marion Logeais, and Florentine Tsayem.

The authors wish to express their appreciation to the co-founders of the programme Françoise Rey of ESSEC and Xavier Hochet of Capgemini Consulting; the early sponsors from ESSEC Hervé Mathe, Christian Koenig and Thierry Sibieude; Aruna Jayanthi, CEO of Capgemini India; and Laurence Chrétien, Vice President and Campus Manager for ESSEC. Their ongoing commitment has been key to the success of the programme and the writing of this book.

They also wish to thank warmly the following Capgemini Consulting coaches and the programme co-ordinator Guillemette Petit, who supported the students with the cases, shared their good and bad times on the field, and conveyed their passion for innovation and for Asia:

Frederic Abecassis, Reda Abid, Zaynab Abouyoub, Sophia Agoumi, Olivier Arnaud-Freaud, Maxime Auzet, Karim Benomar, Alexis Berrie, Gwenael Bouleau, Julien Bourdinière, Céline Breuilh, Thibault Cazenave, Faith Chang, Guillaume Cuzzi, Romain Delavenne, Aurélie Derché, Sylvain Desille, Damien Desmidt, Georges Dry, Claire Duquesne, Mehdi Essaidi, Clément Gendreau, David Giblas, Paul Ghostine, Sara Guillaume,

Xavier Hay, Xian Huang, Seddik Jamai, Leopold Jarry, Thomas Jouffroy, Clemence Lambert, Sophie Larnaudie, Stefan Lavau, Emmanuel Lepeu, Anne-Sophie Leroux, Laure Lucchesi, Barnabé Mantz, Lucie Marelle, Christophe Margaritopol, Nicolas Mariotte, Asma Mhalla, Benoit Napoly, Nam Phuong Nguyen Huynh, Alix Nidjam, Adeline Pairault, Elise Pasqual, Marie Paternault, Sophie Paviet-Salomon, Guillemette Petit, Laure Pressac, Géraldine Richaud, Prerna Shankar, Pierre Songy, Mihail Stoicanescu, Beatrice Thiers, Aurélia Valot, Hermance Verier, Cédric Vialle, Jean-François Vincent, Elizabeth Webb, Hind Yahia, and Karine Zaouche.

Contents

Part E: Small Business with Big Ideas   273

Part A

Introduction

Sustainable Development

How to create and manage a reliable and constantly available water supply in a place with underdeveloped infrastructure and a population unconvinced of its merits? That was the challenge facing **Veolia Water**, a global water services and treatment company, when it undertook a supply project in Karnataka state in South West India.

Veolia has been active in India since 1999 through its subsidiary Veolia Water India, and has been able to take advantage of the Indian government's promotion of private sector involvement in infrastructure projects. Thus the company was selected in 2005 to participate in a 24/7 water supply project in Karnataka state. A continuous and pressurised water supply was implemented in five demonstration zones, located in three cities. The main objective of the project was to establish the feasibility of continuous supply, as many people were convinced it was technically impossible.

This case gives an insight into how, when delivering such an ambitious infrastructure project, an organisation must be innovative on several fronts: Not only on the technical side regarding the implementation, but in communicating with the local population and in pricing the new service fairly for an economically diverse community.

Aside from water, one of the key challenges facing India is providing adequate access to elementary education. Exploring the country's private school market might, at first glance, appear to be an issue concerning the country's elite and privileged few. However, in the case of the **Naandi Foundation** it is just the opposite.

1

Naandi was founded in 1998 at the behest of a Community Public Trust set up by four prominent corporate houses in Andhra Pradesh state. Its mission is to serve under-privileged populations in India through the eradication of poverty and the improvement of those populations' quality of life. One of its main concerns is the protection of children's rights through education.

In India, education represents a way out of poverty, with families — even those who are very poor — willing to make financial sacrifices for their children to access decent schooling. However, the sector faces serious issues: The market is fragmented due to state delimitations; and public schools have evolved to become exclusively aimed at the poorest of the poor, with many of them blighted by constant teacher absenteeism.

The case provides an overview of India's elementary education system, the evolution of its affordable private school market, and looks at what strategies Naandi can employ to establish itself in the market.

In another vast, fast-developing nation, the citizens of rural Tongwei County in China's Gansu province faced many of the same problems as the underserved populations of Karnataka and Andhra Pradesh. They had poor access to education and survived through subsistence farming and remittances from family members who had migrated to cities. A harsh climate and inhospitable land added to their predicament.

However, as a result of the Chinese government pioneering the National Biogas Subsidy Programme, they were given the opportunity to access a reliable source of renewable energy that had the potential to improve both their farming practices and their living conditions.

This third case follows **PlaNet Finance**, a French microfinance organisation with a representative office in China. In a first project in Tongwei, the organisation had provided microloans to farmers so that they could construct individual biogas installations that would allow them to fully benefit from the government programme. PlaNet Finance also sought to provide further training and education, creating what is termed a microfinance 'plus' programme, meaning that its actions are not limited to only providing finance.

PlaNet Finance China began to plan a new project in Tongwei, further expanding on the scale and scope of its original microfinance model. The case raises a number of questions about the role of microfinance in developing economies. Does it promote the goal of self-sufficiency among poor populations? Does the 'plus' element of education and training support that goal or simply make it too expensive to be sustainable? And what role does leadership play in the deployment of such projects?

In all three cases, it is clear that finding the right solutions to big problems, such as providing people with water, energy, and education, requires new ways of thinking.

Chapter 1

Veolia Water India: Bringing a 24/7
Water Supply to the People of Karnataka*

Wolfgang Dick
Financial Reporting and General Management, ESSEC

Patrick Rousseau, Chairman and Managing Director of Veolia Water India (VWI), was impressed by the provocative speech of one of his young employees during the India Urban Space 2007 Summit. More than 150 Indian leaders were looking at a picture of an African country, trying to answer the question "What is the name of this country?" "It is Niger," the young engineer declared. "One of the poorest, tiniest countries in the world. And yet, Niger enjoys a 24/7 water supply. In India, however, a country said to be the new giant superpower, we are not even able to provide this service." Now, in 2009, Patrick still feels the shock among the audience on realising the backwardness of water infrastructure in India. He realised that bringing a 24/7 water supply to India would dramatically help the country's economic development and the health, social, and economic situation of the population. In 2005, VWI had been selected as the private partner of a 24/7 demonstration project in Karnataka state. Patrick would like to use the experience of this project to obtain similar contracts in other Indian cities. Patrick is remembering the beginning of the Karnataka project and the difficulties that VWI faced during the last three or four years, especially in dealing with the population's expectations.

---

*This case was prepared with the support of Alice Chasseriaud, Charles-Henry Babin de Lignac, Simon Hupont, Frédéric Jousset, and Hoa Nguyen and with the collaboration of Capgemini Consulting and employees of Veolia Water India and its partners.

Water in India

Water and Hinduism

Water has a special place in Hinduism as it is believed to have spiritual cleansing powers. India's main rivers are considered sacred because of the many rites they host.

Water Resources

India enjoys three types of water resources: rivers, groundwater and surface water. With an average annual rainfall of 1,170 mm, India is one of the wettest countries in the world. However, there are large variations in the seasonal and geographical distribution of rainfall over the country. For example there is 11,000 mm of rainfall per year in areas like Cherrapunji in the northeast, and only 200 mm per year in Jaisalmer in Rajasthan. Nearly three-quarters of the rain pours down in fewer than 120 days, from June to September.

India's groundwater resources are almost ten times its annual rainfall. Nearly 85% of currently exploited groundwater is used only for irrigation. Besides, groundwater is now the source of four-fifths of the domestic water supply in rural areas, and around half that of urban and industrial areas. However, according to the International Irrigation Management Institute (IIMI), India is using its underground water resources at least twice as fast as they are being replenished.

In terms of surface water, there are 14 major, 44 medium, and 55 minor river basins in the country. The major river basins constitute 83–84% of the total drainage area. This, along with medium river basins, accounts for 91% of the country's total drainage. India has the largest irrigation infrastructure in the world, but the irrigation efficiencies are low, at around 35%.

India has 16% of the world's population but only 4% of the available fresh water on Earth. As a whole, it is not facing a water stress situation yet.[1] Nevertheless, water resources are unevenly distributed over the country and some states (like Rajasthan and Tamil Nadu) suffer from insufficient water resources. Studies indicate that India could become a

---

[1] A water stress situation is identified when a country has less than 1,700 cubic metres per year per capita.

water-stressed country by 2025[2] because of its urban growth and improper water management.

Growing Water Demand[3]

Urbanisation is considered to be both an important component and a natural consequence of Indian economic growth. Since 2002, the annual GDP growth rate has always exceeded 7%, reaching 9.7% in 2006–2007.

A direct consequence of India's expanding urbanisation is a growing strain on civic infrastructure systems, including roads, transportation and water supply networks. By 2030, municipal water demand is projected to grow at a pace of 2% per year on average, to eventually reach 104.9 billion cubic metres.

Individual Water Connection and Public Sources

About 91% of the total urban population has access to water supply, 41% of them with an individual connection and 59% sharing a public source. Numerous illegal connections to the network have been recorded and the absence of monitoring tools makes it impossible to detect them easily. Moreover, networks are old and poorly maintained. Many leaks exist, leading to possible contamination and to a significant wastage of water.

Discontinuous Water Supply

For individual connections as well as for public taps, water supply is not continuous. The length of supply varies. It can happen daily or, in most cases, once every two to three days in a range from one to six hours. In certain areas, supply takes place once a week only. Due to this, the population is cautious and stores water in underground or roof tanks (individual connection) or in jars (public sourcing). Once freshwater is available, stored water is generally thrown away, creating waste.

The supply schedule is irregular: Water can arrive in the middle of the night as well as at mid-day. In some areas, people are aware of the supply schedule, thanks to local newspapers. However, people living in slum areas generally do not get any information regarding water supply schedule.

---

[2] *Source*: India Water Portal.
[3] *Source*: *Urban Water Development in India 2010 (Volume I) — India Infrastructure Research*.

People (most of the time women) often have to miss a working day to collect water, either fetching it at public taps or collecting it and storing it at home. Children may also be in charge of this task; consequently, they have to skip school to collect water. When water comes at night or early in the morning, collection encroaches upon sleeping time.

Impact of Water Supply on Health[4]

Ensuring the quality of water is a major problem for most developing countries, including India. According to a report from the United Nations Environment Programme, more than half of the hospital beds around the world are occupied with people suffering from water-related diseases. These can either be spread directly by contact with contaminated water or through insects and contaminated soils. Symptoms are numerous, from skin irritation to respiratory problems. In fact, 37.7 million Indians annually are affected by water-related diseases, and an estimated 1.5 million children die each year of diarrhea. In addition, there are more than a million cases of malaria each year in India, including around 1,000 deaths.

Until recently, providing safe water was not a priority for the Indian authorities. The water quality standards stated by the Bureau of Indian Standards are relatively lax compared to the WHO's standards. Moreover, complying with these standards is only recommended, not mandatory. Thus, the quality of water in most Indian cities does not meet these requirements.

Water-borne diseases are often due to an inadequate management of water resources: The water distributed has not always been treated correctly. And, supposing that water treatments are correctly done, contamination can still happen in several ways. First, inside distribution pipes: Because of maintenance failures, most of the pipes are porous and have leaky joints. Many impurities can thus infiltrate the pipes, contaminating the water that passes through. Then, discontinuous supply of water allows the introduction of impurities in the pipes as they are not constantly pressurised with water. Waste water management is also an important factor in water contamination. In developing countries, 90% of sewage water is discharged without treatment. This leads to a contamination of water sources, soils, and water pipes.

---

[4]*Source*: "Sick Water?" Report by the UN Environmental Programme.

To prevent water-borne diseases, some people boil or filter water, mostly for drinking and cooking purposes. However, there still seems to be a lack of awareness regarding water-related diseases among the population. Many people use untreated water to wash themselves and sometimes to drink.

Legal and Political Framework

The legal and political framework of water supply is fragmented across central, state, and local levels. The 74th Constitutional Amendment Act (1992) provides the basic legal framework for the Water Supply and Sanitation sector. Water is declared to be a state subject. As such, the urban development departments of the respective state governments have the authority on all issues related to water supply. Thus, municipalities and states are fully responsible for their water supply management. However, the central government tries to promote new methods of infrastructure improvement by giving financial aid.

Pricing and Tariffs[5]

Even though it is commonly presumed in India that water is a free resource, its usage incurs a cost: The cost for collecting the water, treating it, pumping it to the city, storing it, and distributing it to the customers. The cost of water supply has been rising over the years due to various factors such as 'unaccounted for water'[6] and the increasing cost of energy. In Delhi for instance, the cost of production has gone up from Rs. 3.60 (US $0.06) to Rs. 6.97 (US $0.11) per kilolitre between 1998 and 2004.

In India, a great variety of water-charging practices exist. State governments are responsible for tariff structures and for prescribing minimum tariffs. Individual cities have the option of setting tariffs above this minimum level or to stick to it. So far, all Indian cities operate a mix of metered and unmetered tariffs. Except Jamshedpur, no city tests meters on a regular basis for proper functioning. On average, cities only recover 61% of their operational and maintenance costs with the tariffs, the remaining part being recovered through government subsidies.[7] A consequence of these

---

[5] *Source: Urban Water Development in India 2010 (Volume I) — India Infrastructure Research.*

[6] Unaccounted for Water: Water that has been produced and is "lost" before it reaches the customer.

[7] *Asian Development Bank's Benchmarking and Data Book for Water Utilities 2007.*

uncovered costs is poor maintenance of infrastructure leading to a poor quality of service.

Water tariffs in Indian cities are much lower than those in comparable cities in other developing countries. While many surveys show that the Indian population — even the poorest — would be ready to pay more for a good quality water supply service, the main opponents to an increase in water tariffs seem to be the politicians, who fear that their popularity and chances of re-election may be affected.

Financing Needs for Water Supply

Investments to obtain 100% coverage of safe water supply and sanitation services in urban areas by 2021 would require US $38 billion, according to the Central Public Health and Environmental Engineering Organisation. Traditional financing within the water sector consists of various plans and budgetary allocations from the central government. Nevertheless, alternative financing is slowly growing.

- Multilateral agencies such as the World Bank (the world's largest external financier of water supply and sanitation) or the Asian Development Bank.
- Domestic financial institutions such as the Housing and Urban Development Corporation (HUDCO).
- Private sector, whose importance is limited compared to other sectors.

Mobilising funds for water infrastructure projects is still a challenge for Urban Local Bodies (ULB). This is due to the persistence of several disincentives such as concerns regarding municipal agents' financial health and the lack of transparent and accountable municipal structure. As a consequence, the focus on introducing new fiscal instruments, encouraging Private Sector Participation (PSP) and developing commercially viable projects has increased.

On December 2005, the Jawaharlal Nehru National Urban Renewal Mission (JnNURM) was launched by the Central Government to meet the financing needs of urban infrastructure in general and Water Supply and Sanitation in particular. US $22 billion was gathered to develop urban infrastructure in 65 cities. Under this mission, cities could obtain grants ranging from 35% to 90% of their infrastructure project, depending on cities' size and location. State or local governments or private players would contribute the rest.

As the JnNURM is not sufficient to meet all investment requirements linked to water supply and sanitation, the development of private sector participation is essential in order to compensate for the lack of financing.

Karnataka 24/7 Water Supply, a Showcase Project

Karnataka state is situated in the southwest of India. Its population accounts for 5.3% of the total Indian population, and it represents about 6% of the country's surface water resources.[8]

In the early 2000s the government of Karnataka decided to improve the water and sanitation sector in Karnataka state. As a consequence, the Karnataka Urban Water Sector Improvement Project (KUWASIP) was launched. Its main objectives were to:

- Initiate reforms in the urban water sector.
- Demonstrate that sustainable, efficient and commercially-oriented service provision can be achieved through private sector participation.
- Provide the population with a better service that would reduce the different problems linked to water supply (water collection, waiting time, pumping systems, diseases) and improve the impact of water supply in people's daily lives.

The 24/7 water supply project is part of KUWASIP. The Karnataka Urban Infrastructure Development & Finance Corporation (KUIDFC) was appointed as a nodal implementation agency.

The aim of this project is to demonstrate the feasibility of a 24/7 water supply in five demonstration zones in three different cities: Hubli–Dharwad, Belgaum, and Gulbarga. At the time, no efficient 24/7 water supply service existed in India, and the general belief was that such a service was technically impossible to realise. The demonstration zones fulfil the following conditions:

- Represent at least 10% of the population of the city.
- To be representative of the socio-cultural mix of the city, it has to include slums, middle-class and upper-class people.
- The water network of each zone has to be isolated from the rest of the city. The 24/7 project must not have an impact on the water supply of the rest of the city.

---

[8] *Source*: Karnataka website (http://www.karnataka.com/profile/water-resource.html).

This project was funded and financed up to 75% by the World Bank which had been thinking about the development of a 24/7 water supply programme in India for some time and had conducted advanced studies and technical discussions alongside major stakeholders.

Six main actors with different roles and responsibilities were in charge of KUWASIP implementation: KUIDFC (representing the Government of Karnataka), Karnataka Urban Water Supply & Drainage Board (KUWSDB, in charge of providing asset development services), the three Municipal Corporations of the cities involved, and the private operator, as shown in the graph (See Figure 1).[9]

In addition to the 24/7 water supply, it was decided to implement a 24/7 customer service centre to help customers express their problems and feelings about the system and to signal any problem on the network (leakages, low pressure, dirty water, etc.). This centre would also be

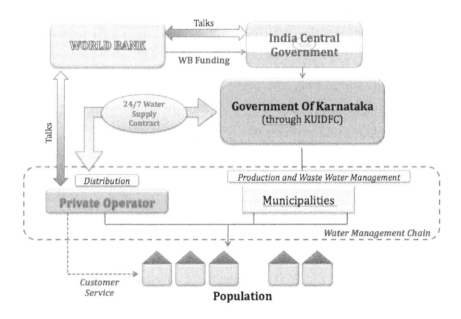

Figure 1

[9]Documentation study of Demonstration Project for providing Continuous (24/7) Pressurised Water Service in the three ULBs in Karnataka State, Final Report (April 2009). Water Sanitation Programme SA.

managed by the private operator and would be situated inside the demo-zones. This service would be one of the first direct relationships between the operator and final customers. More than a useful technical tool, this customer centre was conceived to involve the population in the network maintenance.

Private Sector Participation

The Indian government has long been reluctant to integrate the private sector, especially foreign companies, into public service projects. Indian authorities and the population tend to fear that the intervention of these actors could harm social missions and the population's expectations in the name of profit.

This changed when in its 2002 National Water Policy, the Government of India recommended the intervention of the private sector: *"Private sector participation should be encouraged in planning, development, and management of water resources projects for diverse uses, wherever feasible"*.[10] International institutions (such as the International Monetary Fund and the World Bank), now promote the intervention of private companies as a condition for their loans.

The implication of private companies in the Indian water market has slowly begun to develop through Public Private Partnership (PPP) contracts. PPP allows the two actors, private company, and public authority, to share their financial resources, know-how and experience to improve the provision of basic services to a population. Moreover, PPP contracts offer an alternative to complete privatisation by combining the advantages of the two sectors: The social and environmental responsibility on one hand; and private sector capital, technology, and efficient management on the other.[11] Ownership of the asset remains with the public actor. In addition to the construction and management of the utility, the private company is also involved in the financing part, which is a way for municipalities to remedy the lack of money that characterises the water market in India. PPPs may be structured with different levels of involvement of the private operator.

The KUWASIP would be an important showcase to demonstrate the positive effects of the private sector within the water supply market. The private operator would be in charge of the technical part of the 24/7

---

[10]National Water Policy in India (2002).
[11]United Nations Development Programme PPPSD.

water supply project. A call for tenders was issued by the Government of Karnataka in 2003, and VWI won the bid against six international competitors.

The Private Operator: VWI

VWI already had excellent knowledge of the Indian market and also offered the lowest fee of US $3.6 million for the duration of the contract.

VWI, a subsidiary of the French corporation Veolia Environnement, was created in 1999 as a result of a decision to establish itself in water and wastewater management in India. Unlike other foreign companies, VWI decided to appoint an Indian managing director to better understand the market. The situation is similar for the engineering team. A few French engineers came at the beginning of the project to train their Indian colleagues. Since then, the engineering team has been composed of local engineers who help VWI to better understand the expectations of the population.

Since its creation, VWI has taken advantage of the Indian government's recent push trend to promote private sector participation and has developed its activities in five important projects. VWI has been very successful in meeting the objectives and performance targets of each mission, thanks to its historical know-how around the world.

Even before the Karnataka project, VWI had been talking about bringing a 24/7 water supply to India; it was one of the stakeholders participating in the initial talks with the World Bank. For the company and the institution, developing a method to ensure the supply of safe water to the population was essential. From the beginning, health concerns were key, and the 24/7 water supply was the only way to maintain the quality of water from the treatment plant to the individual tap.

The VWI–Karnataka Partnership

The role of VWI in KUWASIP is determined by a performance-based management contract without commercial risk of revenue collection from customers. VWI's revenues are not correlated to the amount billed to the population for water. The entire financial risk is supported by the Government of Karnataka through the KUIDFC which finances all capital expenditures, given that 75% of the funds come from the Indian central government and this corresponds to the financial contribution of the World Bank.

VWI bears only a negligible political risk: Remuneration is contractually performance-based and no major political decision related to water is likely to be taken during the short duration of the contract. So, the main risk borne by VWI as the private operator is the technical one: Veolia remains responsible in case of any problems on the distribution network.

VWI's mission is to finalise and design the works, prepare the bidding documents, procure contractors, implement works, and operate and maintain the system to supply continuous and pressurised water.

In addition to these objectives, qualitative and quantitative performance targets have been defined by the KUIDFC.

- Metering all connections to measure the consumption of each household.
- Creation of a customer database.
- Minimum of six metre-pressure to serve all houses with a minimum of two storeys without using electric pumps.
- Reduction of the leaks on the water distribution system to 20 litres per connection per day per metre of pressure.
- Establishment of an efficient customer service and billing system: Customer service should be able to respond to each complaint within 24 hours.

VWI receives bulk water from municipalities; its mission is only to ensure the preservation of the level of quality during the distribution phase. Thus, VWI has no power over the quality of water it receives and largely depends on municipalities. However, it commits to warning Indian authorities if this water represents a danger to the population. VWI is responsible neither for the communication plans nor for the setting of tariffs. Nevertheless, for the whole duration of the project, VWI participates in regular meetings with KUWASIP actors and may use its expertise and Indian market knowledge to give advice beyond the technical field.

Dealing with Skepticism and Expectations

The 24/7 project faced much resistance during its implementation. Both KUIDFC and VWI encountered significant difficulties that they had to overcome.

Politicians' Skepticism

At the beginning of discussions, the elected representatives of the chosen cities were worried about the impact such a programme could have on their political image. In the case of a technical failure of the project or of a rejection from the population, they would be the first to face criticism.

Besides, they could not imagine getting all the work done in time. According to them, it was also barely possible to imagine the feasibility of a continuous and pressurised water supply system. They knew how dilapidated the water network was so they were even less prone to take the risk. With good reason, they also wondered how these costs could be recovered without increasing water tariffs. VWI's Patrick Rousseau liked to remind them that the main problem faced in India for the development of utilities programmes is not the 'willingness to pay' of the population but more the 'willingness to charge' of the politicians.

Reluctant Population[12]

Even though the final customers were not asked about their willingness to receive this service, they have become an important part of the pre-implementation of the programme. Like the elected representatives, the population could not understand how such a project could technically be achieved: "How could Urban Local Bodies bring pressurised water continuously when they hardly manage to bring it once a week and when at least one electricity cut per day occurs?"

But what the population feared most was the tariff increase due to this new service. Before the implementation of the program, people in Belgaum paid a flat rate of Rs. 90 (US $1.46) per month whatever they consumed; some others were used to getting free water from public bore wells and stand posts; and others were buying water from private water tanks. People were convinced that having access to the 24/7 system would be too expensive for them. Nevertheless, half of the households declared themselves ready to pay Rs. 50 (US $0.81) on top of their previous bill in order to get this service.

Many of them thought this 24/7 water supply service was superfluous and unnecessary: overall, only a few people (1%) called for a 24/7 water supply. What they expected from the government was a supply with specific timing (67%) and a more regular water supply (from once every five days to once every day). Their expectations were low as they were used to the old system. They only wanted to save time and effort during water collection: 24/7 service was far ahead of their expectations.

---

[12]The statistical data in this paragraph are from Rapid Social Assessment and Communication Strategy, Demonstration Projects and Priority Investments, a survey undertaken by KUIDFC in 2004.

Difficult Economic and Social Conditions

The final customers and their incomes are heterogeneous. For an unskilled worker, the wage in slum areas is around Rs. 3,000 (US $48.60) per month, while it can be much more for middle-class people. It is thus very difficult to plan a recovery cost programme that takes into account this diversity.

What is even more difficult is to set up the project in poor areas: Works will generate problems in the streets; communicating with uneducated people can be difficult; and many people will not accept to pay for a service they did not ask for and believe they do not even need.

Mistrust toward the Private Sector

For the first time in India, a private company would partly subject itself to a public authority for managing a public service. The involvement of the private sector in the management of India's resources still remains a sensitive subject and meets the hostility of some politicians, Non-Governmental Organisations (NGOs) and parts of the population. It is a service Indians consider established and they cannot imagine that a private company will take over and make a profit by distributing water. The fear of a significant rise in the water bill and the fear of full control by a private company over the country's resources and infrastructure is a strong reason for this distrust. Indeed, some politicians and NGOs fear they will lose the control they previously had on this particular matter. All these fears are amplified when it comes to a foreign company managing an essential resource.

Corruption is another a reason why the private sector is not always welcome. A foreign, private company with a strong ethical code might set new rules in order to avoid corruption. Thus, by allowing private companies to step in, corrupt workers may lose some of their advantages. In India, corruption is a real problem: the country is ranked 87th in the Corruption Perceptions Index[13] and it is estimated that about one-third of households paid bribes for a public service in the last year, representing an amount of Rs. 8,830 million (US $143 million).[14] Some projects, such as the introduction of a 24/7 water supply service in Delhi, were cancelled because of strong pressures inside and outside municipal bodies.

---

[13] *Source*: Corruption Perceptions Index by Transparency International.
[14] *Source*: http://www.transparencyindia.org/resource/survey_study/India%20Corruptino%20Study%202008.pdf.

Answering the Population's Expectations

KUIDFC identified several key points in order to make the project a success.

The Social Assessment Survey, a Solid Database

Before implementing the project, KUIDFC undertook a survey in 2004 called *Rapid Social Assessment and Communication Strategy, Demonstration Projects and Priority Investments* to help stakeholders ensure that "the project could deliver sustainable and satisfactory water and sanitation services". The Social Assessment focused on many issues:

- Demographic factors: Number of people, density, age, religion, ethnicity.
- Socioeconomic data: Income, house ownership, media habits.
- Social organisations: Communities, lobbies, social groups, NGOs.
- Expectations and values which could determine if the intended project was needed and wanted.

However, health was not part of the investigation and, according to the population, not an important matter regarding water supply.

An Efficient Communication Plan

The Social Intermediation and Communication Strategy (SICS), a KUIDFC entity, was formed in order to design and manage the communication strategy for the 24/7 project. Great communication efforts had to be made for the project to be accepted by the population.

SICS used the results from the 2004 survey *Rapid Social Assessment and Communication Strategy, Demonstration Projects and Priority Investments* to develop a communication plan. Three NGOs (one for each city) were hired and trained to implement the communication tactics and interact with the population until the beginning of the operations and maintenance (O&M) period:

- **Door to door visits** and **street plays** were given priority in order to warn the poorest, uneducated people about the project's benefits and about good practices regarding water usage and the savings it can allow.
- **Consultation meetings** were organised with opinion leaders, cooperatives, and other neighbouring communities in order to make allies and to convince the rest of the population more easily.

- **Focus group discussions** for women were organised to communicate with those who were often responsible of water collection, i.e., women, and to show them the concrete benefits of 24/7.
- **Discussions with 'anti' group leaders** (such as Communist representatives) were also organised to avoid as much as possible a 'politicisation' of the project.
- **Distribution of IEC** (Information, Education & Communication) materials was organised within schools. Children can be good ambassadors for health and sanitation routines, and can explain basic health principles to their parents.

Socially Fair Tariffs

KUWASIP's bedrock was that everybody would receive the same quality of services, irrespective of the socio-economic status and urban sanitation in which they lived. However, to make this service affordable for everyone, the final tariff had been tailored to the ability of each household to pay. One of the main fears of the population was a rise in their water bill. It was thus essential to set up a tariff in accordance with everyone's willingness and capacity to pay.

On the costs side, one of the conditions of this project was for the KUIDFC to recover at least 80% of O&M costs. The remaining 20% were financed through the municipal budget. To make the project viable in the long term, reaching this target was essential. Pricing was the result of a meticulous study of the population and an advanced analysis by A. F. Furguson & Co, a consulting firm hired by the KUIDFC. VWI was not in charge of setting the price but had a consulting role. The pricing takes into account different factors from capital cost to slab consumption.

The capital cost for the installation of the individual connection is Rs. 3,000 (US $48.60) per household. However, depending on the family's situation, the amount and the details of the repayment would be different:

- When the house is smaller than 600 sq. ft. only Rs. 900 (US $14.60) needs to be recovered, thus the household will have to pay Rs. 30 (US $0.49) per month for 30 months.
- People who already have a connection but live in more than 600 sq. ft. will be charged Rs. 1,500 (US $24.50), i.e., Rs. 30 (US $0.49) per month for 50 months.

Table 1:

Price per KL	Slab Consumption (per month)	Total Price (for maximum consumption per slab)
Rs. 6	0–8 KL	Rs. 48
		(minimum fee, regardless of consumption)
Rs. 10	8–25 KL	Rs. 218
Rs. 12	25–40 KL	Rs. 398
Rs. 20	>40 KL	>Rs. 398

- People who need to be connected to the network and live in more than 600 sq. ft. will be charged for the entire cost: Rs. 30 (US $0.49) per month for 100 months.

In order to recover O&M expenses, a monthly fee has to be paid by the final customers. Each household pays for its own individual connection (the tap outside their house). The choice of a telescopic tariff was quickly made: The price of the first 8,000 litres of water, corresponding to the basic needs of a family, is then much cheaper than the following litres, corresponding to more superficial needs, mostly those of richer people. Thanks to this telescopic tariff, the wealthiest people will pay more so that the poorest can also benefit from the service. A first telescopic tariff was set up at the beginning of the demonstration period, but many stakeholders complained about the high price imposed and the slab system was quickly reviewed; a new range of tariffs was defined after. The telescopic tariff is seen in Table 1.

Irreproachable Service Quality

Originally, in the demo-zones water supply was not continuous and pipelines were under-pressurised and often dirty. Many leakages on the networks were observed as pipelines were generally old and rusted. So, as VWI's aim was to provide the population with good quality water, renovating or changing the existing network was mandatory. Thus, 80% to 100% of the existing network has been changed in order to ensure quality pipelines and networks.

The performance-based management contract signed between VWI and KUIDFC indicates several criteria that VWI should guarantee. Not satisfying these criteria would have an impact on VWI's remuneration:

- **Continuous service without disconnection.** In order to deliver a continuous service without disruption, VWI had to pay particular attention to power cuts. Most cities in India are subject to frequent power failure and, as a consequence, water supply faces many problems. VWI had to make sure stoppages would not occur frequently and aimed at maintaining a maximum of four emergency stoppages per year.

- **Minimum pressure of six metres**, in order to provide water in every building of two floors. This negates the need for electrical pumping systems. The average pressure observed is typically 17.70 metres, far above the performance target.
- **Maintenance of the networks.** VWI is working hard to maintain the quality of its networks. Leakages and pressure are subject to frequent controls to make sure no impurity enters the networks and to reduce the level of unaccounted for water as much as possible. Before the 24/7 project, losses represented more than 50% of input; with the implementation of the project, this percentage has been reduced to 7%.
- **Water quality** is now reaching defined norms. Given the absence of disconnection and the minimum pressure, water is now of high quality and is safe to drink without boiling, filtering or treating it first. Frequent tests ensure the quality of water provided and the efficiency of the networks.
- Adding to this technical success, VWI has set up a very **efficient 24/7 customer service centre**. Responses to complaints are made within a day and addressed within seven days.

Outcomes of the Project

Following its implementation, the 24/7 water supply project is largely satisfying the population. The major outcomes of the project are:

Collecting information about the existing situation of the population, and their needs and expectations as a key factor of success

Thanks to its study, KUIDFC learned useful information about the previous water service, the population's expectations regarding water supply and their opinion concerning 24/7. The information about the degree of willingness to have and to pay for 24/7 service has been strategically important in developing an acceptable offer for the population, especially regarding tariffs.

Using Communication to create acceptance of the project before implementation

Thanks to their knowledge of the people and their practices, NGOs were able to teach the population about the particularities and advantages of the 24/7. They now understand much better the ins and outs of their water supply. In some other cities, like Delhi, this lack of communication had led to the failure of the project.

But a major communication campaign suffered from mistiming. Repair works began in March 2006 whereas the community liaison only began in August 2006. Therefore, in demo-zones, the population was surprised to witness technical works in the street without being informed of the project. That led to some protests, particularly in Dharwad, where works had to stop until the population was informed of the project. According to the three NGOs in charge of communication, the community liaison should have started at least one year before the implementation of the project in order to have time to educate the population and to deliver an effective campaign without any protests.

Increasing school attendance of youth due to time saving

The new service provides the population with a much more convenient way of life as people now have fresh, clean water round the clock with no supply failure. Therefore, a lot of time is saved as people do not have to wait for water or to go to public stand posts to collect it. For some people the time saved is two to three hours daily. For those living in slum areas, this time saved can be up to one to two days per week. This allows for more time for children to go to school and for parents to go to work. Statistics in Hubli–Dharwad show that school attendance has increased from 82% before the implementation of the 24/7 service to 96% after.

Reducing water wastage and electricity bills

All technical burdens that were previously associated with water collection have now become obsolete. Thanks to the minimum pressure of six metres and the set up of a continuous service without water cuts, water storage and the use of electrical pumping systems are no longer needed. As a consequence, water wastage and energy bills have decreased.

Increasing household revenue due to time saving

Due to the increase in working hours and the savings in energy bills, household incomes have significantly increased, especially for those living in poor conditions. After the project was implemented, the World Bank went to the different demo-zones to collect feedback from the population.

One story often recounted by the authorities to promote the project is that of a woman who has seen her household income increase by Rs. 400 (US $6.49) per month. She declared herself ready to pay half of her additional earnings for the 24/7 service.

Declining number of diseases

Chlorine tests and good maintenance of the networks are ensuring that water is now safe to be drunk directly from taps. According to NGOs and doctors, diseases such as skin problems, cholera, infantile diarrhea, polio, and dysentery have begun to reduce somewhat in the demo-zones, though there are not yet statistics regarding the health impacts brought by the 24/7 service.

Similar or even decreasing water bills for the poorest people

People are widely satisfied with the tariff they have to pay. Many of them even claim it helped them to become aware of their consumption and strengthen their responsibility toward water consumption. The water bill has remained similar to what it was before the implementation of this programme. The wealthiest are paying a bit more than before but many people in slum areas have seen their water bill and total cost for water decrease.

Wiping out doubts about 24/7 and PPP by reaching service quality

By reaching all the service quality elements, VWI has managed to provide the population with an impeccable service and has wiped out doubts toward a 24/7 water supply in India.

Proving the technical feasibility of 24/7 in India

Another success factor of this project was the efficiency of the water management process allowed by VWI's experience. If 24/7 did not exist in India previously it was not because of lack of financing or water resources. Indeed the central government has money to allocate to water projects, and the country is not facing a water stress situation yet. The bad quality of service mainly resulted from a lack of competency to set up a well-maintained network between water resources and final customers. The real challenge was to implement an efficient and adapted water management process that could lead to an optimal use of water resources and consequently to an efficient 24/7 water supply service.

It is difficult to change peoples' habits — there is still mistrust

Despite communication and despite the quality of service provided, people generally tend to stick to their usual practices regarding water. Some people are still storing water in case of water cuts. And, those who were filtering, boiling or treating water before are still doing it 'just in case'. If one of the main purposes of the 24/7 water supply is to provide quality water, the behavioural changes that were expected concerning water consumption are not yet totally achieved. The government expected the population to understand the importance of having fresh, clean and drinkable water in their daily life, but people only see the technical and convenience advantages of 24/7 (money, comfort, time saving) and not the benefits for their health and hygiene. That behaviour reflects a general mistrust toward the whole chain of water management.

Distribution quality of water is important, but so too is water production and waste water management

Some customers are not wholly satisfied with the quality of water distributed. In fact, it is not the distribution network that is questioned but rather the water source and the waste water management. Many treatment plants that deliver bulk water to the pipelines are old and some people assume these plants are in poor condition and not well maintained. As a consequence, they believe water does not meet the standards it should. Plus, as India is facing a significant lack of infrastructure in waste water management, many customers and even some NGO volunteers express concerns regarding the possibility of contamination and assume water is not drinkable and safe.

Conclusion

The Karnataka 24/7 water supply project is now seen by every stakeholder as a major innovation in India from a technical, social, and health point of view, as it has significantly improved people's everyday lives. This project is now considered a real showcase and a new starting point in the water supply market. It is used as an example in order to convince other municipalities that were previously skeptical about 24/7 water supply.

VWI has gained awareness and there are now discussions about scaling up the project to entire cities or to replicate it elsewhere, for instance in Nagpur, which has more than 2 million inhabitants.

In the case of a replication, the question of pricing may become a key issue. In the absence of subsidies from the World Bank, where to find other financing sources for future 'bottom of the pyramid' projects? What tariff structure should be implemented? How can VWI manage to be economically viable while staying socially responsible and offering affordable tariffs to a poor population?

Glossary

FIP	Final Investment Plan
GoI	Government of India
GoK	Government of Karnataka
JnNURM	Jawaharal Nehru National Urban Renewal Mission
KL	Kilolitre = 1,000 Litres
KUIDFC	Karnataka Urban Infrastructure Development & Finance Corporation
KUWASIP	Karnataka Urban Water Sector Improvement Project
KUWSDB	Karnataka Urban Water Supply & Drainage Board
NGO	Non-Governmental Organisation
O&M	Operation & Maintenance
PHED	Public Health Engineering Department
PPP	Public Private Partnership
PSP	Private Sector Participation
Rs.	Indian Rupees
SICS	Social Intermediation and Communication Strategy
ULB	Urban Local Body
VWI	Veolia Water India

Bibliography

Websites

- http://www.veoliawater.com.
- http://www.scribd.com/doc/22089310/Indian-Water-and-Wastewater-Treatment-Market Opportunities-for-US-Companies.

- http://www.tted.gov.bc.ca/APTI/Documents/India-Waste_Water_Treatment_Martket.pdf.

Paper Documents

- Socio-Economic, Education, Health, HESCOM bill saved, and other Impact Survey- KUWASIP Project Hubli–Dharwad. Rural & Urban Development Association (RUDA), Dharwad.
- Continuous water supply in Belgaum demo-zones. USWO.
- Continuous water supply in Hubli–Dharward demo-zones. RUDA.
- *Urban Water Development in India 2010 (Vol I & II)* — India Infrastructure Research.
- JnNURM report. Nagpur Municipal Corporation.
- Documentation study of Demonstration Project for providing Continuous (24/7) Pressurised Water Services in the three ULBs in Karnataka State, Final Report (April 2009). Water Sanitation Programme SA.
- Rapid Social Assessment and Communication Strategy, Demonstration Projects and Priority Investments, Final Report (February 2004). Samaj Vikas Development Support Organisation.

Soft Copies

- Les Partenariats Public-Privé en Inde, exemple de l'eau à Nagpur (Mémoire). Flora Berg.
- Survey: 24/7 water supply impact on health, social and economy. Simon Potier.
- Final Report for TA Studies. KUIDFC.
- Tariff Design for continuous water supply in the cities of Belgaum, Gulbarga and Hubli–Dharwad in Karnataka State. FITCHNER Consulting Engineers (India) Pvt. Ltd.
- Water Marketing India report 2009. Global Water Intelligence.
- Expertise et engagement développement durable de Veolia Water AMI-2007 Synthesis.
- Privatisation de la distribution de l'eau potable en Afrique: une aubaine? A. Briand & A. Lemaître.
- Water Privatisation and Implications in India. Association for India's development, University of Texas.
- Moving toward continuous water supply. Experiences from Karnataka. K.A. Joseph.
- The right to water: From concept to effective implementation (2007). UN OHCHR enquiry.
- Veolia Environnement- Financial reports and reference documents 2008 & 2009.

Chapter 2

Naandi Foundation: Delivering High Quality Elementary Education in India*

Wolfgang Dick
Financial Reporting and General Management, ESSEC

"Education costs money, but then so does ignorance".

— Sir Claus Moser.

On an evening in January 2010, Manoj Kumar, the Founder and Chief Executive Officer of the Indian non-profit organisation Naandi Foundation, was coming home from his Hyderabad office. As usual, he greeted Varun, his watchman, and gazed amused at Varun's children playing on the ground. He asked Varun how his children were doing at school, if they were learning anything. Willing to show the importance he was attaching to their education, Varun answered proudly that he had quit soda to save money to keep sending them to school. Varun was proud of the sacrifice he was making for his children to keep them at an affordable private school (APS). Many parents, like Varun, prefer these schools to free of charge government schools because of their better quality. Manoj Kumar realised to what extent education represented a real luxury for lower class Indians. Indeed Varun, who actually had a good position compared to many living in Hyderabad, was forced to abandon a minor pleasure for his children to access what he believed to be good education.

CEO of Naandi Foundation since 2000, Manoj Kumar is strongly involved in education issues, as one of the foundation's missions is to

---

*This case was prepared with the support of Juliette Bouchart, Caroline Conti, Marine Robert, Raphaëlle Sébag, and Nathalie Steege, and with the collaboration of Capgemini Consulting and employees of Naandi Foundation and its partners.

promote child rights in India, and education is a fundamental right inscribed in the Indian Constitution. Manoj Kumar is aware to what extent even elementary education is inaccessible to the poorest of the poor and this is why projects in the field of elementary education represent one of Naandi's main activities. For instance, Naandi provides an extensive after-school tuition programme in government schools and developed an innovative pedagogical model to support it. This know-how could be used in Naandi's own APSs if the foundation decides to launch this initiative, something that has been repeatedly suggested by some of Naandi's stakeholders. However, Manoj Kumar knows the strengths and weaknesses of APSs and had already considered entering the field of private education. He wonders whether Naandi is sufficiently legitimate to offer an innovative model that would enable smaller class sizes and excellent pedagogical quality at an affordable price.

The Education System in India

Structure

The 1950 Constitution of India clearly provided for free and compulsory universal elementary education up to the age of 14.[1] Ever since, elementary education had been structured as follows:

- Pre-primary classes: Nursery, lower kindergarten (LKG), upper kindergarten (UKG), regroups children from three to five years old.
- Primary classes: Classes I to V, regroup children from six to 10.
- Upper-primary classes: Classes VI and VII, regroup children from 11 to 12. Upper-primary schools usually exist in the government school format.
- High school: Classes VIII to X, regroup children from 13 to 15. Children willing to undertake undergraduate studies are obliged to pass the national examination scheduled at the end of class X.[2]

Free elementary education is delivered through government schools. Apart from being free of charge, government schools have the particularity

---

[1] Constitution of India, article 45.

[2] There are numerous curriculum bodies leading to X class-national examinations: Secondary School Certificate (SSC), Central Board of Secondary Education (CBSE) and Council for Indian School Certificate Examination (CISCE). SSC, mainly focused on mathematics, social sciences, sciences, and languages is the most representative of elementary educative schools in India.

of being managed entirely and directly by state government institutions. Thus, public school teachers are directly paid through a government allocated budget; however, on-site management is almost non-existent.

Private schools, on the other hand, are entirely and individually managed on-site and their financial sustainability is theoretically enabled by the collection of numerous fees which vary from one school to another. Even though independent from governmental control, private schools are dependent on state recognition for greater credibility. Unlike the unrecognised ones, recognised private schools benefit from state accreditation and support for national examinations. Some of them, identified as private recognised aided schools, benefit from further governmental support, through grants or allocation of public teachers (See **Exhibit 1** for comparative table).

According to the 1950 Constitution of India, governmental control over education-related legislation is shared between the national government and the respective state government.

National Initiatives

As the Constitution identifies elementary education as a fundamental right for six to 14-year-old children, efforts have been made throughout history to reach 100% school enrolment and attendance. In fact, education has always been a deep concern in this country where issues such as child labour and plurality of languages jeopardise this objective.

The following plans were rolled out to encourage enrolment:

- *Operation Blackboard*
  Starting in 1987, the programme was aimed at increasing human and material resources in primary schools. Following the operation, primary schools were to have at least two rooms, two teachers and a list of essential teaching materials such as chalkboards, chalks, dusters, etc.
- *District Primary Education Programme*
  Launched in 1994, this programme had the objective of universalising primary education. It served the ideal that primary education must be accessible to every child of school-going age and that children must be retained in school once enrolled. Concrete actions of the programme were in the construction of classrooms and new schools, the opening of informal schooling centres, the appointment of teachers and provision of elementary education to disabled children. The programme has been hailed as successful as it enabled the opening of 160,000 standard

and 84,000 alternative schools, and helped more than 420,000 disabled children.[3]

- *Sarva Siksha Abhiyan*
  The 2001 programme set deadlines to ensure school age children completed their elementary education in a timely manner. Sarva Siksha Abhiyan centres were located in areas where schools were insufficient in number. Apart from covering the whole Indian population, the plan put special emphasis on needy parts of the population such as girls, Scheduled Castes and Scheduled Tribes, thanks to specific programmes.

According to 2009 statistics only 4%[4] of school aged children were not enrolled in school. But even if most children are enrolled, the goal of literacy has not yet been reached and is at only 39%.[5] There are two main reasons for this ongoing problem. First, a lack of attendance is partially linked to lingering child labour. At least half of the pupils from rural areas drop out before completing school and 35%[6] of them cannot read their mother tongue in classes III to V. Second, many government schools have a corrupt dynamic where quality is poor and teacher absenteeism high.

As a consequence of the ever-decreasing popularity of government schools, numerous private schools were created by the end of the 1990s.

The Emergence of Private Schools

A study by the World Bank pointed out that on average, 25% of teachers in public schools were absent every day and that only about half of the remaining 75% were teaching.[7]

This seems to be the result of a system paralysed by the teachers' lack of involvement and motivation due to significant job security combined with high salaries.

Ameet Gupta, public teacher in Modern High School's privately aided school commented:

"Public teachers have the privileges both of employment security and attractive salary. In our school, public teachers are paid up to 10 times private teachers' salary. If you consider that government schools do not have any

[3] *India 2009: A Reference Annual (53rd edition)*, 215.
[4] *CIA, World Fact Book.*
[5] The Annual Status of Education Report (ASER) 2009.
[6] The Annual Status of Education Report (ASER) 2009.
[7] Kremer M., Chaudhury N., Halsey Rogers F. *et al.* Teacher Absence in India: A Snapshot. *Journal of the European Economic Association.*

management in field, teachers are absolutely free. Some of them do not see any point in devoting time to children as they will be paid the same as if they were absent. As a result, many of them do not even bother to teach. Teachers' absenteeism and general motivation is a real concern in government schools and partly explains the latest interest for private institutions."

Only one per 3,000 disciplinary measures has been noted in government schools for repeated absenteeism, whereas the rate is 35 per 600 in the private sector. So it seems clear that there is more oversight of teachers in the private sector and in private schools.[8]

The capital of Andhra Pradesh is said to be the biggest private school market in India. Around 5,000 private schools have settled in Hyderabad and among them 3,000 are APSs. All types of private schools are represented, though recognised unaided private schools are the most frequent models. The great majority of them are small entities run by a family and aimed at children living in the neighbourhood. They start as little structures whose goal is to provide a few lessons and then expand due to parents' increasing demand.[9]

Estimates assess the value of India's private education market to go from $40 billion in 2008 to $68 billion by 2012.[10] Even though private schools are believed to be superior in quality compared to public schools, they differ greatly from one another. The market for private schools is indeed extremely heterogeneous; both in terms of costs and quality. The flourishing of all sorts of private schools: Recognised, unrecognised, aided, unaided, has blurred the education landscape and exacerbated the lack of cohesion of the education system.

The aim of the 2009 Right to Education Act is to harmonise the education system and eventually further reduce the proportion of unschooled children. By 2012, unrecognised schools will have to close. Recognised schools, in their turn, will have to reserve 25% of their places to disadvantaged children and will be forced to only hire qualified teachers (See **Exhibit 2**).

Private Schools in Hyderabad, Andhra Pradesh

Description of the Market

There are 73,000 APSs across India; approximately 18,000 of them are located in Andhra Pradesh, and 3,000 of them in Hyderabad, the state

---

[8]Kremer M., and Muralidharan K. *Public or Private schools in India, 2006.*
[9]Gray Matters Capital Foundation.
[10]Lesson Plans, by Anuradha Raghunathan of *Forbes*, 09.11.08.

capital.[11] The sixth largest city in India, it has a population of 6.3 million.[12] Hyderabad is the biggest private school market in India, due to factors such as English medium instruction and religion, that have led 65%[13] of households to choose to send their children to private schools. It thus provides a perfect case to study and build a model of private schooling in India.

Management of APSs

Most APSs are held by individuals who do not necessarily have experience in management.[14] Schools were built, maintained, and managed from scratch. Consequently, precise data on the schools' human resources and financial management are generally not available. Estimates given by school managers reveal the following cost and revenue structure[15]:

- Cost:

  ○ Staff salaries
  They represent 70% of the total cost and are composed of instructional salaries (teachers), administrative salaries (management), and non-teaching staff salaries (mainly cleaners). Teachers from nursery to class V are paid around US $33 to $49 per month for non-trained teachers, compared to US $114 to $130 for trained teachers. For Nursery, UKG and LKG, each teacher cares entirely for one class. From class I to V, there are six subjects and each teacher teaches one or two subjects to three classes. From class VI to X, they teach one of six subjects to two or three classes. Non-teaching staff are paid around US $24 per month.

  ○ Administrative Expenses
  They vary according to the school type. Recognised schools pay specific recognition fees to the government. The amount and regularity depends on government requirements. Recognition fees may amount up to US $2,400 for the first year and US $163 for the following years.

---

[11]Gray Matters Capital Foundation.
[12]Population within the metropolitan area, 4 million in only Hyderabad district (*source*: mapsofindia.com).
[13]Gray Matters Capital Foundation.
[14]Joshi S. Private Budget Schools in Hyderabad City, India. A Reconnaissance Study. Gray Matters Capital Foundation (2008).
[15]These figures are based on a 2010 study conducted on 56 schools located in Charminar and Secunderabad areas of Hyderabad by ESSEC students (Bouchart J., Conti C., Robert M., Sebag R., and Steege N.).

An amount of about $80 a year should be budgeted for various basic teaching materials (chalkboards, chalks, computers, etc.).

o Infrastructure expenses
These depend on the real estate strategy. The purchase price of a building for a medium-sized school is approximately US $114,000, while leasing a classroom costs about US $211 per year. Maintenance costs have to be taken into consideration on a yearly-basis. These can add up to US $163 a year.

o Other expenses may include interest for loans.

- Revenues:

o School fees
They represent the major part of income and include:

■ Admission fees
These are collected when the child is enrolled. They prevent parents from changing school if they are not satisfied. Admission fees for APSs range from US $0.81 to $16.

■ Yearly fees
They are collected every year and increase according to the child's class level. They range from US $29 (nursery) to US $78 (high school).

■ Exam fees
They are collected on a yearly basis and range from US $1.46 to $4.88.

■ Additional fees
They can vary depending on the purpose, for example, computer, maintenance, and library fees. This results in a lack of transparency for parents who do not know exactly what they will pay in total for the whole year.

■ Tuition fees
Depending on the child's ability to learn and the parents' will, tuition fees may be charged for the child to attend extra classes. Tuition fees are assumed to amount to US $2 a year.

■ Transportation fees
Even though in Hyderabad, APSs rarely enrol children from outside their neighbourhood, some of them may offer a fee-paying bus service. Transportation fees are assumed to be US $4 a year.

o Learning material and uniforms. Many schools offer complete book packages and uniforms on the premises. Books are sold at approximately $16.27 per year. The price of uniforms amounts to US $1.62 to $8.14. Uniforms need to be changed twice a year.

o Other sources of income to be considered may be any form of external funds (government grants, investments or donations) and bank loans.

(See **Exhibit 3** for complete financial detailing).

Difficulties that Hyderabad schools' top management have to deal with are both quantitative and qualitative. We can identify three main issues.

First, fee collection is a major problem since many parents have difficulties paying the entire amount of the fees on time. Some schools only collect 50% of their annual fees, with significant impact on cash management. Important capital expenditures must often be delayed due to insufficient funds. This does not only concern computers, but sometimes even doors, walls, toilets or access to drinking water.

Second, school status (i.e., recognition and aid) is frequently linked to the financial situation. Corruption is common: Schools deserving recognition fail due to financial difficulties, while others that do not meet the required conditions obtain it, thanks to substantial bribery.

Finally, there is significant absenteeism and drop out of both children and teachers. The schools' management spends considerable energy retaining children and convincing their parents to do so. The lack of parental involvement is often highlighted. The home environment may not be suitable for studies as parents expect their children to help at home rather than do schoolwork. As for the teachers, many of them are unqualified when recruited. Once trained (training represents additional cost), they often quit their jobs for better wages in more expensive schools. Most of the teachers in APSs are women planning to work for two years before getting married and leaving the profession.

Customer Profile

Parents of children registered in APSs are poorly educated[16] and rarely speak English.[17] Though poor, they do not belong to the poorest people living in India: Despite hailing from and living in slum areas, their limited

---

[16]On an average, parents of children visiting APSs have dropped out of school before class X.

[17]*CIA, World Fact Book*

income is sufficient to send their children to private schools instead of government schools. The family income amounts on an average to INR 4,778 ($77) per month.[18]

Parents are more and more concerned with their children's education as they are aware that it could impact their living conditions in the future. They have high expectations, and therefore accept to spend more than 20% of their monthly income on their children's education[19] (See above and **Exhibit 4** for more details).

Although concerned about their children's level of education, parents do not have the ability to assess the quality of teaching offered by a school. The main criteria for parents in choosing a school are the following:

- The location: The nearer the school, the better it is.
- The teaching of English: Parents tend to favour English-medium schools[20] as they believe children will become fluent by the end of their studies.
- The school's reputation: Word-of-mouth is extremely important when choosing a school since parents encounter difficulties evaluating the quality of teaching.
- The cost of the school is a decisive factor when choosing an APS.

The inability of parents to assess the school's quality of education may lead them to spend a significant portion of their income on education that is not worth it. The only objective evaluation of their children's success is the SSC exam at the end of Xth grade. Students will continue their studies depending on the score they obtain in that exam. Most of the children score between 45 and 60% but more and more of them reach 90%, if not 100%.[21]

---

[18]The average national income amounts to 3,000 INR/month (http://www.expressindia. com/latest-news/Average-Indians-income-crosses-Rs-3000/468084/).

[19]Average for an household of three children on a monthly basis.

[20]English-medium schools have the particularity of teaching subjects in English. Similarly, Urdu-medium schools have the particularity of teaching subjects in Urdu language.

[21]http://timesofindia.indiatimes.com/city/mumbai/SSC-13500-in-city-score-90/article show/6061029.cms.

http://timesofindia.indiatimes.com/city/hyderabad/SSC-Hyderabad-stays-at-the-bottom/articleshow/5966724.cms.

Naandi Foundation

Naandi was founded in 1998 at the behest of a Community Public Trust, set up by four prominent corporate houses of Andhra Pradesh. Each one of them invested US $81,300 and took over the responsibility of managing the trust. The objective of the trust was to create an NGO which could serve as a platform for funds destined to support sustainable development in India.

Ever since, Naandi's mission has been to serve under-privileged populations in India through both the eradication of poverty and the improvement of those populations' quality of life. To do so, Naandi has directed its activities toward three main pillars:

• Protection of child rights through education.
• Creation of sustainable livelihoods for small and marginal farmers.
• Provision of safe drinking water in rural India.

Protecting Child Rights Through Education

• *Ensuring Children Learn (ECL)*
The programme, conducted since 2005 was designed to overcome the difficulties faced by children in government schools. The programme had two objectives. First, providing additional learning inputs and second, assessing their impact on the learning levels of pupils concerned. Sum total, ECL served more than 125,000 children in more than 1,100 schools, all of them located in four Indian states.[22]

Naandi Foundation's intervention at ECL proved to be successful: Data collected in Hyderabad and Mumbai showed that children's learning levels had improved by almost 40% in one academic year and that children following the programme performed better on an average than children who didn't.[23] Through this programme, Naandi developed a methodology and tools to teach children. They created instructional material that the government certified and now use on a large scale.

• *Nanhi Kali*[24]
Given the ongoing cultural difficulties for girls to attend school, Naandi has developed a programme entirely dedicated to underprivileged girls

---

[22] Naandi Foundation (http://www.naandi.org/what_we_do/learn_7a3.aspx?VerticalId='1&ProgramId=2).
[23] Naandi Foundation.
[24] Naandi Foundation (http://www.nanhikali.org/nanhikali/about_ nanhi_ kali.aspx).

called Nanhi Kali. A total of 48,364 girls were studying under Nanhi Kali in 2009 from classes I to X.

- *The Mahindra Pride School*
  The school offers training to underprivileged students from Scheduled Castes and Tribes to help them get jobs and perform well at work. The final objective is to give their families a chance to step out of poverty.
- *Naandi Learning Institute (NLI)*
  Naandi has created the NLI for learners to come at times that suit them to improve a range of skills such as language, mathematics, English, and sciences. Naandi has reading materials and reference books, which learners can use for training.

Naandi's Strengths and Threats

Naandi certainly has several advantages if it were to enter the APS market. However, those advantages are accompanied by threats.

First, thanks to the ECL program, Naandi developed a partnership with the government. Naandi Foundation thus has a network within government representatives. As a consequence, it might be easier, administratively speaking, to create a new model and to obtain recognition. On the other hand, there is the risk that this partnership associates Naandi's actions with the government whose schools do not have a good reputation.

Second, Naandi has gained a lot of experience and knowledge, thanks to its training programme. Its free educational programme based on its own innovative pedagogical model has proven to be successful. These programmes are offered free of charge in government schools. Providing the same service in private schools and charging for it might be difficult to promote. There is also the risk that this programme may not be considered as worthwhile.

Naandi has already run a number of significant projects from scratch. Starting not only one but a chain of APSs could be managed by an experienced team. However, serious financial risks must be taken into account. Solutions to reduce cost or to increase revenues will turn out to be necessary. Some options are to centralise costs through wholesaling or the creation of a centralised training centre for teachers (See **Exhibit 5** for financial details).

Naandi is partnering with important investors; its brand is already strong and is still gaining in reputation. Nevertheless, failure of a significant project like this one could impact the good reputation of existing projects.

Last but not least, Naandi is a non-profit organisation managing non-profitable projects. Attracting investors for the APS project may be tricky as these investors might expect a financial return on their investments.

Strategic Challenges and Opportunities

Manoj Kumar is perfectly aware that APSs are not as affordable as their name suggests: The fees represent a big part of household expenditure for families (See **Exhibit 4**). In addition, the quality varies significantly from one to another. Consequently, the term APS does not refer to a homogenous type of school, teaching technique or teaching materials. It only refers to a segment of the education market: Schools for poor people impoverishing themselves further without having any guarantee of the quality of their children's education.

Manoj Kumar thus believes there is a place for a structure combining affordable prices with high quality of education and is considering entering the market so as to promote both quality and affordable private education to the majority of poor people.

Exhibit 1: Differences between School Types.

	Government Schools	Private Recognised Unaided	Private Recognised Aided	Private Unrecognised
Management	Government	Private entrepreneurs or families or network of schools	Private entrepreneurs or families	Private entrepreneurs or families
Funding	Government	Fees only	Fees and sometimes government subsidies	Fees only
Profile of teachers	Public teachers Can stay for more than 20 years	Mostly women around 20 years old Stay 2/3 years until marriage	Sometimes combination private/public teachers. Mostly women around 20 years old Stay 2/3 years until marriage	Mostly women around 20 years old Stay 2/3 years until they get married
Salaries of teachers	Evolve with experience. From 20,000 to more than 40,000 INR/month	Around 2,000 to 5,000 INR/month	Around 1,000 to 3,000 INR/month	Around 1,500 to 3,000 INR/month
'Hidden' fees	Everything is taken care of by the government	— Admission fees — Books — Tuition — School bus — Computer — Library — Uniform — Exam fees …	— Admission fees — Books — Tuition — School bus — Computer — Library — Uniform — Exam fees …	— Admission fees — Books — Tuition — School bus — Computer — Library — Uniform — Exam fees …

(*Continued*)

Exhibit 1: (*Continued*)

	Government Schools	Private Recognised Unaided	Private Recognised Aided	Private Unrecognised
Quality of facilities	Concrete buildings but overcrowded rooms.	Some schools have the commodities needed for a proper teaching, others are in much lower condition	Most of the schools are offering all the commodities needed for proper teaching	Schools in much lower condition. Sometimes no walls, no doors, no water, no toilets
Quality of teaching	Huge absenteeism among teachers	Teachers present but depending on the condition of the schools, the environment may not be favourable for teaching and learning	Depends on the management of the school. If strong, government teachers will be here and teach as well as the private teachers; if not, absenteeism of government teachers	Teachers present but depending on the condition of the schools, the environment may often not be favourable for teaching and learning
Perception by parents	Government schools are perceived as bad schools. Last resort for the poorest families or families not willing to pay for education	Well perceived	These schools are still perceived as linked with the government and are thus considered with caution by parents. However the working environment is adequate and is appealing to parents.	Private unrecognised schools are not the best solution but they are a compromise between private recognised schools and government schools in terms of fees and of quality.

Source: Survey in 56 schools conducted in November 2010 by ESSEC students (Bouchart J., Conti C., Robert M., Sebag R., and Steege N.) in Hyderabad, Andhra Pradesh (India)

Exhibit 2: New Regulation, the Right to Education Act.

Right to Education (RTE) Act

 A new opportunity to improve private schools or unachievable goals?

Some Mandatory Norms...	... And Punishments
- 25% of government sponsored seats in private schools - Minimum for teachers' wages and training (at least training for higher secondary school certificate but different norms for each class) - The obligation to build new infrastructures (playgrounds, 1 classroom/teacher) - Must have a school library with books, newspapers, magazines on all subjects - Availability of drinking water	- If it doesn't gain approval within 3 years => the school shall "cease to function" - Huge fine for the owner who runs a school with no certificate

Future?	⇒	Higher bribes?	⇒	Higher cost for APS?	⇒	Some APS will have to close ?

Exhibit 3: Comparison of the Financial Data between the Private School Models.

Criteria	Private Recognised Unaided	Private Recognised Aided	Private Unrecognised
Admission fees* (INR)	500	750	0
Nursery fees (INR/year)	1,800	240	0
Primary fees (INR/year)	2,700	600	600
Upper-primary fees (INR/year)	3,000	960	840
High school fees (INR/year)	4,800	1,560	840
Exam fees** per session (INR every 3 months on an average)	175	330	0 (are not allowed to do the SSC exam)
Tuition fees (INR/year)	125	90	90
Transport fees (INR/year)	250	500	0
Books (INR/year)	1,000	450	450
Average change of uniform/year	3	3	3
Uniform fees (INR)	450	300	600
Additional fees*** per year (INR)	175	—	—
Instructional salaries (INR/year)	49,500	16,800	24,000
Administrative salaries (INR/year)	120,000	60,000	60,000
Non-teaching staff salaries (INR/year)	18,000	9,600	9,600
Teaching material (outside books) (INR/year)	5,000	5,000	5,000
Maintenance (INR/year)	10,000	10,000	10,000

Source: Survey in 56 schools conducted in 2010 by ESSEC students (Bouchart J., Conti C., Robert M., Sebag R., and Steege N.) in Hyderabad, Andhra Pradesh (India). Values indicated are medians.

*Admission fees are paid by the parents when they enrol the child in a school. They are one-time fees but they can be equivalent to three months of monthly fees.

**Exam fees are fixed at 175 INR by the government. However, children enrolled in unrecognised schools shall pass the exam at a recognised school and thus pay sometimes up to three times the regular fee.

***Additional fees may include library fees, use of computer fees, etc.

Exhibit 4: Hyderabad Households Expenditures Related to Education.

										Mean
Household										
Number of children	3	3	4	5	3	1	5	2	2	**3**
Income of the household (INR/month)	3,000	5,000	3,000	6,000	5,000	4,000	7,000	4,000	6,000	**4,778**
Monthly Fees										
Monthly fees for all the children (INR/month)	300	500	700	900	425	100	650	170	300	**449**
Percentage of the income (%)	10	10	23	15	9	3	9	4	5	**10**
Other Costs										
Admission fees (INR)	0	600	0	100	300	250	100	250	0	**178**
Uniform fees (INR/year)	1,500	1,500	2,000	1,500	1,500	500	2,500	1,000	1,000	**1,444**
Book fees (INR/year)	3,000	6,000	5,000	5,000	3,000	800	5,000	525	2,000	**3,369**
Term fees (INR/year)	900	1,500	1,650	2,700	1,275	300	1,950	510	900	**1,298**
Total other fees (INR/year)	5,400	9,600	8,650	9,300	6,075	1,850	9,550	2,285	3,900	**5,290**
Total Costs										
Cost for a year (INR)	9,000	15,600	17,050	20,100	11,175	3,050	17,350	4,325	7,500	**11,683**
Percentage of the annual income (%)	25	26	47	28	19	6	21	9	10	**21**
Cost for a year for one child (INR)	3,000	5,200	4,263	4,020	3,725	3,050	3,470	2,163	3,750	**3,627**
Percentage of the annual income for one child (%)	8	9	12	6	6	6	4	5	5	**7**

Source: Survey conducted in 2010 in Little Century High school in a slum area of Hyderabad, Andhra Pradesh (India) by ESSEC students (Bouchart J., Conti C., Robert M., Sebag R., and Steege N.).

Exhibit 5:   Impact on Cost Structure of a Chain-Based Model.

Reduction on teaching material (INR/year)	−1,000
Gain in commission on books	+3%
Training centre costs (INR/month)	47,000

Source: Estimations based on a 2010 study of 56 schools in Hyderabad, Andhra Pradesh (India) by ESSEC students (Bouchart J., Conti C., Robert M., Sebag R., and Steege N.).

References

CIA, World Fact Book.

Constitution of India.

India 2009: A Reference Annual (53rd edition).

Joshi S. Private Budget Schools in Hyderabad City, India. A Reconnaissance Study. Gray Matters Capital Foundation (2008).

Kremer M., Chaudhury N., Halsey Rogers F. *et al*. Teacher Absence in India: A Snapshot. *Journal of the European Economic Association*.

Kremer M., and Muralidharan K. *Public or Private schools in India, 2006*.

Naandi Foundation Nanhikali website: www.nanhikali.org/nanhikali.

Naandi Foundation website: www.naandi.org.

Raghunathan A. Lesson Plans. *Forbes*, 09.11.08.

The Annual Status of Education Report (ASER) 2009.

Chapter 3

PlaNet Finance China: New Models of Microfinance in Tongwei*

Thomas Jeanjean

Accounting and Management Control Department, ESSEC

In November 2010, Gabrielle Harris, Executive Director of PlaNet Finance China, a representative office of the international non-governmental organisation (NGO) PlaNet Finance, was reading an article reviewing the development of the *Zhōngguó Wǔnián Jìhuà*, China's 12th Five-Year Plan[1] (2011–2015). While China increasingly "considers its development strategy more from a global"[2] viewpoint, it seeks to "rebalance economy, environmental and social performance, and to reflect a global perspective".[3] As Gabrielle watched the flocks of pigeons flying around in Beijing's winter sun, she reflected with satisfaction on the relevance of PlaNet Finance's two largest projects to China's most recent and upcoming Five-Year Plans. Both plans emphasised the importance of increasing per capita income, green development, dealing with climate change issues, fostering independent

---

*This case was prepared with the support of Marie Camille Cornel, Aurélie Derché, and Quentin Dumouilla, and with the collaboration of Capgemini Consulting and employees of PlaNet Finance and its partners.

[1]China's Five-Year Plans, 中国五年计划 in simplified Chinese or *Zhōngguó Wǔnián Jìhuà* in pinyin refer to a series of economic initiatives established by the Chinese Communist Party every five years.
[2]Xinhua, People's Daily Online, 2010. China listens to global experts for new five-year plan. *People's Daily Online*, [online] January 20. Available at: <http://english.people.com.cn/90001/90778/90862/6873408.html> [Accessed December 10, 2010].
[3]C. Lawrence Greenwood, vice president of the Asian Development Bank (ADB), cited in Xinhua, People's Daily Online, 2010. China listens to global experts for new five-year plan. *People's Daily Online*, [online] January 20. Available at: <http://english.people.com.cn/90001/90778/90862/6873408.html> [Accessed December 10, 2010].

innovation and closing the gap between the rich and the poor as well as between rural areas and the fastest growing urbanised regions[4,5] (See **Exhibit 1**).

Following the results of the first project in providing renewable energy to the inhabitants of Tongwei County in Gansu Province, the upcoming second project aimed to take this one step further, continuing with green technology but placing the emphasis on entrepreneurship and innovation. As she gazed out onto the vast metropolis and the mountainous backdrop, Gabrielle went over the plans for the upcoming Tongwei II project. She reflected on the funding challenges, the obstacles and the opportunities which this project presented.

An avid sinophile, Gabrielle first moved to China in 1980 to undertake Postgraduate studies in the History Department of Nanjing University. She was one of the first Westerners to arrive after the opening up of the People's Republic of China, and one of the first women. Since then, she has always worked in China, in various positions and industries. Before joining PlaNet Finance China, Gabrielle was an entrepreneur: As the designer and general manager of her own jewellery startup, she worked in a joint venture with Chinese workshops. Through her years of experience living and working in the country, Gabrielle Harris has not only become fully bilingual, but also familiar with China's administration and regulations. Her knowledge of Chinese culture and of the dos and don'ts in the Chinese political and business arenas is invaluable for her function as executive director at PlaNet Finance China, particularly when dealing with local governments and associations in rural China.

Gabrielle joined PlaNet Finance in November 2005 to design and direct innovative development projects to spread the power of microfinance as a tool to combat poverty in both rural and urban China. Since joining, she has sought out means to alleviate poverty in a more comprehensive way by associating it with other factors through microfinance plus[6] programmes

---

[4]Xinhua, People's Daily Online, 2010. China listens to global experts for new five-year plan. *People's Daily Online*, [online] January 20. Available at: <http://english. people.com.cn/90001/90778/90862/6873408.html> [Accessed December 10, 2010].
[5]National Development and Reform Commission (NDRC), People's Republic of China. *The Outline of the Eleventh Five-Year Plan for National Economic & Social Development of the People's Republic of China Profile.* [online] Available at: <http:// en.ndrc.gov.cn/hot/t20060529_71334.htm> [Accessed December 10, 2010].
[6]There is a distinction to be made between microfinance, microcredit and microfinance plus, this is covered in the microfinance section of this case. Microfinance plus refers

(see **Exhibit 2**). PlaNet Finance China has developed a particular focus on microfinance plus environment through the introduction and development of renewable energy technologies to rural populations with the support of microfinancing efforts. The particular focus in this domain was the Tongwei I project. Launched in 2006, Tongwei I served to accompany the Chinese National Biogas Subsidy Programme and aid the successful implementation of biogas facilities as a suitable source of renewable energy in individual households in Tongwei County.

Following the end of the first project and the discovery of new areas in need of aid, Gabrielle Harris and the PlaNet Finance China team decided to continue their development work in Tongwei County to further develop Tongwei I and seek to spur entrepreneurial efforts in the development of renewable energy technologies.

Following their cooperation from 2007–2009, renewable energy company Areva agreed to work with PlaNet Finance again, but through their subsidiary, Areva Renewables. However, in the summer of 2010, when the project had already begun, Areva decided to sell this subsidiary and the new owners were not interested in honouring the original commitment because it would not be using Areva's large-scale biomass technology. As a result, Areva Renewables was now no longer able to finance the Tongwei II project as of November 2010.

Gabrielle found herself facing several issues concerning the Tongwei II project. Not only was her major pre-occupation how to replace the lost co-financing for Tongwei II in a less than favourable global economic context, but following the findings of her most recent trip to Tongwei County, and against the backdrop of the fast-changing economy of Southeast Gansu, she was seeking to ensure that PlaNet Finance China and the Tongwei Rural Development Association (TWRDA)[7] identified and served the *real* poor.

---

to activities which local microfinance institutions (MFIs) may offer to complement the microloans such as entrepreneurial, life skills, and farming training, information on health, nutrition, and sanitation, advice on improving living conditions and the importance of educating children, etc. Microfinance plus is based on the idea that to overcome poverty the poor require more than access to capital.

[7] The Tongwei Rural Development Association (TWRDA) is a local Tongwei MFI which partnered with PlaNet Finance China for the two Tongwei Projects. Established in 1996, the TWRDA's government status is unique. It is the only authorised branch of the Tongwei County government External Aid Office. There are very particular rules in China concerning foreign funding for community organisations. Money can only enter the county through the External Aid Office who can only transfer it to the TWRDA. The TWRDA is made up of a team of eight with a mixture of microfinance specialists,

These recent developments meant that Gabrielle and Alison Schmidt, the Deputy Project Manager for Tongwei II, needed to adjust the choice of villages and possibly one of the township areas for Tongwei II.

Sitting at her desk, Gabrielle analysed the results of the first Tongwei project, wondering how PlaNet Finance China could capitalise on the innovative elements of Tongwei I and apply the experience and lessons learned to move forward with Tongwei II. She questioned whether Tongwei II's scope was sufficiently broad to fulfil its mission, or whether it needed to be narrowed in order to reduce the funding issues and remain in line with the more purely microfinance view of the wider PlaNet Finance organisation.

Microfinance

Defining Microfinance

Microfinance is a development tool designed to reduce poverty. It is defined as *"the practice of providing financial services, such as loans as low as $100, savings and insurance to very poor individuals and families who traditionally have no access to credit to help them grow tiny businesses or engage in other productive economic activities. This process enables the working poor to become more self-sufficient and in turn, improve the lives of family members, communities and whole societies"*.[8]

Two types of institutions can provide microfinance services: Microfinance Institutions (MFIs) and private commercial banks. MFIs include credit and saving cooperatives, NGOs and non-bank financial institutions (some have transformed from NGOs into regulated institutions). Private commercial banks and parts of state-owned banks can also provide microfinance services: Indirectly by providing funds to MFIs or directly by launching a microfinance branch.[9]

The origin of microfinance goes back to the early 1970s when pioneer NGOs like the Boston based ACCION International and the Bangladesh based Grameen Bank, led by Muhammad Yunus, started issuing microloans

---

administrative staff and management. They work with a wide range of international partners who contribute to the economic and social development of Tongwei County, each of the partners is involved in a specific program. The TWRDA's main partners are PlaNet Finance, United Nations Children's Fund (UNICEF), United Nations Population Fund (UNPFA), and Grameen Trust.

[8]ACCION, 2010. About ACCION: What is the difference between microfinance and microcredit. [online] Available at: <http://www.accion.org/Page.aspx?pid=1648> [Accessed December 3, 2010].

[9]*ibid.*

to deprived areas in Brazil and Bangladesh. Today, more than 150 million people benefit from microloans. Around 80% of microfinance clients are women as they generally achieve better repayment rates and traditionally have less access to money. Today, it is estimated that more than 500 million people could be potential clients.[10,11]

The Application of Microcredit

Microcredit is generally applied as follows: Small loans are provided to clients at cost recovery interest rates, ranging from 20% in most cases to over 100% a year depending on the country.[12] The loan period runs from six months to a year on average with a high reimbursement frequency (usually on a weekly basis) starting immediately after the loan is taken out.[13,14,15]

The loans can be granted to individuals in two different ways. The most widespread process is group lending. Group lending is *"a mechanism that allows a number of individuals to gain access to microcredit by providing collateral or guaranteeing a loan through a group repayment pledge. The incentive to repay is based upon peer pressure; if one person in the group defaults, the other group members make up the payment amount"*.[16] In the case of a default in the group, all of the members are considered insolvent and will be denied future loans. This process reduces high transaction costs resulting from managing several microloans.[17] The second microcredit loan process is *"individual lending whereby microcredit is provided to one client and other people are not required to provide collateral or guarantee a loan"*.[18]

---

[10] PlaNet Finance, 2010. Microfinance: Key Figures. [online] Available at: <http://www.planetfinancegroup.org/FR/chiffres_cles.php> [Accessed December 3, 2010].

[11] Hagiu, A., and Corsi, E., 2009. *PlaNet Finance: Broad Scope in Microfinance, 708441.* Boston: Harvard Business School Publishing, p. 2.

[12] Duflo, E., 2009. Microcrédit, miracle ou désastre? *Le Monde,* January 12, 2009.

[13] Armendariz, B. and Morduch, J., 2010. *The Economics of Microfinance.* 2nd ed. Cambridge: The MIT Press, p. 4.

[14] Swibel, M., 2008. Microfinance Fever, *Forbes,* [online] Available at: <http://www.forbes.com/forbes/2008/0107/050.html> [Accessed December 3, 2010].

[15] PlaNet Finance, 2010. Microfinance: Overview. [online] Available at: <http://planetfinancegroup.org/FR/microfinance.php> [Accessed December 3, 2010].

[16] ACCION, 2010. About ACCION: What is the difference between microfinance and microcredit. [online] Available at: <http://www.accion.org/Page.aspx?pid=1648> [Accessed December 3, 2010].

[17] Hagiu, A., and Corsi, E., 2009. *PlaNet Finance: Broad Scope in Microfinance, 708441.* Boston: Harvard Business School Publishing, p. 2.

[18] ACCION, 2010. About ACCION: What is the difference between microfinance and microcredit. [online] Available at: <http://www.accion.org/Page.aspx?pid=1648> [Accessed December 3, 2010].

From Microcredit to Microfinance

The success of microcredit paved the way for microfinance as the high repayment rates obtained by NGOs (above 90%)[19] attracted governments along with corporate donors, despite the fact that MFIs were not able to cover their costs and had to rely on subsidies and grants. Microcredit became even more attractive when some microloan providers, such as the Bank Rakyat Indonesia (BRI) Unit Desa (a branch of the state-owned bank) restructured in 1984. This proved that microcredit could be a sustainable business. From then on many banks developed a microcredit branch aimed at reaching financial sustainability through inter-bank borrowing and operations on capital markets. *"Over time, the microfinance industry recognised that the poor who lack access to traditional formal financial services required a variety of financial products to meet their needs, not just microcredit. So microcredit evolved into microfinance in the 90s. Microfinance includes a broader range of services, such as loans, savings, insurance and transfer services (remittances) targeted at low-income clients."*[20] Simultaneously, many MFIs decided to become for-profit, regulated, financial institutions allowed to take deposits and to take advantage of commercial funding sources and thus become less dependent on unpredictable donor financing.[21]

The Evolution of Microfinance

Throughout the 1980s, MFIs realised that some of their fundamentals needed questioning. Microfinance mostly promoted family-based enterprises striving to make profit, rather than companies that could create jobs. Indeed, group lending might have some advantages and fit first-time clients. However, microfinance as it stood was not necessarily the most appropriate loan mechanism for better-off clients seeking larger loans. Indeed, as group members do not want to cover another member in the case of failure, they are more likely to focus on safe and small investments and refrain from engaging in entrepreneurship. Group members have no

---

[19] Hagiu, A., and Corsi, E., 2009. *PlaNet Finance*: *Broad Scope in Microfinance, 708441*. Boston: Harvard Business School Publishing, p. 2.

[20] ACCION, 2010. About ACCION: What is the difference between microfinance and microcredit. [online] Available at: <http://www.accion.org/Page.aspx?pid=1648> [Accessed December 3, 2010].

[21] Hagiu, A., and Corsi, E., 2009. *PlaNet Finance*: *Broad Scope in Microfinance, 708441*. Boston: Harvard Business School Publishing, p. 2.

incentive to engage in risky and ambitious projects if they cannot pocket the gains due to others' potential failures.

In addition, the microfinance industry has witnessed some cases of 'free-riding' whereby one failure incentivised other group members not to reimburse their share and to keep the money. Other studies show that there is no real difference in terms of repayment rates between group lending and individual lending.

As a result of these evolutions the Grameen Bank chose to stop group lending in some cases in 2002. Clients no longer face a mutual sanction in the case of failure but they are encouraged to continue meeting on a regular basis to foster mutual aid. The Grameen Bank also widened the repayment periods from weekly to monthly to encourage clients to invest in productive activities that are profitable in the longer term.[22,23]

Debates in the Microfinance Industry

There are a number of ongoing debates in the microfinance industry. First, there is criticism of the high interest rates (usually more than 20%) charged to microfinance clients, who are poor by definition. According to MFIs these high interest rates are necessary as they result both from the high transaction costs of managing many microloans (operating costs reportedly account for an average of 25% of a MFI's portfolio *versus* 5–7% for a commercial bank)[24] and from the risk of lending money to very poor people which is high too. The Finance Minister of India, Pranab Mukherjee, urged state-owned banks providing funds to MFIs to *"consider a covenant in future loan agreements with microfinance institutions, mandating that interest rates be capped at 24%"*.[25] This was after several suicides among microcredit beneficiaries were reported in Andhra Pradesh, mainly due to recollection practices of microfinance companies

[22]Duflo, E., 2009. Microcrédit, miracle ou désastre? *Le Monde*, January 12, 2009.
[23]Giné, X., Jakiela, P., Karlan, D., and Morduch, J., 2009. Microfinance Games. [online] Available at: <http://karlan.yale.edu/p/mfgames_1may09.pdf> [Accessed November 29, 2010], p. 32.
[24]PlaNet Finance, 2010. Microfinance: Overview, [online]. Available at: <http://planet financegroup.org/FR/microfinance.php> [Accessed December 3, 2010].
[25]Kazmin, A., 2010. Microfinance: India considers rate cap on loans to poor. *The Financial Times*, [online] November 17. Available at: <http://www.im4change.org/rural-news-update/microfinance-india-considers-rate-cap-on-loans-to-poor-by-amy-kazmin-4407.html> [Accessed December 7, 2010].

who borrow money from commercial banks at 10–15% and then lend it at 30%.[26]

In terms of the process, the best approach to provide microloans is still being discussed: Should one develop local MFIs close to poor people who mainly live in rural areas where no financial services are available; or should one develop microcredit activities in banks located in cities? Banks have the liquidity needed and MFIs have the rural network required to reach the poor. However, the fact that MFIs can be the 'last mile link' for banks has been questioned in the aftermath of the suicides in India. *"If the banks are able to go direct, they can lend at lower rates, and that over time is fundamentally a more stable system, but going from past experience, the banks seem to lack the DNA to achieve that,"*[27] says Alok Prasad, former India country director of the Citi Microfinance Group, and now the chief executive officer of the Microfinance Institutions Network (MIN), a body representing 44 for-profit MFIs in India.

Additionally microfinance is criticised for not serving the poorest people given that only people who are able to generate revenues are eligible for a loan.

The Move toward Microfinance Plus

Muhammad Yunus based the fundamentals of microfinance on the presumption that credit constraints alone, not skills, were the obstacle faced by the entrepreneurial poor: *"I firmly believe that all human beings have an innate skill. I call it the survival skill. The fact that the poor are alive is clear proof of their ability. They do not need us to teach them how to survive; they already know. So rather than waste our time teaching them new skills, we try to make maximum use of their existing skills. Giving the poor access to credit allows them to immediately put into practice the skills they already know."*[28]

The majority of the microfinance industry focuses on providing microloans alone: *"Much of the microfinance industry focuses on the*

---

[26] *ibid.*
[27] *ibid.*
[28] Yunus, M. and Jolis, A., 2003. *Banker to the Poor: Micro-Lending and the Battle Against World Poverty*. Dhaka: PublicAffairs, p. 140.

infusion of financial capital into micro-enterprises, not human capital, as if the entrepreneurs already have the necessary human capital."[29] Recent developments in the industry have led to microfinance plus as many loan providers believe training sessions accompanying the loan can prove profitable, although no results in terms of rise in income have been highlighted. Such training sessions are meant to help people who are interested in setting up a business to gain the necessary skills and to help existing small entrepreneurs improve their skills. Training is on running a business, dealing with banks or potential investors, basic accounting and entrepreneurial skills to help people set up or improve their business plan.[30,31,32] Now some microfinance providers, like PlaNet Finance China, have broadened the range of training content they offer to fight poverty in a more comprehensive way: "*With Microfinance Plus Programmes, PlaNet Finance China can leverage the Microfinance Institutions' network and resources to tackle other critical issues such as health, environment, education and rural areas development.*" (see **Exhibit 2** for examples)[33]

Applying Microfinance Plus to the Tongwei Projects

The main question concerning microfinance plus is the extent to which it is a sustainable business model. Traditional microfinance strives to cover its costs and sometimes struggles. Adding a non-financial element would mean an increase in expenses which could result in higher interest rates. The cost of microfinance plus is one of the questions Gabrielle Harris asked herself in her quest for funding. She needed to find a way to justify that "*at best,*"

---

[29]Karlan, D. and Valdivia, M., 2010. Teaching Entrepreneurship: Impact of Business Training on Microfinance Clients and Institutions, [online]. Available at: <http://karlan.yale.edu/p/TeachingEntrepreneurship_revision_jan2010.pdf> [Accessed November 29, 2010].

[30]Klinger, B. and Schündeln, M., 2010. *Can Entrepreneurial Activity be Taught? Quasi-Experimental Evidence from Central America.* Boston: Harvard Business School Publishing, p. 2.

[31]Yunus, M. and Jolis, A., 2003. *Banker to the Poor: Micro-Lending and the Battle Against World Poverty.* Dhaka: PublicAffairs, p. 140.

[32]Karlan, D. and Valdivia, M., 2010. Teaching Entrepreneurship: Impact of Business Training on Microfinance Clients and Institutions, [online]. Available at: <http://karlan.yale.edu/p/TeachingEntrepreneurship_revision_jan2010.pdf> [Accessed November 29, 2010].

[33]PlaNet Finance, 2010. What We Do: Microfinance Plus Programs. [online] Available at: <http://www.planetfinancechina.org/what-we-do/mpp> [Accessed December 3, 2010].

the interest from the microfinance loans covers the salary of loan officers and admin staff.[34] She wondered whether the extra expenses incurred by microfinance plus make the activity profitable enough to cover the costs. Currently the Tongwei Projects are able to place emphasis on education and training in addition to providing microfinance loans because they *"are nicely-funded European Union (EU) projects. This allows the financing of training sessions, attention from the MFI, etc. However, it would be difficult to move this project elsewhere"*[35] without similar subsidies from a third party, reckons Gabrielle Harris.

PlaNet Finance

Jacques Attali, founder and first president of the European Bank for Reconstruction and Development, first proposed the concept of PlaNet Finance in a seminar for the Aspen Institute, a Washington, D.C.-based NGO dedicated to fostering enlightened leadership and open-minded dialogue.[36]

PlaNet Finance is not a religious association and it does not work on behalf of a specific government, company or country. Founded in October 1998, it is an international NGO that aims to alleviate poverty worldwide through the development of microfinance. It seeks to become a microfinance platform that brings together the various actors in the sector and, simultaneously, serves to pool the resources needed to develop microfinance.[37]

Since its foundation, PlaNet Finance has attracted the interest of the private and the public sector. It receives contributions (in cash and in kind) from numerous international firms and organisations. PlaNet Finance built up its portfolio and presence gradually and now has a wide international reach with offices in 80 countries and 266 employees of 45 different nationalities. The firm has a diversified set of revenues, yet it

---

[34]Interview with Mrs Gabrielle Harris carried out by ESSEC students Marie Camille Cornel, Quentin Dumouilla and Aurélie Derché in the PlaNet Finance China in Beijing on the November 17, 2010.

[35]Interview with Mrs Gabrielle Harris carried out by ESSEC students Marie Camille Cornel, Quentin Dumouilla and Aurélie Derché in the PlaNet Finance China in Beijing on the November 17, 2010.

[36]Hagiu, A., and Corsi, E., 2009. *PlaNet Finance: Broad Scope in Microfinance, 708441*. Boston: Harvard Business School Publishing, p. 6.

[37]PlaNet Finance, 2010. PlaNet Finance: Overview. [online] Available at: <http://www.planetfinancegroup.org/EN/qui_sommes_nous.php> [Accessed October 7, 2010].

remains heavily dependent on external sponsors such as Dexia, Capgemini, Organisation Internationale de la Francophonie (*via* the Fonds Francophone des Inforoutes), The World Bank (*via* InfoDev), and private donors.

PlaNet Finance has a unique business model, combining social business activities and non-profit activities.[38] According to François Durollet, Managing Director of PlaNet Finance, *"PlaNet Finance holds a unique position in the sector as the only organisation that combines non-profit and social business activities within the same group. This model gives PlaNet Finance the flexibility to design innovative projects"*.[39] Another innovative element of the PlaNet Finance model is that all of its *"new ideas are initially set up in the non-profit part of the organisation, which acts as an incubator. Once these activities become sustainable, they can become social businesses. At this point in the process, PlaNet Finance seeks either equity or technical partnerships with external organisations"*.[40]

PlaNet Finance is involved in most of the activities which surround microfinance, such as consulting, ratings and investment funds. In addition to its financial services, PlaNet Finance engages two types of non-financial services. The first is highly technical: It investigates ways in which MFIs can improve their activities through up-scaling, downscaling and the opening of greenfield institutions. The second element is the development of microfinance plus which involves combining microfinance with other activities such as gender empowerment, production optimisation, the search for new markets, and the organisation of microentrepreneurs into cooperatives so that they can develop strong positions in the market.[41]

PlaNet Finance China

PlaNet Finance China, the representative office in Beijing, has been involved in the Chinese microfinance sector since 2003. It is a non-profit, tax-exempt organisation that works for sustainable social and economic

---

[38] MicroCapital Team, 2010. MEET THE BOSS: François Durollet, Managing Director of PlaNet Finance. MicroCapital.org, the candid voice for microfinance [online] February 22, 2010. Available at: <http://www.microcapital.org/meet-the-boss-francois-durollet-managing-director-of-planet-finance/> [Accessed on December 6, 2010].

[39] *ibid.*

[40] MicroCapital Team, 2010. MEET THE BOSS: François Durollet, Managing Director of PlaNet Finance. MicroCapital.org, the candid voice for microfinance [online] February 22, 2010. Available at: <http://www.microcapital.org/meet-the-boss-francois-durollet-managing-director-of-planet-finance/> [Accessed on December 6, 2010].

[41] *ibid.*

development in China by supporting and promoting the microfinance sector.

PlaNet Finance China currently has a six-person full-time team comprising a mix of Chinese and international staff. It is split into two activity lines: Projects and back office support (See **Exhibit 3** for a full organisational chart). Zhang Han, the rural microfinance expert and Alison Schmidt, the deputy project manager, oversee the project work. Alison joined PlaNet Finance in March 2009 as deputy to Gabrielle to focus on managing the implementation of the Tongwei II Project. She complements Gabrielle who is the brains behind the operation in its day-to-day development. In addition to Zhang's responsibilities as a consultant and microfinance trainer, he works with Gabrielle and Alison on the microfinance and staff training sides of the Tongwei projects. Zhang also coordinated the development of the microloan products for Tongwei I and will do so for Tongwei II. The back office team provides support for the projects, research, grants and financing as well as ensuring the smooth running of operations. PlaNet Finance China has implemented projects in rural and urban China, serving local microfinance programmes and financial institutions in more than 20 Chinese provinces and cities. The Tongwei Projects are its largest in recent years, and they take up much of team's time and resources.

PlaNet Finance China seeks to strengthen microfinance delivery in two ways:

(1) Provide growth assistance to small MFIs that are trying to get loan services to farmers and entrepreneurs in the central and western areas of China.

(2) Assist existing regulated financial institutions to efficiently extend their loan portfolio to small loans, using best practice credit and risk management strategies and technologies.

In its microfinance plus work, PlaNet Finance China tries to bring donor resources to poverty-stricken areas to address certain weaknesses (e.g., access to market information, lack of coping mechanisms for agriculture in a changing climate, lack of micro-entrepreneur training resources, etc.). At the same time it works to improve and diversify the performance of the local microfinance organisations leveraging PlaNet Finance China's technical services. Under conditions of increasing urbanisation in western China, PlaNet Finance China is facilitating training on individual lending which can complement the older group-lending models.[42]

Tongwei County

Tongwei is one of 58 counties in Gansu province, located in the heart of China. It is home to 464,400 citizens, most of whom are farmers living in villages.[43] Tongwei's population is mainly poor, and Tongwei is classified by the Chinese government as a 'poverty county'.

Poverty in Tongwei County is caused by several factors. The main one is lack of education. In the vast majority of cases, people drop out during middle school.[44] Women rarely go to school at all. Incomes are both low and irregular. Indeed, the annual average net income per household in Tongwei is CNY 1,390 (US $200),[45] whereas the annual average income per household for the whole of China is around CNY 8,000 (US $1,300).[46] Moreover, the revenue generated by the sale of crops comes only once a year, as does the income sent by migrant workers who have moved to cities. The revenue sent home by migrant workers constitutes the main income of rural households. Households with members who work away receive between CNY 6,000 and 15,000 (US $950–$2,400) per year per household, depending on the number of migrant workers in the family.[47] This income is not included in official data because it is considered as a secondary activity, the main one being agriculture. However, this source of revenue is important to farmers as they rarely produce enough food to sell surplus and everything is used for personal consumption. As a

---

[42]PlaNet Finance China, 2010. PlaNet Finance China: Origins and Philosophy. [online] Available at: <http://www.planetfinancegroup.org/EN/qui_sommes_nous.php> [Accessed October 7, 2010].

[43]Renewable Energy Project for Tongwei County, Gansu Province. [online] Available at <http://www.planetfinancechina.org/what-we-do/microfinance/tongwei> [Accessed November 30, 2010].

[44]Usually, Chinese children go to middle school, or Zhongxue (中学) between the ages of seven and 12.

[45]Renewable Energy Project for Tongwei County, Gansu Province. [online] Available at <http://www.planetfinancechina.org/what-we-do/microfinance/tongwei> [Accessed December 1, 2010].

[46]China Average Salaries and Expenditures. [online] Available at: <http://www.world salaries.org/china.shtml> [Accessed December 6, 2010].

[47]Interview with farmers carried out by ESSEC students Marie Camille Cornel, Quentin Dumouilla and Aurélie Derché with the translation assistance of Gabrielle Harris and Alison Schmidt in Wancha and Xinsi villages, on November 10 & 12, 2010.

result, the majority of farmers have no agricultural income and need to send family members away to work in construction or factories in order to survive.

As Tongwei is located in the middle of mainland China, the weather is particularly cold in winter and dry all year round. Living conditions are harsh as heating houses with coal is expensive (US $72 per ton in 2006).[48] The land is also very hilly, which necessitates terrace cultivation and increased difficulty for any automated work. Therefore, most of the field work is done manually or with the help of livestock. Because of the topographic situation, the soil is highly erodible and poor in nutrition. Farmers plough a large proportion of their cash into chemical fertilisers in order to maintain productivity.

The National Biogas Subsidy Programme

The harsh living conditions as well as the 'poverty county' status of Tongwei, led the Chinese central government to select Tongwei for its National Biogas Subsidy Programme.

The main purpose of this programme is to provide enough materials and training to farmers so they can build an individual biogas pit for their homes. A biogas pit, or biodigester, is a pit where villagers put animal, human and vegetation waste. This matter is then partly turned into biogas, thanks to a fermentation process. Biogas is a mixture of methane and carbon dioxide which can be burned for heating or, in the case of Tongwei I, cooking. Once the Biogas is extracted, the remaining matter in the pit, called the slurry, can be used as a biological fertiliser.

The National Biogas Subsidy Programme is an innovative means of providing rural populations with energy. It is designed to help farmers cut their fuel and chemical fertiliser expenses while providing them with a source of renewable energy. The objective is also to help the villagers, particularly women, save time on cooking, as they no longer need to collect fuel and light fires. This in turn, is supposed to increase productivity.

Not only is biogas the cheapest renewable energy source on the market[49] but it also pushes people to recycle organic waste rather than cut down

---

[48]Li, G., Niu S., Ma, L., and Zhang, X., 2009. Assessment of environmental and economic costs of rural household energy consumption in Loess Hilly Region, Gansu Province, China. *Renewable Energy*, June 2009, 34(6), p. 1441.

[49]Interview with Mr He Qingchun, director of the Energy Office of Tongwei, carried out by ESSEC students Marie Camille Cornel, Quentin Dumouilla and Aurélie Derché with

trees. The National Biogas Subsidy Programme also has an environmental purpose, even though the emphasis is on economies of time and money for the farmers. Biogas is indeed 'greener' than coal or other traditional energy sources as its environmental cost, CO_2 emissions, are the lowest per cubic metre.[50] It may appear somewhat ambitious to try to convince one of the poorest counties in China to turn green, but energy is one of the most basic leverages one can use against rural poverty, as "supply and demand of rural energy sources is a complex issue of interconnecting ecology, economy and society".[51]

There are two key phases in the construction required to fully exploit and reap the benefits from the biogas installation: The digester and the three-in-one conversion involving the installation of the animals' pen and a human toilet (See **Exhibit 4**). The total cost of the full system is between US \$500 and \$600.

According to the Tongwei Energy Office,[52] 280 Tongwei villages have benefited from the National Biogas Subsidy Programme since 2006, and 16,300 biogas pits have been built throughout the county.

Through the programme, a subsidy of US \$190 to \$240 covers the provision of specialised equipment (tubing, valves, meter and fluoride filtration) as well as the cost of technical supervision, but the farmer must bring the building materials. Anyone living in one of the villages selected by the government programme can benefit from it.

Of course, this means that those living in the villages in Tongwei County which were not selected for the programme do not subsidised access to biogas pits. It also means that the three-in-one conversions have to be financed by the villagers. This further construction costs approximately

---

the translation assistance of Alison Schmidt in Tongwei Energy office, on November 11, 2010.

[50] $1m^3$ of Biogas combustion emits 1,172.5 g of CO_2, compared to 1,487 g for 1kg of coal, in Li, G., Niu S., Ma, L., and Zhang, X., 2009. Assessment of environmental and economic costs of rural household energy consumption in Loess Hilly Region, Gansu Province, China. *Renewable Energy*, June 2009, 34(6), p. 1443.

[51] Li, G., Niu S., Ma, L., and Zhang, X., 2009. Assessment of environmental and economic costs of rural household energy consumption in Loess Hilly Region, Gansu Province, China. *Renewable Energy*, June 2009, 34(6), p. 1444.

[52] Interview with Mr He Qingchun, director of the Energy Office of Tongwei, carried out by ESSEC students Marie Camille Cornel, Quentin Dumouilla and Aurélie Derché with the translation assistance of Alison Schmidt in Tongwei Energy office, on November 11, 2010.

US $320 depending on the size of the pit and the animal pens.[53] Therefore, it can take some time before the beneficiaries can collect the extra funds required to fully reap the benefits of their new biogas installation.

Introducing Tongwei I: The Renewable Energy Project for Tongwei County, Gansu Province

The Tongwei I project started in 2006, when Gabrielle Harris travelled to Gansu province and was first made aware of the National Biogas Subsidy Programme. Gabrielle remembers: "*At that time, PlaNet Finance China was looking for a good capacity-building project, and seeking to help a small organisation which was stuck.*" They started to evaluate the needs of TWRDA, which was already known to Zhang Han because PlaNet Finance had previously donated a computer to them. Coincidentally, PlaNet Finance in Paris was approached by Areva because they were interested in financing a renewable energy project. PlaNet Finance China won the deal against PlaNet Finance Brazil. This accumulation of circumstances is what led to the cooperation of PlaNet Finance China and the TWRDA on the Tongwei I Project.

The mechanisms, Actors, and Activities of Tongwei I

Funding mechanisms (See Exhibit 5)

The Tongwei I project benefited from several types of funding. Areva provided US $63,000, which was to be used for project-related fees, such as the TWRDA staff and loan officers' salaries. In November 2007, PlaNet Finance China applied for an EU grant for Tongwei I, and won US $300,000. Meanwhile, PlaNet Finance obtained a donation of US $57,000 with the intended purpose of providing a rotating fund to finance microloans for renewable energy projects (See **Exhibit 6** for more details on finances).

Actors and activities (See Exhibit 7)

The microloan products were designed after market research was conducted in Tongwei and analysed in Paris. PlaNet Finance China then submitted

---

[53]Lomboy, C. and Gaeng, P. PlaNet Finance Technical Advisory Services (Asia), Inc., April 2009. Microfinance & Renewable Energy: Using Microfinance to Increase Access to Renewable Energy in Tongwei County, Impact Assessment, p. 2.

the proposed interest rates to TWRDA for approval. Two products were designed this way for the Tongwei I project. The first one was an eight-month loan of US $320 at a 6% interest rate, the other one was a 12-month loan of the same amount at an 8% rate. The loans were distributed following the group lending mechanism. The borrowers gathered every month to pay one-twelfth (in case of a 12-month loan) of the interest, and reimbursed the capital at the end of the loan period. In case of a late payment, a penalty interest rate of 14% was applied.

According to PlaNet Finance and the policy of most MFIs, these microloans were only granted to women, who valued them greatly as they rarely had access to money and had high reimbursement rates. In Wancha Village, 53 of the 56 clients who obtained loans were women; the exceptions were for households with special conditions such as widowed men.[54] Zhang Han provided TWRDA staff with training on microfinance in general and on these two products in particular, as well as advice on what to do if a client did not pay back. This kind of situation was largely avoided due to the group lending methodology. Clients formed groups with other women in order to apply for a mutual guarantee loan. If one of them failed to reimburse the loan, the others would have to pay for her. This limited the risk of untrustworthy clients, as people would group only with those they trusted. Moreover, given the fact that this project took place in small villages, neighbour pressure made people keener to make payments on time.

Eight villages from the government programme were chosen to host the Tongwei I project. In each village, one loan officer was appointed by TWRDA to inform the villagers of the availability of microloans to complete the government subsidy and build the three-in-one conversion units. The loan officer then helped the villagers to apply for the loan, and collected their file to transmit to TWRDA with his recommendations on the potential clients. This loan officer was often the Secretary General of the village, which conferred on him some authority. TWRDA then decided whether to grant the loan, according to criteria such as income, household activity, experience and reputation.

---

[54] Interview with Mr Wan, Wancha Village Secretary General and Tongwei I Loan Officer, carried out by ESSEC students Marie Camille Cornel, Aurélie Derché, and Quentin Dumouilla with the translation assistance of Gabrielle Harris, in the communal buildings of Wancha Village, on November 10, 2010.

Tongwei I Added Value to the National Biogas Subsidy Programme

The main added-value of Tongwei I is that it allowed people benefiting from the National Biogas Subsidy Programme to have quicker access to the three-in-one conversion, thanks to traditional microloans. But Zhang Han insists that Tongwei I's *"business model is totally different from traditional microfinance."*[55] Tongwei I is unique in that it not only provided financial help to complete a government programme, but it also focused on training around the biogas pit and its agricultural uses, bringing teaching methods which were innovative for rural China. A strong accent was put on how to operate the biogas pit safely and efficiently to avoid shortages, especially in winter when temperatures fall and the fermentation process in the biogas pit slows down. PlaNet Finance China insisted on providing comprehensive training to ensure their clients got the most possible out of their biogas pit installation.

Training sessions were led by Energy Office technicians, whose teaching methods were improved and supervised by PlaNet Finance China and TWRDA. The Energy Office technicians spent more time in Tongwei I project villages than in villages who only benefited from the National Biogas Subsidy Programme. They adapted their teaching methods following tips from PlaNet Finance China. For example, they were more careful in checking if the participants clearly understood the process, by asking them questions and feedback on what they had learned, encouraging them to repeat their lesson and teach others. Additionally, when Gabrielle noticed that women were uncomfortable in the learning environment as many had not been to school, she adapted the setting by adding tea and snacks, which made the women feel more comfortable. PlaNet Finance China encouraged the Energy Office trainers to change their methods from passive listening to active participation. This approach proved a success, according to Mr He Qingchun, Head of the Energy Office: *"Villages that have not benefited from PlaNet Finance customised training often do not know all the advantages they can gain from biogas and biofertiliser."*[56]

---

[55]Interview with Mr Zhang Han, Rural Microfinance Expert of PlaNet Finance China, carried out by ESSEC students Marie Camille Cornel, Quentin Dumouilla and Aurélie Derché in PlaNet Finance China office, Beijing, on November 17, 2010.
[56]Interview with Mr He Qingchun, director of the Energy Office of Tongwei, carried out by ESSEC students Marie Camille Cornel, Quentin Dumouilla and Aurélie Derché with

At the same time that the microloans were granted in selected villages, PlaNet Finance also organised road show campaign around Tongwei County to visit 32 villages that did not benefit from its loans. The road show covered environmental themes, such as waste management, environment conservation and yield improvement enabled by natural compost in agricultural production. It aimed to make farmers aware of issues related to sustainable development and renewable energy sources and show them how they can easily apply it to their daily lives.

Tongwei I Results

Eventually, 430 clients in eight villages benefited from the Tongwei I project. The results of Tongwei I can be best put into context through the comparison of two villages. One, Wancha, benefited from the National Biogas Subsidy Programme and from Tongwei I microloans. The other, Xinsi, was just recently selected for the government programme, but has not yet received any microloans. In Wancha village, a number of substantial improvements were made.

(1) A lot of time was saved on cooking. Women no longer have to collect harvest waste, wood, use coal or light fires for each meal. Additionally the gas cooking process is much more convenient. "It was a revolution in the kitchen," reckons Mr Guo, a farmer from Wancha village whose wife benefited from a microloan. The harvest waste can now be used to feed livestock, implying that further substantial savings can be made on feeding the cattle.[57] According to a survey implemented in late 2008 by PlaNet Finance China, the time dedicated to fuel collection dropped from 2.24 hours a day in the warm season to 0.92 hours and from 3.27 hours a day in the cold season to 2.01 hours.[58] As a result, women saved an average of 1.5 hours and half a day, which can be used for cultivation, but also for leisure, the children's education and sometimes

---

the translation assistance of Alison Schmidt in Tongwei Energy office, on November 11, 2010.

[57]Interview with Mrs and Mr Guo, beneficiaries of a Tongwei I microloan, carried out by ESSEC students Marie Camille Cornel, Quentin Dumouilla and Aurélie Derché, with the translation assistance of Gabrielle Harris, in Wancha Village, on November 10, 2010.

[58]Lomboy, C. and Gaeng, P., PlaNet Finance Technical Advisory Services (Asia), Inc., April 2009. Microfinance & Renewable Energy: Using Microfinance to Increase Access to Renewable Energy in Tongwei County, *Impact Assessment*, p. 37.

for other small scale professional activities: Mrs Wei uses her spare time to make hats to sell at the market.[59]

(2) The sanitation of households strongly improved as the gas made for a cleaner environment. There is no longer coal smoke in the kitchen and surroundings, which has improved the health of the villagers (although biogas is not used for heating and coal is still used a lot in winter). Of the people interviewed in Planet Finance China's impact survey, 58% noticed less coughing and lung problems.[60] Sanitation also improved regarding human and animal excrement as proper means of disposal now existed in the villages.

(3) The fertiliser resulting from the biogas pit proved very useful and most households used it for their crops, resulting in improved quality and a larger quantity. Fertiliser reportedly helped production improve by 15−20%, which was a pleasant surprise as it was unexpected that biofertiliser would be more efficient than the chemical one.[61] Moreover, some people who did not have enough to eat before, have now reached self-sufficiency and can start selling part of their production: "Life is pretty good now," says Mrs. Guo. Some people even started growing new crops which would not have survived without the fertiliser.[62]

(4) Some savings in fertiliser expenses were noticed and resulted in a small increase in disposable income. The consumption of fertiliser decreased by approximately 25% but the expenses remained relatively stable as fertiliser only accounts for US $32 per year per farmer.[63] It was reported that it was the innovative approach to training that led to the increase

---

[59]Interview with Mrs Wei Xu Lan, beneficiary of a Tongwei I microloan, carried out by ESSEC students Marie Camille Cornel, Quentin Dumouilla and Aurélie Derché, with the translation assistance of Gabrielle Harris, in Wancha Village, on November 10, 2010.
[60]Lomboy, C. and Gaeng, P. PlaNet Finance Technical Advisory Services (Asia), Inc., April 2009. Microfinance & Renewable Energy: Using Microfinance to Increase Access to Renewable Energy in Tongwei County, *Impact Assessment*, p. 37.
[61]PlaNet Finance Technical Advisory Services (Asia), Inc., November 2009. Final narrative Report. Microfinance & Renewable Energy: Using Microfinance to IncreaseAccess to Renewable Energy in Tongwei County, Impact Assessment, p. 11.
[62]Interview with Mrs and Mr Guo, beneficiaries of a Tongwei I microloan, carried out by ESSEC students Marie Camille Cornel, Quentin Dumouilla and Aurélie Derché, with the translation assistance of Gabrielle Harris, in Wancha Village, on November 10, 2010.
[63]Lomboy, C. and Gaeng, P. PlaNet Finance Technical Advisory Services (Asia), Inc., April 2009. Microfinance & Renewable Energy: Using Microfinance to Increase Access to Renewable Energy in Tongwei County, *Impact Assessment*, pp. 17, 29.

in efficiency and use of fertiliser. The Tongwei I clients were the most well-educated on biogas in Tongwei County.

(5) Savings in energy were significant as far as coal was concerned. An average of US $64 to $80 was saved per year for each household, thanks to the biogas installation. This is significant considering the total coal budget for households in the county is about US $140.[64,65]

(6) The general **conditions of women** also improved since the microloans were only given to women. The loans helped change the position and perception of Wancha village's women, both in the household and in society.

As a result of these changes the villagers who benefited from Tongwei I are eager to learn about other new projects to improve their living conditions. "*They now have running water in part of the village, and would be interested in having solar water heaters which highlights the new hopes and expectations brought by Tongwei I*," says Mr Wan, the Loan Officer and Secretary General for Wancha village.[66]

As a basis for comparison, a taste of what life was like before Tongwei I, can be given by Xinsi, a candidate village for Tongwei II. Indeed, the testimony of Mrs. Wang illustrates the plight of her fellow villagers. She said she only uses her agricultural production for self-consumption and therefore has no real income from agriculture. Harvest waste is the main source of energy she uses for cooking and it takes her about two hours a day to collect fuel for cooking and heating. She has no cattle because she lacks appropriate facilities. She explains that the quality of the soil is poor and that they have to use chemical fertilisers which are expensive. Although she is a recent beneficiary of the National Biogas Subsidy Programme and is having a biogas pit built, Mrs. Wang's story

---

[64] PlaNet Finance Technical Advisory Services (Asia), Inc., November 2009. Final narrative Report. Microfinance & Renewable Energy: Using Microfinance to Increase Access to Renewable Energy in Tongwei County, *Impact Assessment*, p. 11.

[65] Lomboy, C. and Gaeng, P. PlaNet Finance Technical Advisory Services (Asia), Inc., April 2009. Microfinance & Renewable Energy: Using Microfinance to Increase Access to Renewable Energy in Tongwei County, *Impact Assessment*, p. 17.

[66] Interview with Mr Wan, Wancha Village Secretary General and Tongwei I Loan Officer, carried out by ESSEC students Marie Camille Cornel, Aurélie Derché, and Quentin Dumouilla with the translation assistance of Gabrielle Harris, in the communal buildings of Wancha Village, on November 10, 2010.

highlights the benefits of Tongwei I in helping people achieve better living conditions.[67]

The Transition to Tongwei II

Tongwei II was born out of Tongwei I as expressed by Gabrielle Harris: *"My frustrations with Tongwei I and what we had not accomplished drove Tongwei II."* The question of Tongwei II comes back to her vision of poverty and her toolbox for addressing it (See **Exhibit 8**). In Gabrielle's vision, the most powerful tool to combat poverty has always been the question "why". *"Why is this place poor? Why don't these people process their raw materials and get more value from their crops? Why can't they grow better crops? Why don't they send their children to school? Why are their soils so thin and dry? What is the matter with that grandmother over there, and why can't she go see the doctor"?*[68]

Gabrielle's determination to achieve poverty reduction and her personal involvement in helping Tongwei County out of poverty are what led to the existence of PlaNet Finance China's Tongwei II project. Against all odds she and her team pressed for a grant from the European Comission and, to everyone's surprise, obtained it.

In Tongwei I, PlaNet Finance China sought to push farmers out of poverty through the use of microfinance loans for biogas pits and the implementation of extra interactive training sessions to stimulate the farmer's independence and reflection. Thus PlaNet Finance China *"gained a deep understanding of the local development and environmental challenges that weigh heavily on the Tongwei community"*.[69] Through Tongwei II, PlaNet Finance and TWRDA seek to take poverty reduction and sustainable development in Tongwei County one step further, continuing to support the National Biogas Subsidy Programme. Through an emphasis on microfinance plus, PlaNet Finance China and TWRDA will *"focus on increasing financial inclusion, further incorporating renewable energy*

---

[67] Interview with Mrs Wang, beneficiary of the National Biogas Subsidy Programme, carried out by ESSEC students Marie Camille Cornel, Quentin Dumouilla, and Aurélie Derché, with the translation assistance of Alison Schmidt, in Xinsi Village, on November 12, 2010.

[68] Harris, G., 2010. Breaking down the Walls of Poverty, TEDx Great Wall Beijing, *World without Walls*. May 20, 2010, p. 4.

[69] PlaNet Finance China, 2010. From Rural Isolation to Market Integration (Tongwei II). [online] Available at: <http://www.planetfinancechina.org/what-we-do/tongwei-ii> [Accessed December 6, 2010].

technology into daily life, developing Tongwei's nascent green industries,and finding ways to add value to raw commodities within the greater Tongwei farming communities".[70]

What Tongwei II Entails

Where Tongwei I sought to bring renewable energy to those farmers who could not afford the technology investment required, Tongwei II aims to take Tongwei County from rural isolation to market integration. It will build on Tongwei I by continuing to help the local government of Tongwei County improve the living conditions of its rural population by better utilising the county's resources and talents all the while building its own green development path to increase the county's GDP.

Increase in scale

Tongwei II will enlarge the scale of Tongwei I in two ways: Loans and geography. In Tongwei II, PlaNet Finance China and TWRDA aim to provide 1,200 biogas microfinance loans and 1,800 productive loans intended for clients wishing to develop economic activity. To distribute these loans, they will target 27 villages in five townships, as opposed to eight villages in Tongwei I. With Tongwei II, the scale of the project will increase from 430 to 3,000 clients. When asked about the challenge regarding the increase in scale, Mr Sun Guodong, Director of TWRDA, replied that considering there are 60,000 people in Tongwei County who have microfinance needs, 3,000 does not seem large in comparison and thus is a reasonable amount for TWRDA.[71]

In terms of geography, Tongwei II will extend its work to Cheng County, which lies 400 km south of Tongwei in the Longnan area of Gansu province. The area suffers from the aftermath of the 2008 earthquake which significantly damaged its infrastructure and homes. Cheng County has a population of 263,000, of which 219,000 are farmers who reside within 17 townships and 96 villages. Approximately 70% of the farmers currently live in relative to extreme poverty (earning between US $100 and $130 per year). It is believed that Cheng County's weather and water

---

[70] *ibid.*

[71] Interview with Mr Sun Guodong carried out by ESSEC students Marie Camille Cornel, Quentin Dumouilla and Aurélie Derché with the translation assistance of Alison Schmidt in the TWRDA offices in Tongwei on November 11, 2010.

conditions are suitable for biogas development and PlaNet Finance China would like to replicate the successful model of Tongwei I.[72] *"With loans for biogas technology implementation, residents of Cheng County can take advantage of renewable energy technology while simultaneously building the local economy and improving the currently very-poor living conditions"*.[73]

To support this increase in scale and geographical extension, several plans have been established. Firstly, TWRDA will recruit and PlaNet Finance China will help train new loan officers who will work at a township level. Secondly, there will be representatives in each village responsible for helping with the operational aspects of the loans. PlaNet Finance China has adjusted Zhang Han's time so that he can spend more time on Tongwei II, coordinating the various parties and improving staff expertise. Furthermore, PlaNet Finance China plans to directly employ two independent auditors to check on compliance.

Increase in scope

In addition to improving the living conditions of the poor rural populations through the financing of the three-in-one conversions, Tongwei II places emphasis on talent management and improving the economic development of the region. In Cheng County, for example, PlaNet Finance China will establish a microcredit training platform to enable the ultra poor to use their talents and develop activities to improve their living conditions.

Tongwei II also aims to promote greater financial inclusivity by offering different types of loans from those proposed in Tongwei I. PlaNet Finance will open up new microfinance loan centres in five townships to provide small general business and renewable energy loans to the township residents as well as to the outlying village population.

Differentiation from Tongwei I

Tongwei II aims to increase access to fundamental needs such as finance, energy and decent employment. The objective is to teach the farmers and villagers how to use the biogas technology at their disposal in the most

---

[72] PlaNet Finance China, 2010. From Rural Isolation to Market Integration (Tongwei II). [online] Available at: <http://www.planetfinancechina.org/what-we-do/tongwei-ii> [Accessed December 6, 2010].
[73] *ibid.*

efficient way possible, leaving more time to think about productivity gains and to take advantage of the potential of the agricultural market. The main activity and differentiating factor of Tongwei II is the establishment of the Rural Business & Innovation Centre (RBIC), an information source, knowledge centre and incubator for the commercialisation of agricultural commodities and development of new products. Tongwei II clearly differs from Tongwei I in that it aims to promote and support entrepreneurial behaviour, whereby villagers can dare to innovate and thus increase their earning potential. In time, this model should move farmers toward more economic diversification and autonomy, as many areas today still rely heavily on government subsidies.

Introducing the RBIC

The RBIC is the extension of the innovative aspect of the Tongwei I project, taking the development of new forms of adult education and the development of entrepreneurship one step further. The idea for the RBIC stems from the concept that there can be very tall walls around local cultural traditions that set behaviour. In Tongwei I, it was observed that people naturally follow tradition and individuals replicate the behaviour of their peers and it takes a very brave, independent person to do things differently. In Tongwei II, PlaNet Finance China intends to leverage its role as a non-Chinese NGO to stimulate the locals and push them to dare: *"International organisations give go-getter locals an excuse for going against tradition: In the trade, we call this 'launching a pilot'."*[74]

The RBIC is believed to be the first ever of its type in China. The RBIC will include several sections (See **Exhibit 9**) with the aim of pushing entrepreneurs forward and providing them with the tools and support they require.

To break down these walls and ensure that the RBIC is as successful as it can be, Gabrielle realises that a lot of external aid, local relationship-building, and personal involvement on her behalf will be required. As advocated by C.K. Prahalad in his work *"The Fortune at the Bottom of the Pyramid"*, PlaNet Finance China is convinced that *"private sector*

---

[74]Harris, Gabrielle Harris (2010). Breaking down the Walls of Poverty, TEDx Great Wall Beijing, *World without Walls.* May 20, 2010, p. 5.

involvement is a crucial ingredient to poverty alleviation"[75] and that it is crucial to the success of the RBIC. Gabrielle is ready to spend one week a month in Tongwei to ensure that the RBIC serves its purpose as an entrepreneurial incubator and truly changes the way villagers think.

Expectations for Tongwei II

The expectations for Tongwei II are vast. Potential clients hope to save time and money through microfinance loans for biogas and improve their sanitary conditions. The local government expects a lot from the RBIC, hoping that it will help kick start some local economic activities and that it will improve the farming techniques of locals. Additionally, through the link with the European Commission, the local government hopes that it will facilitate exchanges with other areas of the world and their know-how. Overall, the enthusiasm, hopes, and expectations for Tongwei II are very high.

Obstacles Ahead and Eventual Opportunities

Gabrielle Harris and Alison Schmidt realise that there are many obstacles ahead of them regarding the launch of Tongwei II and the construction of the RBIC.

The main worry faced by PlaNet Finance China in November 2010 was the funding of the Tongwei II project. As seen in Tongwei I, though microfinance plus is very beneficial, it is also extremely costly. PlaNet Finance China had secured US $800,000 from the European Commission. This amount was to cover 75% of the 42-month long Tongwei II Project. Following the drop-out of Areva, PlaNet Finance China needed to find a new sponsor urgently.

With the increase in the scale of the project from 430 clients in Tongwei I to 3,000 clients in Tongwei II, there is no doubt that it will be necessary to train the local microfinance team to handle more work with the same human resources. Gabrielle realises that the quality of the training and framework offered to the microfinance staff is pivotal to the smooth-running of the purely microfinance aspect of Tongwei II.

---

[75]Prahalad C.K., 2010. *The Fortune at the Bottom of the Pyramid*, 5th Anniversary Edition. New Jersey: Pearson Education, Inc., Wharton School Publishing, p. 33.

Another obstacle has been finding the extra funding to build a centre that can really serve the people of Tongwei and live up to the expectations. The current budget for the building covers the refurbishment of an existing building; however as there is no building available, the decision has been made to construct one and PlaNet Finance has paid US $16,000 to the Tongwei county government to cover land costs of the plot. The local Tongwei government is also heavily involved in the financing of the project and has contributed US $35,000 to cover the remainder of the land costs. Though having a purpose-built facility would be a great opportunity, it will take more time and capital to build from scratch.

Additionally, PlaNet Finance China realises that they rapidly need to start to link RBIC with local industry in order to get them working together and promote RBIC as a place for research and development and encourage the creation of new inventions. If PlaNet Finance China is successful with this, it will ultimately create a unique NGO–Government–Private sector link, something extremely beneficial for the local economy and which the Chinese government is extremely keen to foster.

In light of these two obstacles and of the challenges ahead, Gabrielle continued to push her team to find alternative solutions for the successful deployment of Tongwei II.

Most notably, a novel financing opportunity lay ahead of PlaNet Finance China in Tongwei County: The possibility to link the microfinance loans for the biogas installations to carbon credits. This innovative model, which PlaNet Finance China is looking into with The Microcarbon Foundation, will form a new kind of financial model which could be replicable not only in Tongwei but in other countries. However, in order to know whether this can move forward, they must wait for the outcome of the United Nations Framework Convention on Climate Change (UNFCCC) starting in November 2010.

Conclusion

Tongwei II is most likely the last project that PlaNet Finance China will execute in Tongwei County. Future projects will build on the knowledge and capacity acquired through these two large-scale projects. According to PlaNet Finance policy, PlaNet Finance China's team and resources will have to move on to a new poverty area in China. Gabrielle's main regret is that PlaNet Finance China does not have more resources available for the microfinance loan funds to serve more people with biogas.

PlaNet Finance China reflects positively on the effect it had on Tongwei County through its Tongwei I project. The team can see the multi-faceted impact that the project has had on the participating villages. The overall feedback from clients has been positive, showing good fieldwork by the loan officers trained by PlaNet Finance China in explaining the projects to the beneficiaries. The main innovation of the programme was bringing intensive, repeated participatory training sessions in microfinance, biogas and agriculture to this rural area of China. The knowledge enthusiastically shared by the villagers and their eagerness to participate, question and seek solutions shows the strong educational impact which PlaNet Finance China has had.

This positive reflection on Tongwei I fuels the commitment of PlaNet Finance China in the development and execution of the Tongwei II project. Through Tongwei II PlaNet Finance China will be taking the positive aspects of Tongwei I, further aiming to help boost Tongwei County out of its geographical and economic isolation.[76]

The questions that lay ahead will determine the success and execution of Tongwei II. Additionally, they will have a deep impact on the orientation of PlaNet Finance China's future actions. In sticking with her poverty-reduction ideals, Gabrielle must continue to think about and adapt her approach to microfinance, whether it means sticking to microcredit or emphasising support through microfinance plus. The team needs to reflect on the financing of its projects and their sustainability, whether this means increasing interest rates, finding new sources of financing, or simply more grants. This leads to the question of the sustainability of the activity. As an NGO, should PlaNet Finance China even seek to achieve sustainability? Should PlaNet Finance China's projects aim to financially help as many people as possible, or rather should they help fewer people, but with a broader help programme, not limited to loans? All of this links back to re-thinking PlaNet Finance China's mission and vision and linking it to a question of scope *versus* scale.

With the experience of Tongwei I and vision of Tongwei II in mind, Gabrielle reflected on the key success factors of Tongwei I and how

---

[76]PlaNet Finance China, 2009. From Rural Isolation to Market Integration: A Pilot Partnership. *European Commission Grant Application Form (Parts A and B) Non-State Actors and Local Authorities in Development Actions in partner countries (In-country)*. May 7, 2009, p. 7.

she could use them to move Tongwei II and her quest for funding forward.

Exhibits

Exhibit 1.1: Elements from the Outline of the 11th Five-Year Plan for National, Economic and Social Development of the People's Republic of China.[77]

China's 11th Five-Year Development Plan includes the following chapters:

(1) Guiding Principles and Development Goals.
(2) Building a New Socialist Countryside.
(3) Optimising and Upgrading Industrial Structure.
(4) Accelerating the Development of the Service Industry.
(5) Promoting Balanced Development Among Regions.
(6) Building a Resource-Conserving and Environment-Friendly Society.
(7) Implementing the Strategy of Developing China through Science and Education and the Strategy of Strengthening China through Tapping Human Resources.
(8) Deepening Institutional Reform.
(9) Carrying out an Opening up Strategy Featuring Mutual Benefits and Win-Win Situation.
(10) Building a Socialist Harmonious Society.
(11) Promoting Socialist Democratic Politics.
(12) Promoting Socialist Cultural Development.
(13) Strengthening National Defence and the Army.
(14) Establishing and Improving the Implementation Mechanism of the Plan.

---

[77]National Development and Reform Commission (NDRC), People's Republic of China. *The Outline of the Eleventh Five-Year Plan for National Economic & Social Development of the People's Republic of China Profile.* [online] Available at: <http://en.ndrc.gov.cn/hot/t20060529_71334.htm> [Accessed December 10, 2010].

Exhibit 1.2: Building a New Socialist Countryside.[78]

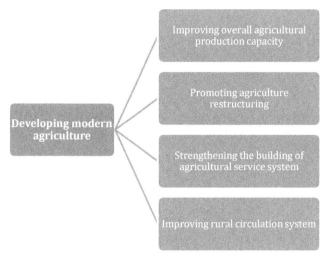

(a) Developing Modern Agriculture.

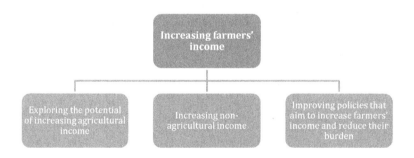

(b) Increasing Farmers' Income.

[78]National Development and Reform Commission (NDRC), People's Republic of China. *The Outline of the Eleventh Five-Year Plan for National Economic & Social Development of the People's Republic of China Profile.* [online] Available at: <http://en.ndrc.gov.cn/hot/t20060529_71334.htm>[Accessed December 10, 2010].

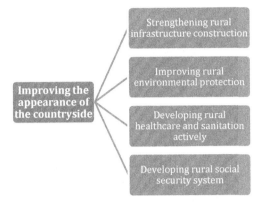

(a) Improving the Appearance of the Countryside.

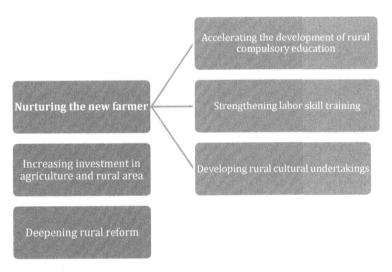

(b) Further Development of Rural Areas.

Exhibit 1.3: Building a Resource-Conserving and Environment-Friendly Society.[79]

(a) Fronts of Resource Conservation and Environmental Protection.

Exhibit 2: PlaNet Finance China's Microfinance Plus Programmes.

Below are the various types of microfinance plus (MF+) programmes which PlaNet Finance China has implemented in China since its launch:

MF + Rural

Leveraging the existing MFIs' infrastructure to enable better development of rural areas.

MF + Health

Leveraging the existing MFIs' infrastructure to implement awareness and disease prevention campaigns: Work with pharmaceutical companies to devise sustainable pilot projects to improve healthcare access for lower income populations: To explore microinsurance mechanisms for healthcare coverage.

MF + Education

Leveraging the existing MFIs' infrastructure to provide training to microentrepreneurs, especially women.

MF + Environment

Leveraging the existing MFIs' infrastructure to implement programmes raising awareness and making positive impact on areas of renewable energies, waste management and biodiversity.

---

[79]National Development and Reform Commission (NDRC), People's Republic of China. *The Outline of the Eleventh Five-Year Plan for National Economic & Social Development of the People's Republic of China Profile.* [online] Available at: <http://en.ndrc. gov.cn/hot/t20060529_71334.htm> [Accessed December 10, 2010].

Exhibit 3: PlaNet Finance China Organisational Chart.

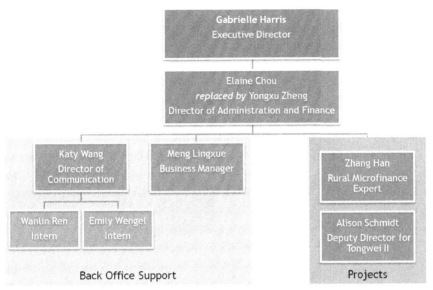

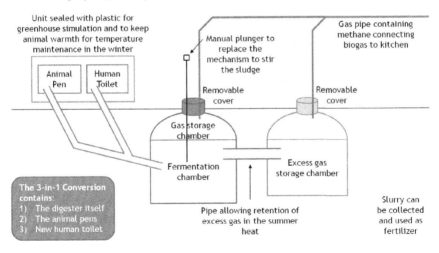

Exhibit 4: The Biogas Pit Mechanism.

Biogas digesters utilize the anaerobic digestion of manure, harvest and human waste to produce methane, a high-quality cooking fuel.

Exhibit 5:   Tongwei I Financing Mechanisms.

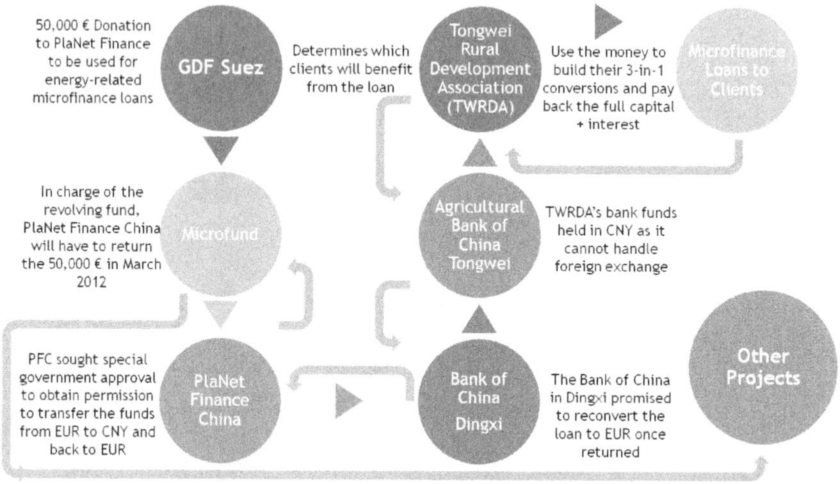

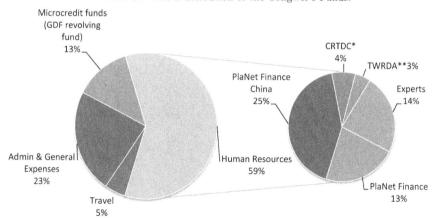

Exhibit 6:   The Distribution of the Tongwei I Funds.

Note: *CRTDC = China Rural Technology Development Centre.
**TWRDA = Tongwei Rural Development Association.

Exhibit 7:   Tongwei I Actors and Activities.

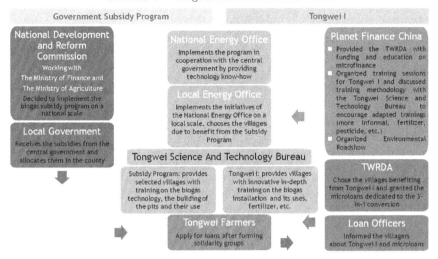

Note: TWRDA = Tongwei Rural Development Association.

Exhibit 8: The Walls of Poverty.[80]

The "walls of poverty" illustrated below were defined by Gabrielle Harris for a speech given on:

Wall 1: Illiteracy

- You cannot read, so walls run in every direction around you.
- People can tell you anything they like about your rights and you can only believe them.

Wall 2: Lack of Information

- There is no information pinned on the wall to spark new ideas.
- Information is not available to help you use the resources you have.
- You are nowhere near a market for your product and even if you were closer, you do not know what the prices are.
- You know nothing of new trends changing the world outside the wall.

Wall 3: Cashless in a World with No Credit

- You have no cash to wall off the effects of the next emergency.
- You do not have enough cash at any time to buy materials at better pricing levels, so the only way to be competitive is to not charge your labour.
- You have overdue debts and threats are mounting.

Wall 4: Sense of Collective Organisation is Weak

- You work alone because you fear competition and you have no leverage with buyers; you have never heard of cooperatives; the middle men will try to do everything to keep things that way and producers beat each other on price and get poorer with each sale.

Wall 5: A Degrading Environment

- You have little water but a lot of dry land with poor soils, you live high above the water table, so irrigation is impossible; fertility is going down fast, the evaporation rate is impossibly high and more of the topsoil gets blown away during the winds of spring.

---

[80]Harris, G., 2010. Breaking down the Walls of Poverty, TEDx Great Wall Beijing, *World without Walls*. May 20, 2010.

Exhibit 9: The Rural Business and Innovation Centre (RBIC).[81]

The RBIC will comprise of several sections:

(1) An open-door knowledge centre, printed materials/computer-based/instructional videos library open to all members. The knowledge centre will double up as an information centre for enquiries concerning the local investment environment, regulations, etc.

(2) A kitchen/lab for:
   (a) Experimenting with crops grown using more organic growing practices.
   (b) Experimenting with cash crop introductions adapted to local growing conditions.
   (c) Trialing design of finished food product development and branding to build a small business for a local entrepreneur/create jobs for local people at an established company.

(3) A training centre for would-be entrepreneurs and 'green collar' jobs.

(4) A showcase for renewable energy technologies.

(5) A microfinance service counter to provide financing for small-scale renewable energy technology investments, and more.

(6) An open area for technical training (agricultural, veterinary and green jobs) which will also be a venue for cross-disciplinary brainstorming.

---

[81] PlaNet Finance China, 2010. From Rural Isolation to Market Integration (Tongwei II). [online] Available at: <http://www.planetfinancechina.org/what-we-do/tongwei-ii> [Accessed December 6, 2010].

Part B

Introduction

New and Old Media

Yek Mobile is a high-tech startup created in Shanghai in 2010 with the objective of developing iPhone and other smartphone applications for advertising. It was founded by Zhijian Zhang, an engineer who returned to China following Postgraduate studies in the US. After meeting up with his high school friend Li Zhu, the two came up with the idea of a business that would leverage the growing demand for smartphone apps in brand marketing.

The company quickly gained a foothold in this promising market and has grown rapidly as a result. In the first instance, Yek's clients have been mainly fashion and luxury brands. But now its leaders have to decide which market to focus on in the coming years, taking into consideration their current clients, competitors and the market's growth potential. They are looking to move into digital marketing and must consider how to operate in this fiercely competitive segment.

The case follows the challenges Yek faces as its leaders develop the business model to respond to market forces. It looks at the specific challenges of growing a startup in China and provides a perspective on the conditions that inform innovation in China.

It is worth noting that two years after the original case, ESSEC students undertook a second project for Yek, this time looking at the company's opportunity for global expansion. This trajectory perfectly illustrates the rapid pace of development in China's high tech sector.

The second case in this section picks up the story of **StarryMedia** in 2012, another Chinese startup looking to make its mark in the high tech sector. The unique social media landscape in China presents an exciting opportunity for entrepreneur Brian Xin. After working in technology businesses in the US, Brian has moved back to China to create his own venture. His new company aims to leverage social media to provide marketing research, a relatively new and untested business model in China. But while Xin may be ahead of the curve in seeing the opportunity, his company faces a number of challenges.

The case tackles the problem of 'e-readiness' or how an advanced technological offer may not be a good fit for the market. It describes the innovative business model of a startup in China, and provides an insight into the government's policy toward entrepreneurs. It also continues the discussion begun in the previous case of Yek Mobile, about the nature of digital innovation in China.

In the third case, we meet the founders of **Mozat**, a plucky, Singapore-based game company. Following some early success in Saudi Arabia, they decide it's time to tap into the relatively uncharted market for mobile gaming in the Middle East and North Africa, navigating tricky cultural territory on the way.

When considering innovation in business, it can be easy to forget that not every company is part of the digital realm. Such is the case of **Priya Entertainments**, a successul Indian cinema company based in Kolkata. Founded in 1959 with a single screen, it has been a family business for three generations and now oversees six single screens and two multiplex theatres in West Bengal.

Its current managing director, Arijit Dutta, is dealing with a number of issues that are critical to the continued success of his business: The changing tastes of the local population, the cultural dynamics of the heterogeneous Indian movie industry, and the threat posed by the widespread availability of pirated DVDs.

As with each of the entrepreneurs featured in this section, Arijit Dutta must think of new and innovative ways to market his service in the context of people's fast-changing media consumption habits.

Chapter 4

Yek Mobile: Launching an Innovative High-Tech Startup in China*

Li Yan

*Department of Information Systems,
Decision Science and Statistics, ESSEC*

Yek Mobile is a Chinese startup in the mobile marketing business which was founded in 2010. It specializes in mobile application development for iPhone and Android devices. Recognised as one of the Top 10 Strategic Technologies for 2010 worldwide, mobile applications show a huge growth potential, with numerous companies striving to be present on this new advertising platform.

> "*The quality of the experience of applications on these devices, which can apply location, motion and other context in their behaviour, is leading customers to interact with companies preferentially through mobile devices. This has led to a race to push out applications as a competitive tool to improve relationships with customers and gain advantage over competitors whose interfaces are purely browser-based.*"
>
> — Gartner[1]

Nevertheless, it is not yet definite whether Yek Mobile will focus on mobile application development in the future, since the CEO is exploring other opportunities, such as digital marketing services or location-based services

---

*This case was prepared with the support of Vincent Boche, Kevin Guieu, Clément Janicot, and Vincent Vainunska, and with the collaboration of Capgemini Consulting and employees of Yek Mobile and its partners.
[1]Gartner Identifies the Top 10 Strategic Technologies for 2011, Gartner press release, October 2010. http://www.gartner.com/it/page.jsp?id=1454221.

(LBS).[2] Since Yek Mobile is moving fast on a promising market, the management team will have to decide which market to focus on for the coming years, given their current clients, their competitors and the market's growth potential.

About Yek Mobile

The name of the company is a tribute to Friedrich Hayek, the 20th century Nobel Prize-winning economist, whose liberal ideas are upheld by Yek Mobile team. Zhijian Zhang, the founding CEO (founders also include Li Zhu, Yek Mobile's Sales Director, and Bing Shi, Chief Strategy Officer), graduated from Peking University, also known as the Chinese Harvard. Zhang earned a Graduate degree from the Singapore–MIT Alliance (SMA) programme. After being rejected by US immigration to enter the US for further studies at Stanford University, he went back to China, where he started working for a large company. Two weeks later, his high school friend, Li Zhu, came to him with a business idea. Overnight, they decided to establish a company, which became the first firm co-founded by the two friends in the mobile industry (See **Appendix 1**).

Yek Mobile, their third company, was created in March 2010, with the objective of developing iPhone and other smartphone (mainly Android-based) applications for clients who want to advertise through this new channel. Since its inception, the company has grown rapidly. The company now has 25 employees (See **Appendix 2**), and will soon grow out of the capacity of its current office, only eight months after its establishment. Yek Mobile is located in the Incubation Center of the Pudong Software Park at Zhangjiang High-Tech Park in Shanghai, a selective office location with financial support from the Chinese government.

The startup has three main activities: Mobile application development, digital marketing services, and promotion through LBS as well as social network services (SNS). In terms of its value offering to customers, mobile application development aims at combining technology and creativity to engage end-users of retailers (Yek's clients) and provide a rich, interactive mobile experience. The digital marketing activity's objective is to promote clients' mobile applications, making more end-users install and use

---

[2]LBSs are information services accessible with mobile devices through the mobile network and utilising the ability to make use of the location of the mobile device (Virrantaus *et al.*, 2001).

the applications. The third business line, LBS and SNS, is less present in the business mix for the time being. Both services aim at helping retailers (apparel and fashion/luxury brands) boost their sales using cutting-edge technologies such as Augmented Reality (AR).

Yek Mobile's Clients

Yek Mobile's clients are mainly in the apparel industry. The choice to focus on this industry stems from the CEO's conviction that apparel and fashion companies are more prone to avant-gardism or innovativeness in their marketing strategies. In addition, they usually have large marketing budgets compared to other industries. It is also related to the founders' *Guanxi* (personal network) in the apparel industry.

Yek Mobile's first big account was Metersbonwe, the largest apparel company in China, boasting a network of over 4,000 stores. Yek Mobile provides Metersbonwe with a complete solution regarding their mobile marketing needs. First, they developed mobile brand applications to advertise Metersbonwe's different brands[3] on iPhone and Android devices. For instance, one application reports daily local weather and dresses models with Metersbonwe clothes according to the weather on the mobile screen. The brand's presence on this new advertising channel makes them look young and dynamic in the eyes of their customers, most of whom are fashionable youngsters.

Second, Yek Mobile developed a mobile store application for all Metersbonwe brands. The store is called Bang-Go[4] and is integrated with Metersbonwe's existing online store with the same name.

Finally, Yek Mobile is promoting Bang-Go websites (both mobile and PC Internet versions) through an affiliate network, placing advertisements for Bang-Go stores on websites, blogs and various applications. Through a tracking system in banner ads, Metersbonwe is informed of the sales made through Yek Mobile ads. In addition, Yek Mobile is utilising public relations efforts to promote Metersbonwe. For instance, they made the Metersbonwe application one of the two featured during the official launch of Wo Store,[5] China Unicom's[6] own app store (for Android and Nokia smartphones).

---

[3]Metersbonwe, Me & City and AM–PM.
[4]www.bang-go.com.cn.
[5]http://store.wo.com.cn.
[6]China Unicom is one of the leading mobile operators in China with 150 millions GSM subscribers.

Metersbonwe is thought to be a long-term partner of Yek Mobile for their mobile marketing needs.

> *"Mobile marketing is really customer-oriented. We know who is using the mobile so we have much more information about the customers. Thus, it is easier to launch communication campaigns that are well-targeted. Chinese people use their mobile a lot and many of our customers have a smartphone, so it is a huge opportunity for consolidating our business. Considering those facts, I think that mobile is the future of marketing."*
>
> — Min Jie, CEO, Bang-go.com and CIO & VP, Metersbonwe.

A new client for Yek Mobile is vancl.com, China's top online clothes seller, which sells its own products and distributes other brands. Yek Mobile will develop mobile applications and a Wap site (mobile commerce) to move vancl.com onto the mobile channel. Thus, Yek Mobile counts among its clients the largest online clothes store, as well as the largest apparel retailer in China. In addition to these clients, the startup is also working with Li Ning, a major sports clothing brand with over 8,000 stores, founded by an Olympic champion in China.[7]

Yek Mobile is also present in other industries, and one of its major clients is Remy Martin China, a French spirits company.

> *"At present, we rely mainly on SMS advertising as a mobile marketing strategy, but I think mobile applications are the future of mobile marketing. Our objective with mobile applications is to improve brand awareness of Remy in China. To do so, applications should be useful, funny and designed in a way that people will stick on using it."*
>
> — Honest Huang, Digital Marketing Manager, Remy Martin China.

Yek Mobile developed one application called Graffiti for Remy Martin (See **Appendix 3**). It is designed to be used at promotional events on iPads, where the customer takes a picture of himself and sends it to his friends with the Remy Martin event invitation attached to it. Remy Martin is also working with Yek Mobile on an application replicating a drinking game with dice, to be used in bars and pubs.

Yek Mobile's Revenue Model

Yek Mobile not only develops applications, but has also tried numerous business models since its inception. Along with development fees, the

---

[7] www.lining.com.

company is exploring a revenue-sharing model with some of its clients. This model is widely used in online advertising.

Application Development Pricing Models

Yek Mobile has two different revenue models for application development. First, it invoices its clients based on the number of hours forecast to be spent on the project (time-based pricing). In this model, Yek Mobile also charges maintenance fees each year, amounting to around 10% of the initial development fee.

Second, for the new client, vancl.com, it has introduced another pricing model, which is related to the number of application installations by customers (installation-based pricing). Each time a client downloads and installs the application, Yek Mobile gets a corresponding fee.

> *"I thought about shifting the pricing strategy to a more scalable revenue model because, after all, this is the way Bill Gates got rich!"*
>
> — Zhijian Zhang, CEO, Yek Mobile.

Revenue-Sharing Pricing Model

For digital marketing and mobile store development, Yek Mobile uses a revenue-sharing model with its clients, where Yek's revenue is linked to the sales achieved through the mobile store or ads on Yek's affiliate network.

Presentation of the Market

Mobile Phone Users

After a contraction in 2009, the worldwide mobile phone industry gained 21.7% growth in the first quarter of 2010, thanks to the progressive global economic recovery and the booming demand for smartphones (up 56.7% from Q1 2009).[8, 9]

As for China, the number of mobile phone users reached 805 million in June 2010, with a growth of 15.85% over the previous year, according to China's Ministry of Industry and Information Technology (MIIT).[10]

---

[8] http://www.palminfocenter.com/news/6470/worldwide-mobile-phone-market-grows-22/.
[9] http://www.palminfocenter.com/news/6460/global-smartphone-market-grows-57/.
[10] http://www.digitimes.com/news/a20100804VL200.html.

Among those 805 million users, 25.2 million (i.e., 3.1%) were using 3G smartphone devices, a constantly growing market in which the country will invest 120 billion Yuan (US $19 billion) in 2010, according to Zhang Feng, an official at MIIT.[11]

In most developed countries in Europe and North America, the mobile phone market penetration rate averages or exceeds 100%, meaning that some people possess more than one mobile phone. In these countries, replacement sales are the main growth factor. Innovative products such as smartphones represent the future of the market.

By contrast, in developing countries the market has a strong potential for growth. The mobile market penetration rate in China was only 60.5% in June 2010; continuous growth and fierce competition are therefore to be expected in years to come.

In China, Nokia dominates the mobile phones market, with a 47% share in 2009. But it is positioned in the low-end market, and smartphone companies' market shares are increasing at fast pace (See **Appendix 7**). Yek Mobile is currently focusing on iPhone and Android devices, representing 18% of the market. The iPhone, which is very expensive in China (US $735), is winning market share very rapidly (14% in 2009). Android phones are more affordable, and also show a steady growth.

Mobile Marketing

The Mobile Marketing Association (MMA) defines mobile marketing as *"a set of practices that enables organisations to communicate and engage with their audience in an interactive and relevant manner through any mobile device or network".*[12]

As mobile phones, especially smartphones, offer countless communication possibilities, they naturally became part of the marketing media. Marketers and companies try to attract new customers in several ways: SMS/MMS, Wap/mobile Internet ad banners and posters, Internet search (paid mobile Internet search listings), ad insertion into SMS, mobile TV, radio, and applications. In addition to these, mobile advertising innovations have recently appeared: quick response (QR) code scanning, mobile coupons, advertising through mobile social networks, dedicated smartphone applications, etc. (See **Appendix 6**).

---

[11] http://news.xinhuanet.com/english2010/sci/2010-07/20/c_13406639.htm.
[12] http://mmaglobal.com/news/mma-updates-definition-mobile-marketing.

The market for mobile advertising is very promising as it is relatively inexpensive. In the US, the cost per year for application development and agency costs averages $500,000, compared with the approximate $130,000 spent for a single 30-second network TV spot. Mobile advertising also enables countless innovations (tailor-made ads, LBS, etc.), and often has a viral effect. However, as of today, there are no effective metrics that can measure the campaigns' impact. Besides, issues regarding consumer privacy have been raised as mobile marketing is developing.

Recent forecasted data released by Informa Telecoms & Media indicates mobile advertising revenue will reach US $20 million by 2015. Much of that growth will come from India and China, giving Asia-Pacific 30.9% market share, while North America will register 18%, Europe 8.6% and Latin America 6.4%.[13] The mobile marketing industry is no longer in an experimental state. It is quickly maturing.

The Chinese mobile advertising market has changed considerably since Chinese operators launched 3G services in May 2009. Now, SMS advertising is still the most widely used mobile advertising method. It represented an estimated 40−50% of China's mobile advertising revenue in 2007. But, it is not about SMS 'spam' anymore.

> *"Unlike email marketing, the Chinese government has already officially banned SMS spamming since March 2008. The response rate to a pure push SMS campaign is also extremely low, at less than 0.1%.[14] However, push to a client's existing database is okay, and it is a great way to do CRM. The response rate is much higher in this case, usually more than 25%."*
>
> — Lucy Lee, Business Development Director at Phonevalley China.[14]

Along with SMS advertising, smartphone applications nowadays stand for the future of mobile marketing. They enable companies to reach directly the wealthy and educated part of the population, especially iPhone owners.

> *"People in China are receptive to the fashionable aspect of mobile phones. Possessing a smartphone is a way of displaying one's success, and wealthy Chinese are prone to pay quite a lot of money to acquire one."*
>
> — Min Jie, CEO, Bang-go.com and CIO & VP, Metersbonwe.

---

[13]http://www.mobilemarketingwatch.com/mobile-advertising-revenue-to-grow-tenfold-by-2015-to-24-1b-focus-on-china-india-11354.
[14]http://www.imediaconnection.com/content/24695.asp.

Yek Mobile is developing on iPhone because its users constitute a valuable market that shows great promise of growth in China. Besides, iPhone owners are good targets for Yek Mobile's clients such as Remy Martin,[15] whose customers are well-to-do Chinese who are likely to own a smartphone, especially an iPhone.

> *"In China there are a total of 7 or 8 million iPhones, of which 50% come from Hong Kong. iPhone and smartphone owners have much bigger purchase power. This is why we target them."*

— Honest Huang, Digital Marketing Manager, Remy Martin China.

Presentation of the Competition

Industry Chain and Mobile Marketing Agencies

The mobile marketing industry chain goes from the advertisers to the customers, through several intermediaries (See **Appendix 9**). Mobile marketing agencies can deliver three types of services:

- Conceptualisation of general mobile marketing strategies.
- Implementation of advertising and CRM strategies.
- Application development.

Yek Mobile is mainly involved in application development, but would also like to act more as a mobile marketing consulting firm in the near future.

There are four types of competitors for Yek Mobile in the mobile marketing field:

- Traditional marketing agencies.
- Mobile marketing agencies.
- Mobile application developers.
- LBS agencies.

Traditional marketing agencies have been a little slow in getting on the mobile marketing bandwagon. Agencies like WPP, Publicis, and IPG are now active in this market in China.

Mobile marketing agencies are the direct competitors of Yek Mobile. They propose mobile marketing solutions to their clients and develop the applications internally. Madhouse is one of the leaders in this market.

---

[15]Third cognac brand in China (20% market share).

Founded in 2006 in Shanghai, Madhouse focuses exclusively on mobile media and advertising.

"Madhouse is one of our competitors. They develop applications, but they outsource a lot. They could become clients of Yek for the development part."

— Zhijian Zhang, CEO, Yek Mobile.

There are numerous mobile application developers in China and the competition is fierce in this segment.

Augmentum is one of the leaders in the Chinese market. Founded in 2003, it now boasts more than 1,000 employees worldwide with four development centres in China. One of its businesses specialises in mobile application development. However, application developers are not really competitors of Yek Mobile as they do not propose marketing solutions but only develop applications for marketing agencies.

Similarly, there are very few LBS agencies in China currently, and they only compete with Yek Mobile in one segment: Location-based promotion and marketing. Bedo and Gypsii are two emerging LBS leaders in China, in a market that was estimated at US $80 million in 2007 (for LBS market in total, marketing LBS being only a small part of it). This innovative market is growing rapidly and fiercer competition is also to be expected. Yek Mobile is likely to be part of it.

Growth Rhythm of the Mobile Marketing Industry

In 2010, the mobile marketing industry in China is very competitive, with a lot of different players. Yek Mobile is one of numerous successful startups, benefiting from the huge market potential. Most brands in China do not have any smartphone applications or specific mobile marketing feature yet. But this situation may not last for long.

Research from Informa Telecoms & Media estimates that *"much of the future growth in mobile advertising will stem from movements made by big-name players such as Google and Apple"*.

"Successful companies that have unique and attractive technology for mobile advertising will become takeover targets for companies such as Google, Apple, Nokia and Yahoo."

— Shailendra Pandey, Senior Analyst with London-based consultant Informa.

Competitive Advantage of Yek Mobile on Every Single Market: Industry Price with Better Quality and Networking as a Way of Earning Contracts

Yek Mobile does not intend to boast lower prices than its competitors.

> *"We have prices at the level of the industry, but we provide higher standards of quality. The fact that we develop for iPhone also proves more valuable for our clients because it is more fashionable. But we still keep the price at the industry level. It is very important for us."*
>
> — Zhijian Zhang, CEO, Yek Mobile.

Yek Mobile proposes a cost per sales (CPS) revenue sharing model (See **Appendix 8**). They charge the client for the mobile application development part, within a fixed remuneration contract. A second contract is about the marketing activity. Once the application is launched, Yek Mobile gets a percentage of the sales made through the application.

Compared with its competitors, Yek Mobile also benefits from the tremendous social network of the two co-founders, both seasoned entrepreneurs who benefit from experience, business acumen and contacts with Chinese businessmen and companies.

> *"Fifty percent of our time is spent finding new clients. We target clients among the consumer brands and we use our social network. Having Metersbonwe as one of our clients is also a great asset in prospecting."*
>
> — Li Zhu, Sales and Business Development Director, Yek Mobile.

Every significant contract signed by Yek Mobile stands as a showcase and attracts new clients. Thus, in this industry, networking appears to be as important as devising innovative business models as a way to success.

Is Yek Mobile an Innovative Company?

Points of View of Two CEOs

Even at an early age, the Chinese are not encouraged to innovate. The educational system is almost fully test-oriented. The system is evolving nowadays; however, one or two decades ago, there was nothing about invention or creation in school education. It was only about learning, remembering and repeating. Thus, one should not be astonished about the way innovation is perceived in China.

The term *Shanzai* means 'mountain village' or 'mountain stronghold' in Chinese and is a direct reference to piracy. It is also a way of describing and characterising what innovation in China is. B2C (brought to China) and C2C (copied in China) are well-known jokes in the business world and are the terms that describe innovation best in a Chinese context. *"Copying what is done westwards"*[16] is a way of innovating by adapting to the local market. So in a lot of cases, innovation in China is not radical but something that is more incremental. But, is this real innovation?

Joseph Schumpeter is a pioneer in the analysis of how innovation is applied to the economy; he described innovation as *"the main engine of growth"*.[17] According to him, innovation is not an invention (radical) anymore but *"something that comes from the users' requirements. It is a bridge from users to technology, and from technology to users"*.[18]

The fact that innovation is now a multiple process requiring interactions between companies and customers is new for most companies. The best example is perhaps Google. Baidu is the Chinese Google, the copied one. How did it beat the worldwide number one search engine in China? The answer is quite simple: Baidu knows the market; it had and still has a better understanding of Chinese users' requirements. Even if it has the same design, there are some dramatic differences. Baidu has more promotional links and the language is different and more suited to Chinese. In fact, what is most interesting is that Google China often copies Baidu on these aspects in order to strengthen its presence in China.

That is how a new innovation process is taking root in China, which is called the 'ping-pong' conception of innovation. A first company, X, which is Chinese, copies a second one, Y, which is, let's say American, and adapts its concept or product to the Chinese market. But after that, Y will try to copy the innovations that X used to adapt the product to the Chinese market.

In China, currently there is an obvious lack of a legal system that can protect innovative companies in certain domains, such as new technology, for their inventions. As a consequence, companies have no motivation to invest money in research and development (R&D) because they will be copied very rapidly and they will not have the time to recover their R&D costs. In this sense, innovation is not rewarded in China.

---

[16]Min Jie, CEO, Bang-go.com and CIO & VP, Metersbonwe.
[17]An Introduction to Economics with Emphasis on Innovation, Pol, E Carroll P, 2006.
[18]XieDianxia, founder of www.iknowing.com.

"To make money in China, you have to be fast to the market. Innovation takes a lot of time and resources".

— Zhijian Zhang, CEO, Yek Mobile.

Technology companies such as Yek Mobile are afraid of being copied by other competitors; even their clients are worried that Yek Mobile may provide similar products or services to their competitors.

"Sometimes our clients are afraid to be copied; for example, we have signed with Metersbonwe a clause that stipulates that we would not work for their three most important competitors."

— Zhijian Zhang, CEO, Yek Mobile.

It seems to be the companies' duty to protect themselves with contracts in such a scenario. As soon as they have a creative supplier, they want it to be totally dedicated to their cause.

Moreover, one of the best ways to innovate in China is not by creating a new product but by thinking of an innovative business model and, of course, by adapting a brilliant idea to the Chinese market.

For instance, 360.cn is considered innovative in China because of its business model. It provides free antivirus software to everyone (it earns money through advertising), which is something that is totally new for the Chinese market. Of course, 360.cn is a copycat of software that already exists in Europe (Avast, for instance) but it is truly an innovative business model that has profoundly changed the Chinese antivirus software market.

The aim of Yek Mobile is to follow roughly the same strategy.

Yek Mobile's Way of Innovation, a Pragmatic Approach

Young and dynamic as it is, Yek Mobile is not radically innovative. However, the management team is fully aware of the dramatic need to be innovative in the future if they want to grow and be successful. The market on which Yek Mobile is evolving is highly competitive and will be even more so in the years to come. So, if Yek Mobile wants to survive and thrive, they must be innovative and should be able to differentiate the company from the rest.

Although not radically innovative, Yek Mobile is creative. The inspiration mainly comes from two sources. First, Yek Mobile's business is driven by its clients. Whenever a client asks them for something that is original, they are compelled to create it. Second, Yek Mobile uses quality brainstorming as a way of creation: Not only formal brainstorming in a meeting room, but also passive brainstorming which means that every single employee is encouraged to send to everyone what he finds innovative. This source of inspiration mainly comes from Western blogs. Yek Mobile is trying to develop an innovative business model inspired by what is successful in the West. For instance, the success of the company Foursquare is one of the reasons why Yek Mobile is trying to position itself in the LBS market. Once again, Western innovation is adapted to the Chinese market.

Yek Mobile also transforms and upgrades what it takes from the West. It is hard to call it only incremental innovation as Yek Mobile goes far beyond this. The management team does not simply copy an idea and adapt it to the local market but also makes some drastic changes and improvements.

For instance, Yek Mobile is the first application developer to use a game engine to upgrade the reality and user experience of its applications. A game engine is software that is used to create videogames, and could be either 2D or 3D. Yek Mobile used a 2D game engine to create applications for clients such as Me & City in order to give the user the impression that he or she is in a real city. Thanks to this application, the customer is able to wander in a London-style town and enter different buildings, check the weather, watch videos, and have an overall experience of what it is like to be in that place.

Three Strategies for Yek Mobile's Future

Considering all the aspects presented, the senior management has mapped out strategies to steer the company's growth in the future. During the first nine months since its inception, Yek Mobile did not want to limit itself to a specific field. To be able to identify opportunities, it wanted first to understand the market and the customer needs. After almost a year, it is definitely the time to make a choice. When Zhijian Zhang thinks of the present situation, he visualises three different possibilities to manage the activity portfolio. First, he can specialise only in application development. Second, focus only on marketing. The third is for the company to do both. At this time, it is hard for him to know which one is the best option and he is somewhat anxious about it. The consequences of his choices will have a major impact on the future success of his company. The organisation of the company, the type of people to hire, how much money to invest in as capital, and other factors, depend heavily on the strategic choices he is going to make.

Concentrating on Application Development

The first strategy is to position the company at the low end of the industry chain. From this perspective, Yek Mobile will only be a mobile application developer for iPhone, iPad, and Android. It means that they will have to let go of other activities such as digital marketing. Yek Mobile has already signed contracts to develop mobile applications for two prestigious Chinese firms, Vancl and Metersbonwe. With these names, it will be easier to convince other big companies to work with them.

> *"Yek Mobile could become the specialist for the development of high quality applications for big companies, particularly in the apparel industry."*
>
> — Zhijian Zhang, CEO, Yek Mobile.

Zhijian Zhang considers the main advantage of this strategy to be the tremendous number of potential clients. Big companies want to develop their own applications but most of them do not have the capabilities to do it in-house and will have to outsource. Zhijian Zhang also visualises having clients such as Western companies that would like to outsource the development of an application in China because the cost is much lower than in Europe or the US.

On the other hand, the competition in this segment is fierce, with numerous companies and even freelance students who are able to develop applications at a low price. Even if Zhijian Zhang trusts the skills of his employees and their capacity to rapidly create high quality applications, he is a bit worried about the competition.

Focus on Marketing

The second strategy is to focus on the high end in the industry chain of mobile marketing. In this scenario, Yek Mobile will be a marketing agency specialising in new media and mobile marketing. The company will completely stop developing applications. If a client needs an application to implement its new media marketing strategy, Yek Mobile will outsource the development of the application to third parties, while simply concentrating on the definition and the implementation of the marketing strategy. Traditional marketing agencies could become their clients since they tend to outsource tasks concerning new media because they do not have the capabilities in-house.

The main advantage of this strategy is that, in the marketing segment, the profit margins are much higher and the competition is less intense compared to the application development segment.

"The budget devoted to mobile applications is much lower than that of e-marketing in the vast majority of big companies. When we understood that, we thought that specialising in this market could be an efficient solution for our company."

— Zhijian Zhang, CEO, Yek Mobile.

When asked about the trends in the application development market, the answer is quite clear.

"The competition is stronger in the application development market; that is also a reason for us to move up the industry chain since we don't want to end up in price competition with application developers."

— Zhijian Zhang, CEO, Yek Mobile.

However, when the company was created, marketing was not its core business and the top management has more experience in mobile application development. Even if the competitors are fewer in the marketing segment, Yek Mobile will have to hire people who have a marketing background and let go of those engineers currently working in the application development department.

Application Development + Marketing

The last strategy is an intermediate solution. In this scenario, Yek Mobile will pursue its two main activities: The development of mobile applications and the implementation of new media marketing strategies. With this strategy, Yek Mobile will contact clients and propose mobile application development services, Yek Mobile's core expertise, which has already attracted prominent clients such as Metersbonwe and Vancl. Using this application development service as a door-opener, Yek Mobile's sales team will meet with potential clients. The team will then propose a package which includes not only application development but also mobile and Internet marketing services.

"In the end, we want to offer more value to our clients by providing them with a comprehensive solution — a packaged solution."

— Zhijian Zhang, CEO, Yek Mobile.

There are currently no companies that propose the same package on the Chinese market. The main advantage of this strategy is that it allows Yek Mobile to easily convince potential clients with their expertise in mobile application development and then to benefit from the high margins of marketing services.

On the other hand, what concerns Zhijian Zhang the most is that with this strategy, Yek Mobile will not be profitable on the application development segment. Indeed, application development is a service sold at a low price as an incentive for clients to do mobile marketing with Yek Mobile. The loss on the application development should be compensated by the high margins of the long-term marketing contracts. However, Zhijian Zhang understands the challenge of convincing clients to commit to long-term contracts. Still, Yek Mobile will have to invest in people with a marketing background if they decide to follow this strategy.

It is time for Zhijian Zhang to make a final decision.

Appendices

Appendix 1: Background of the Founders of Yek Mobile.

Zhijian Zhang: CEO, Serial Entrepreneur and expert in mobile app and game R&D.

- B.Sc in Electronics from Peking University in 2001.
- R&D Engineer for Alcatel Shanghai Bell and Microsoft China through 2001–2002.
- M.Sc in Innovation in Manufacturing Systems and Technology from Singapore–MIT Alliance (SMA) in 2003.
- Co-founder of Shanghai Mobile Creative Info Tech providing wireless value-added services (VAS) for cell phone users in China since 2004.
- Acquired and sold Zhejiang Mek Tech Info Tech Co. Ltd., through 2005–2009.
- Mobile Creative was acquired by a Chinese company in 2008.
- Co-founder of Yek Mobile in 2010.
- Eight years experience in leading the R&D team that develops 100 + mobile applications and games.

Li Zhu: VP of Sales and Marketing, Serial Entrepreneur and expert in marketing mobile applications.

- Co-founded Shanghai Xindong Info Tech Co. Ltd., (Service4Media.com) in 2001. The company was acquired by Index Group (Japan) in 2005 for US $40 million.
- Co-founder of Shanghai Mobile Creative Info Co. Ltd., 2004.
- CEO of Zhejiang Mek Info Tech Co. Ltd., from 2005–2009.
- Eight years experience in marketing mobile applications and games.

Appendix 2: Organisational Chart.

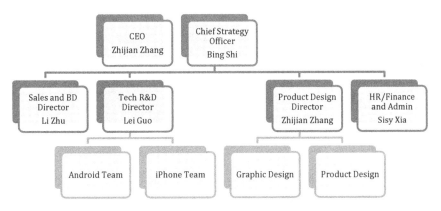

Appendix 3: Example of Application Developed for Remy Martin China.

Appendix 4: Repartition of Client Portfolio.

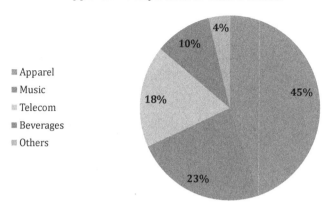

- Apparel
- Music
- Telecom
- Beverages
- Others

Appendix 5: Yek Mobile Cost Structure Analysis, First Six Months, in K¥.

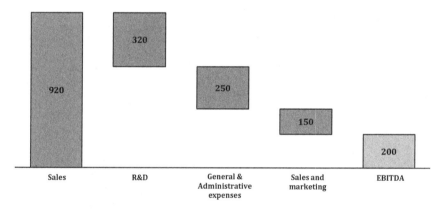

Appendix 6: China Advertising Industry: Circa 250 billion ¥ (from Research and Markets, 2007).

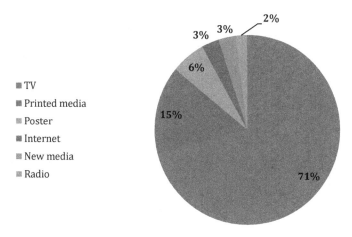

- TV
- Printed media
- Poster
- Internet
- New media
- Radio

Appendix 7: Repartition of Chinese Smartphone Market, 2009 (from Research and Markets, 2007).

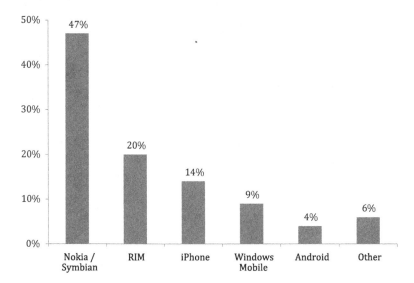

Appendix 8: Pricing Strategy of Yek Mobile (CPM: Cost per Mille/CPC: Cost per Click//CPA: Cost per Action/CPS: Cost per Sale).

	Mobile app development	Digital marketing service	Location based (LBS) Social Network (SNS) Promotion and Marketing Apps
Overview	• To combine technology and creativity to engage end user and to provide a rich, interactive mobile experience	• To market both clients' mobile apps and brands/products and services	• To help retailer (apparel and fashion/luxury) boost sales using most cutting edge technologies: LBS/SNS/Augmented Reality
Pricing	1. App Development Fee 2. CPA (cost per download)	1. CPM / CPC / CPA 2. CPS	1. CPS (cost per sales, revenue sharing model) 2. CPM / CPC / CPA

Appendix 9: Industry Chain, From the Advertiser to the Customer.

Appendix 10: Adaptation as Innovation (a Metersbonwe Shirt).

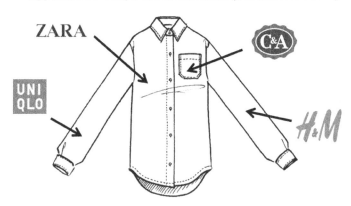

Chapter 5

StarryMedia: Bridging the Gap between Innovation and Market Needs*

Li Yan

Department of Information Systems,
Decision Science and Statistics, ESSEC

Brian Xin was comfortably settled in an armchair at StarryCoffee, drinking his latte as usual. He liked to sit there, taking a break and putting things into perspective. His wife had opened StarryCoffee a year ago, on the first floor of the building where his technological company, StarryMedia, was headquartered. Besides providing the employees of Zhangjiang High-Tech Park in the Pudong area of Shanghai with delicious meals and coffees, the café served as the perfect lab for Brian to try out the new features of his product. Brian Xin co-founded StarryMedia in 2009 with Tim Gong, a colleague of his whom he knew from a previous job at Linktone.[1] The two engineers had seen the potential of the Internet in collecting the data that netizens share and the value that such data could provide to businesses. Therefore, they had decided to develop the tools necessary to bring this huge opportunity to local merchants. In their late thirties, they left their jobs[2] to focus on this startup venture.

In 2012, after three years of technological development, it was time for StarryMedia to prove itself valuable, especially as the second round of

---

*This case was prepared with the support of Ana Aliyari, Alexandre Basbous, Sylvain Désille, Laëtitia de Larturière, and Marie Leport, and with the collaboration of Capgemini Consulting and employees of StarryMedia and its partners.
[1]Linktone is a provider of wireless media, entertainment and communications services for the China market.
[2]Appendix 1: Brian Xin's résumé.

funding was imminent and would determine the future of the company. The business model had already enthused many acquaintances who saw the real potential of the idea. However, the kick-start was not as smooth as expected, and Brian was thinking over the observations that both his Vice President of business development (BD) and Vice President of operations had reported to him: Their clients did not fully understand or appreciate the features StarryMedia provides.

About StarryMedia and Xingdian.com

StarryMedia before Xingdian

Brian thought back to how it had all started back in 2009. So much had been achieved and many decisions had reshaped the original idea into the current model of StarryMedia.

When he was working as the Chief Technology Officer for MSN China, Brian was struck by the fact that most information collected on user habits by the MSN search engine was not re-used, even though the analysis of such data could lead to great business opportunities. Thus was born the idea of online surveys: StarrySurvey. Do-it-yourself, and consequently low-cost, StarrySurvey was conceived to make marketing research easily available to SMEs and any individual wishing to use a free and efficient survey tool. In addition, users could join StarryPanel, a database of users to whom targeted surveys could be sent, based on their profile.

Xingdian as an O2O Solution

However, limited success of StarrySurvey and StarryPanel led the entrepreneurs to shift their development direction. In March 2012, StarryMedia finally unveiled its Xingdian platform, which was later followed by its mobile-based equivalent, Xingdian Life. Xingdian is based on the concept of O2O, meaning 'Online to Offline' or 'Offline to Online'.

A broad definition of O2O businesses can be summed up as purchasing products or services online and then consuming them in a brick-and-mortar store. It is different from traditional e-commerce since O2O does not involve the back-end logistics of delivering products to customers' doorsteps.

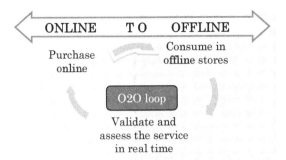

Generally speaking, O2O commerce bridges the gap between the physical and the digital world by creating an ecosystem that connects isolated retailers of goods and services to online platforms and tools so as to widen their access to end-consumers. For customers, they benefit from discounts, have access to premium services, and can discover new products. This type of O2O business has been very popular in China and is exemplified by Groupon. The company's success proved the potential of connecting Internet users to local brick-and-mortar services. However, Brian saw a major flaw in the Groupon model and other large vertically integrated e-commerce platforms such as Taobao, the Chinese e-commerce behemoth. The information collected on purchases made by end-users was kept by the e-commerce platforms without being shared with the retailers that were selling on the platforms. The data, which was jealously guarded, was then sold to manufacturers and marketing research companies at a steep price.

Right from the start, Brian was convinced that the future of O2O commerce was to create a mutually beneficial environment for merchants and end-consumers where the former would have access to the habits and patterns of online consumers' behaviour. In this way, merchants would be able to focus their marketing efforts based on consumer data analytics, while end-consumers would benefit from receiving advertisements and offers that would more closely fit their needs.

Xingdian from the end-consumers' perspective

Back to Xingdian: How did Brian design the value proposition for end-consumers and merchants?

Step1 Purchase the product or service on PC web or mobile phone

Step2 Receive a QR code for the purchase

Step3 Take the code to consume the product or service in the offline store or give the code to a friend as a gift

Step4 Review the product or service online and share shopping experience on social media websites

Step5 Collect digital stamps as a reward for purchase and accumulate enough stamps to redeem gifts later

Figure 1   End-consumers' Shopping Process on Xingdian.

End-consumers visiting Xingdian or Xingdian Life, either directly from the website/mobile app or landing there *via* external links, benefitted from discount coupons for services on a user-friendly platform. The fluid process a consumer follows on Xingdian is illustrated in Figure 1.

In addition to its pleasant interface, Xingdian had other attractive features for its end-customers. When they bought coupons on the platform, they could pay with pre-purchased "StarryPoints", avoiding the need to use a credit card or Alipay account for each transaction, making it quicker and safer. After the purchase, when the consumer went to the offline store to collect the product or service, the quick response (QR) code was easily verified at the retailer's outlet, thanks to the Xingdian scanner device that merchants had installed in their shops. Xingdian lent this device to them.

Xingdian from the merchants' perspective

Xingdian provided merchants with a complete end-to-end service that could be divided into four main steps:

- Merchants could promote themselves by initiating marketing and sales activities on the platform such as distributing coupons, launching flash sales and organising marketing surveys with gifts to respondents.
- They could share these specific actions instantly, with one click, to all their social networking sites (SNS) accounts in order to broaden their reach and communication.
- Xingdian is also a landing platform, meaning that all brands and Xingdian consumers can go directly to the platform to process their transactions.

- Along the transaction process, data on user behaviour and profiles are collected and added to a database. Merchants could leverage the advanced data mining tools embedded in the platform to monitor the progress of the marketing and sales activities, and to better understand their customers. To that end, merchants had access to a dashboard on their personal page on Xingdian. This dashboard would answer questions such as "How many coupons have been sold so far?", "How many respondents have answered the survey so far?", "What are the specificities of my customers on Xingdian?" The dashboard also gave precise information about the distribution of users depending on the different SNS they used to reach Xingdian.

Brian chose to position Xingdian with O2O businesses because this would help him to avoid dealing with the complicated and costly step of back-end logistics support. While the purchase was done online, customers had to personally go to the shop, either to collect their product or to consume it on the spot. Whatever the case, consumption and collection were always conducted by the customers themselves. That was why the first three targeted industries were the food and beverage industry, the lifestyle industry (beauty and personal care) and the entertainment industry (events and ticketing).

Xingdian's Revenue Model

Xingdian is in the early stage of business development (BD) to attract merchants to their platform and the sales team need more time to reach critical mass. They usually pushed for one-year contracts with the merchants they recruited. The deal did not involve any entrance fees for the merchants. This policy led to a revenue model based on the 'freemium' concept, where there were only three ways StarryMedia could generate revenue:

- By getting 5–10% of all merchants sales revenue on Xingdian;
- By making merchants pay a small fee when they required Xingdian's operation department to set up their campaigns or design their coupons on the platform; or
- By helping merchants develop e-commerce capabilities, which resulted in the integration of a selling tool on their website.

At the end of 2012, the third method was seen as a short-term solution to generate revenue. For the first method, the merchants' sales on the

Xingdian platform had not yet reached a fully satisfactory level. For the second method, the setup fee could only partially cover the operation department's expenses and could not be considered a sustainable source of revenue.

Xingdian's Internal Organisation

By the end of 2012, StarryMedia had 26 people under its employment (See **Appendix 6**), most of whom had worked hard on the technical development of the product and on improving the user-friendliness of the platform. Led directly by Tim Gong, they acted relentlessly to find new ideas for Xingdian and to cater to the needs of new clients. Tim felt that StarryMedia should keep its technological edge over its competitors. Besides the R&D team, the BD team had four members, led by Hai Tao, and the operations team had two members, led by Hai Yang.

The Challenges and Opportunities of the O2O Market in China

The Internet penetration rate in China had skyrocketed from 10% to 40% of the population, representing an increase from 111 million netizens in 2005 to 538 million in 2012, in absolute values. This upward trend is expected to continue. With regards to the O2O business, it is seen as a complementary part of offline shopping. The total amount of O2O business in China was RMB 100 billion (US $16 billion) in 2012, when it was estimated to be only RMB 56 billion (US $9 billion) the previous year. The investment of venture capital is following the same trend as the first 11 months of 2011; more than RMB 1 billion (US $160 million) had been invested into the O2O market.

This growth led the major players of the Internet market in China, Alibaba and Baidu, to invest massively in this sector. The O2O business in China is expected to skyrocket as its growth is closely intertwined with the success of mobile Internet, which is spreading rapidly across the country.[3] In 2012, mobile devices overtook home computers as the means to access the Internet, totalling 388 million users. Following this trend, mobile shopping was also taking off rapidly.

---

[3] *Chinese Internet giants see huge potential in O2O*; www.wantchinatimes.com.

Chinese Competitors in the O2O Sector

The mobile instant messaging application WeChat by Tencent had long adapted its strategy to the shift into the O2O business, as it already allowed businesses to communicate directly with their fans through its platform. Baidu had set up an online, location-based service that enables its users to locate the closest offline stores. This application was an extension of its map service and was expected to generate O2O revenue. Baidu's bet was that a richer map experience could expand both its customer base and its offline business base. But the O2O market in China was still dominated by Chinese startups like Dianping, Jiepang, Buding or Dingding, which provided users with O2O services and enjoyed a very large base of merchants in Shanghai. Take Dianping, China's leading local lifestyle platform, for example. Over the years, it had become a top-of-mind player on the O2O market for lifestyle coupons,[4] with over 40 million unique users in 2012. Thanks to a virtuous circle, almost all the major brands in the lifestyle sector were present on this platform, where they advertise their brands.

Chinese e-Shoppers

Today, several profiles have been identified to describe Chinese e-shoppers. According to a Bain Consulting study, we could describe four kinds of profiles: 'Bare minimum', 'digital leaders', 'value seekers' and 'old-school'.

- The 'bare minimum' makes up the biggest surveyed group (34%) and broadly represents users who surf but do not have enough income yet to spend online, such as students. They are to be closely watched as they will start spending online when they gain enough disposable income.
- The 'digital leaders' represent the second-biggest group with around 30% of those surveyed. Aged around 35-years-old, they are the users with the highest income among Chinese netizens (around US $5,500 monthly). What they want from online consumption is quality, convenience and service. As such, they are attracted by both renowned brands and good deals. They use Alipay, online banking and cash on delivery to pay for their online purchases.
- The 'value seekers' represent 20% of those surveyed and are a smaller demographic group compared to the digital leaders. They are younger (in their twenties) with less income. 'Value seekers' are mainly interested in

---

[4] *Dianping's mobile apps record over 40 million unique users*; www.prnewswire.com.

good bargains in cosmetics and clothing, which means that their decision is made according to price and word-of-mouth. Surveys show that their preferred platform is Taobao and they prefer to pay with Alipay.

- Those in the 'old-school' group (the remaining 16%) find online shopping complicated and somewhat dangerous. They spend a very small amount of money online (US $500 a year, on an average) and prefer to use their time shopping in a physical store with their family, regarding the activity as a form of leisure. The only way to increase their involvement with online shopping is to create confidence among them through the provision of well-organised platforms with easily definable products.

Given the glittering opportunity represented by online shopping in the early days, many companies jumped onto the e-commerce bandwagon. In time, the market consolidated and one e-tailer dominated the sector, Taobao, which was the first online platform that included multiple stores in China, and was considered the biggest retailer in the country. More products were purchased on Taobao in 2012 than from China's top-five brick-and-mortar retailers combined, making it possible for Taobao to reach the impressive figure of RMB 1 trillion (US $160 million) in revenue for the year. It boasted more than 800 million online products, of which 48,000 were sold per minute. Other e-tailers existed but they had to bridge the gap that existed between their services and the market leader's.

StarryMedia Faces Fierce Competition in Spite of an Innovative Value Proposition

The fragmentation of the O2O landscape made it difficult to identify StarryMedia's direct competitors. Considering Xingdian's activity as a whole, the combination of market research, marketing campaign management and O2O platform services is a unique proposition. However, taken separately, there are many features on which Xingdian can be challenged. Brian knew the uniqueness of the business would be revealed only when merchants adopted the complete end-to-end process of its value proposition. The real challenge was to find the right approach and marketing message to convince merchants to adopt the platform.

End-consumers

As an O2O platform, Xingdian.com deals with both the expectations of the end-consumers and those of the merchants. As of October 2012, Xindian had

200,000 end-consumers. Surveys had shown that consumers usually found Xingdian when searching on the Internet using keywords such as 'coupons' or 'flash sales'. As with any e-commerce platform, users would then assess the reliability of the website, how intuitive it is ·to navigate, the range of products, price positioning, convenience of delivery or consumption, geographical coverage and customer service. If the platform passed the test of being trustworthy and valuable, it was likely to attract consumers. Research had shown that the satisfaction rate for online shopping among Chinese consumers was high, with 85% of them saying that online buying was as good as or even better than offline shopping,[5] with 93.8% of first-time buyers becoming repeat buyers.[6] The remaining tasks for e-tailers were to attract consumers and win their loyalty by offering superior products and services.

Merchants

From the merchants' point-of-view, they were mainly interested in the short-term impact on the revenues brought about by an e-commerce platform. Thus, online presence to them meant gaining visibility for their brands and generating traffic for their stores. They conceived the Internet only as a complementary channel for sales and branding, apart from the brick-and-mortar points of sales. Many were not ready for the leap forward, and were resistant to launching 100% digital promotion campaigns or doing data-mining of consumer behaviours through online tools. Many Shanghainese merchants only started to try e-commerce at the end of 2010 through group-buying websites by offering coupons or vouchers.

When merchants were approached by StarryMedia sales people, the only thing they cared about was the sales volume through Xingdian, and they often considered it as another Groupon or Meituan, or an advertising platform. But Xingdian's features differ very much from the aforementioned platforms.

- Group-buying websites: Merchants often compared Xingdian to another group-buying platform such as Meituan, China's number one group-buying player, which was much bigger than Gaopeng (the Chinese branch of Groupon). But Xingdian didn't resort to the group-buying process as

---

[5]Bain & Company, *China e-commerce: Heading toward RMB 1.5 Trillion*, 2012.
[6]McKinsey Insights China, *Digital nation on the rise: Profiting from China's Internet revolution*, 2010.

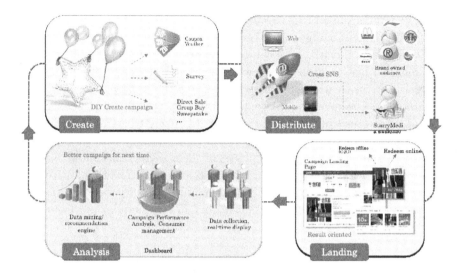

Figure 2　End-to-End Solution for Merchants.

it positioned itself as a self-service platform that offered a close-loop end-to-end solution for merchants to create, distribute and manage promotions, close deals and analyse consumer behaviour data (as shown in Figure 2). Xingdian chose not to go to the group-buying market, since the success of this market had proven to be very limited, as emphasised by the failure of Groupon in China. However, merchants didn't seem to understand Xingdian's advantage over group-buying websites.

- Advertising platforms: Dianping was the top-of-mind advertising platform, and many merchants had already done business with this Chinese startup. However, for Dianping, merchants had to pay to be ranked higher on the Dianping page, and they did not have full control of the management of their online campaign. Xingdian's advantage over this type of website was obvious: It was not just an advertising platform, but a much more comprehensive tool that empowered merchants to design, manage and monitor their own online promotion campaigns, and evaluate the results with sophisticated analytics tools provided by Xingdian. Again, merchants didn't seem to appreciate these features.

There was a lot of confusion in the minds of merchants about all these new methods of digital promotion and they preferred e-tailers with whom they could associate a simple and specific characteristic, such as Meituan for group-buying, and Dianping for online advertising. It seemed that the end-to-end solution offered by Xingdian was too comprehensive and too overwhelming for merchants to understand and too many features embedded in the platform had also blurred its core value. Furthermore, the self-service features on Xingdian required merchants to be sophisticated users of digital marketing and sales tools, which was not the case at all. The roots of this perception gap were crucial to the ongoing adoption of this innovative digital sales and marketing tool in the Chinese market.

Assessment of the Readiness of End-Consumers and Merchants to Adopt O2O

The Chinese had proved their interest in O2O deals. The 200,000 consumers that StarryMedia had gathered on Xingdian without much effort in just six months proved this trend. Price was once the determining criteria for O2O shopping. However, a trend has emerged to show that price, while remaining important in the decision-making process, was surpassed by the shopping experience. Chinese consumers conducted O2O shopping primarily for convenience and product assortment (62%), and not only for price (41%).[7] This trend had urged merchants to come up with more interesting product offerings and more value-added services. Xingdian was there to help match the end-consumers' demand with the O2O deals provided by the merchants.

Moreover, StarryMedia had engaged in mobile development since its early days, spearheaded by Xingdian Life. China is experiencing a massive adoption of smartphones, which goes hand-in-hand with the installation and use of many mobile applications. Smartphones provide users with ever-expanding possibilities in the fields of interactivity, geographical localisation, means of payment and coupon wallets, and this could be a decisive competitive advantage to businesses and, of course, to the success of Xingdian.

Assessment of the Readiness of Merchants to Adopt Digital Marketing Research and Campaign Management Features

Chinese merchants had expressed their interest in the online channel to attract new customers. Alick Zhou, the CEO of IPSOS China, confirmed that:

> *"Digital marketing in China is definitely a hot issue and the latest growing economic trend. However, the market is still very young and*

---

[7]McKinsey Insights China, *Digital nation on the rise: Profiting from China's Internet revolution,* 2010.

a lot of people have no sense and feeling for digital marketing research.
These are the challenges for StarryMedia."

The feedback from the StarryMedia sales team indicated that merchants generally signed a contract to join Xingdian for short-term consideration since it would generate more traffic in stores and increase sales volume. They did not consider the positive impact of learning how to take advantage of the DIY online marketing tools that would be useful in the long run.

Nonetheless, Mr Zhou from IPSOS China acknowledged that it was only a matter of time before digital marketing tools would be understood and adopted by merchants, and that China was on the verge of a web revolution that would disrupt traditional lifestyles.

The Challenge for StarryMedia

Even if time would invariably drive merchants to understand how they could benefit from the full potential of the digital marketing and sales tools, StarryMedia could not wait. Stagnation was a dead end for startups. Companies like StarryMedia had the opportunity to stand out because they were front-runners. Innovation was crucial, not only because it was the best defence against the threat of copycats, a common phenomenon in China due to weak regulations on intellectual property and patents, but also because it was a necessity to keep China's fast-learning netizens on tenterhooks.

Brian had received feedback from the sales team that it was difficult to recruit merchants because the number of end-consumers on the platform was not large enough, a fact also contributing to the inactive usage of Xingdian by existing merchants. Brian immediately thought of Taobao, the number one online shopping website in China, which managed to capture 60% of market share in just two years. Its strategy took into account the price sensitivity of online shoppers (no up-front fees, hard-discounted prices), which was the dominant factor in 2000. Taobao quickly reached a critical mass and created network effects by locking in a huge number of end-consumers and pulling in a huge pool of merchants at the same time. At this point, Xingdian was quite weak in the number of end-consumers, even though it boasted 200,000 users who had joined the platform without any specific marketing effort being launched.

A revolutionary idea needs daring early adopters in order to flourish. These market leaders pave the way for new innovations by setting a trend that is quickly imitated by more common users. StarryMedia needed the early adopters to set the trend. However, the benefits of StarryMedia's technological advancements and digital marketing tools would take time to materialise, while merchants were focused on quick results.

Currently, Brian's conundrum could be summed up as follows: Should his teams take more time to make existing merchants understand Xingdian's value proposition and to make them feel committed and satisfied with the platform first? Or should they first target the quantitative objective and place a priority on reaching a critical number of merchants on the platform to create network effects as Taobao did?

Brian finished his coffee, walked to the cashier with his smartphone, logged into his Xingdian Life mobile app account, and purchased one more latte. The waitress scanned the QR code and served him right away. He was always delighted by how easily it worked.

Restructuring the Team to Tackle the Problems

In order to tackle the current problems, Brian decided to shift the company's strategic focus from its original emphasis on technological development to BD and operations. Two new departments were created. The BD department would be responsible for quickly expanding the merchant network on Xingdian and they would be fighting as the pioneer soldiers in the field to conquer one merchant after another and occupy the market as much as possible. The Operations department would then take care of the merchants recruited by the BD department through day-to-day interactions to walk them through the end-to-end digital marketing and sales solution provided by Xingdian, to make sure that they understood everything they could achieve through Xingdian, to encourage them to actively use the platform, and to seek assistance whenever they needed it.

So far, the BD team had done a great job, having contracted more than 60 merchants, representing 260 stores in Shanghai in just three months. The objective was to reach 200 merchants for more than 500 stores by the end of 2013. The BD team had evaluated this objective using the following category system:

o T category = top-of-mind brands (currently 3–5% of the portfolio).
o A category = small, trendy chain stores (70% of the portfolio).
o B category = local stars (20% of the portfolio).
o C category = single stores.
o D category = others, and mainly e-commerce websites.

While the focus was on categories 'A' and 'B', 'T' was very much valued because securing contracts with brands such as McDonald's or Starbucks would immediately boost Xingdian in terms of visibility. Thus the objective was set to 10−15% of the portfolio for T-category brands. Yet, there were pros and cons from targeting these influential retailers. On the one hand, their popularity was likely to attract end-consumers and other merchants, creating network effects similar to Taobao's during its take-off stage. On the other hand, they were too big to pay attention to the other features available on Xingdian other than the selling platform, resulting in them not making full use of the solution.

The four sales people in the BD team divided the merchants as follows: One was in charge of merchants in the CBD Pudong area as a whole to leverage on synergies in this specific district. Another was responsible for beauty sector merchants in Shanghai. A third looked on the food and beverage sector in Shanghai to leverage the sector's synergies. Finally, there was the Vice President, who completed the team by focusing on the biggest brands. They organised their work, spending four days a week out in the field, guided by these grids. The method they used to approach merchants was to identify store personnel who showed an interest in Xingdian. They talked to the store manager and tried to arrange a meeting with a decision maker. Although each situation was different, the sales team noticed that high-level managers who had decision-making power were usually more willing to accept the Xingdian platform. In contrast, store managers were more reluctant to implement the system as they had been approached by many group-buying platforms and they thought this was just another one without understanding the uniqueness of Xingdian's offer. That could be quite an obstacle to the commitment of the merchants as it might result in store-level people being unaware of how to validate coupons using the Xingdian Scanner, as some 'mystery visits' had shown.

Once the contract was signed, the file was transferred to the Vice President of operations, Hai Yang, who was in charge of progressively educating the merchants on the features they might be interested in. Hai Yang would create an account on the platform for the merchant and email a short PowerPoint presentation to the merchant to explain the functions.

Currently, StarryMedia did not have a standardised process to communicate with the merchants. Thus it was sometimes unclear who was accountable for the relationship between StarryMedia and the merchants. There were also no fixed procedures in place to advise on how regularly the operations department should interact with merchants, what topics to discuss, how to assess the level of satisfaction of merchants and what to do to improve it.

The biggest headache for Hai Yang was that most of the merchants only used Xingdian as a platform to distribute coupons without trying out its more advanced DIY features (as shown in Figure 2), such as conducting marketing research surveys with their end-consumers, consolidating Web, mobile and SNS channels in order to distribute sales information, or leveraging the cutting-edge data-mining techniques provided by Xingdian to analyse consumer data in order to gain better insights. Without being aware of all the features, merchants could not see the innovativeness of the Xingdian platform, and would therefore only consider it as another Groupon.

Even if, during meetings they had with the salesperson before signing the contract, the merchants had received a detailed explanation of how the platform would work, they were unable to comprehend the features offered by Xingdian fully or were blocked by technical difficulties in usage. At the beginning, they would not hesitate to call StarryMedia for assistance, but their interest would wane as time went by. Furthermore, if they could not see the immediate results brought by Xingdian in terms of sales increase or improvement in online visibility, they might gradually give up on the platform.

Every month, Hai Yang would call the merchants and proceed to check on their use of the platform over the period. She used this monthly call as an opportunity to promote the Xingdian features that the client might be interested in. However, she often found the merchants too occupied with other matters to follow her through the process. Brian thought:

> *"The current business model would not be scalable. We have positioned ourselves to be a DIY platform, on which the support team would not need to intervene too much in the setup of promotions and the daily management of merchant accounts. We simply don't have the manpower to support merchants in this way."*

It seemed Xingdian had two major problems:

- The technological solution they offered was much more advanced than what the market needed. This explained why most of the merchants did not pay attention to most of the features.
- The DIY tools were not intuitive enough to be used by the merchants themselves without assistance from Xingdian. This explained why a small

group of merchants who were interested in trying the advanced features would weary and give up.

Brian and his team could spare no effort in tackling the second problem by carefully listening to merchants' concerns and improving the platform's ease of use.

But the first problem might be out of the team's control. History has seen a lot of good innovations fail, not because of technological issues but because of their bad timing to market: They were too advanced to be appreciated. Brian needed to think thoroughly if there was really a mismatch between what his company was offering and what the market needed. If there was, how could he bridge this gap? By trimming down the current features of the Xingdian platform into a simplified version to cater for what the market appreciated?

Brian had finished his second latte. There was no time to waste. He had to find answers to these strategic questions and point out a clear direction for his team to follow.

Appendices

Appendix 1: Brian Xin's Resume.

Education

- **Tsinghua University**: 1988–1996, China.
  Bachelor and Master's degree in Electric and Electronics Engineering and Biomedical Engineering.

Professional experience

- **StarryMedia (2009–now)**, China: Founder and CEO.

- **MSN China (2007–2009)**, China: CTO.

- **iKang (2006–2007)**, China: CTO.
  Pioneer in web medical management, equivalent of the US-based WebMD and United Healthcare.

- **Linktone (2005–2006)**, China: VP Technology.
  Provider of wireless media, entertainment and communications services in China.
  - Headed the entire technology department and business intelligence unit (LDC, web development headed by Tim Gong, mobile business)
  - Built the "Super Girl Show" project, 1st SMS-based voting system in China for the Chinese version of "American Idol".

- **Cadence (2003–2005),** USA: Member of the consulting staff.
  Number one in electronic-designed automation software.
  ○ Created an Open Access Database and built a standard for EDA Database.

- **Creation of Rival Watch (1999–2003),** USA: Co-founder and CTO.
  Provider of B2B intelligence.

- **Dactron (1996–1999),** USA.
  Startup specialising in industrial controllers using DSP (Digital Signal Processing) technology in San José.

- **ZTE (1996–1997),** China.
  The second-largest Chinese Telecom Infrastructure Provider.
  ○ Built the ISDN terminals.

Appendix 2: StarryMedia.com.

Appendix 3: Xingdian.com.

Appendix 4: Organisation Chart.

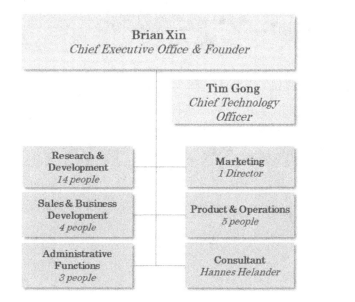

Appendix 5: Category of Xingdian's Clients (Merchants).

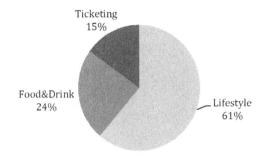

Appendix 6: Number of Netizens in China.

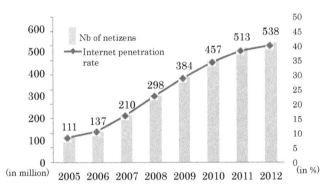

Source: CNNIC.

Appendix 7: Repartition of Netizens in China by Age (In Million).

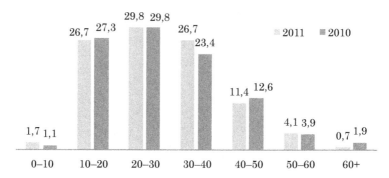

Source: CNNIC.

Appendix 8: Repartition of Netizens by Means of Access (In Million).

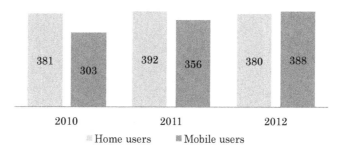

Source: CNNIC.

Appendix 9: Utilisation Ratios of Various Network Applications during 2010 and 2011.

Application	2011		2010		
	Users (10,000)	Utilization ratio	Users (10,000)	Utilization ratio	Annual growth rate
Instant messaging	41510	80.9%	35258	77.1%	17.7%
Search engine	40740	79.4%	37453	81.9%	8.8%
Online music	38585	75.2%	36218	79.2%	6.5%
Online news	36687	71.5%	35304	77.2%	3.9%
Online video	32531	63.4%	28398	62.1%	14.6%
Online games	32428	63.2%	30410	66.5%	6.6%
Blog/personal space	31864	62.1%	29450	64.4%	8.2%
Microblog	24988	48.7%	6311	13.8%	296.0%
E-mail	24577	47.9%	24969	54.6%	-1.6%
Social networking website	24424	47.6%	23505	51.4%	3.9%
Online literature	20267	39.5%	19481	42.6%	4.0%
Online shopping	19395	37.8%	16051	35.1%	20.8%
Online payment	16676	32.5%	13719	30.0%	21.6%
Online bank	16624	32.4%	13948	30.5%	19.2%
Forum/BBS	14469	28.2%	14817	32.4%	-2.3%
Group buying	6465	12.6%	1875	4.1%	244.8%
Travel booking	4207	8.2%	3613	7.9%	16.5%

Source: CNNIC.

Appendix 10: Uses of the Internet in China.

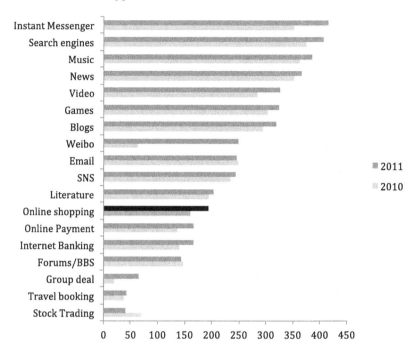

Appendix 11: A 9-Block Canvas[8] to Sum up Xingdian's Value Proposition.

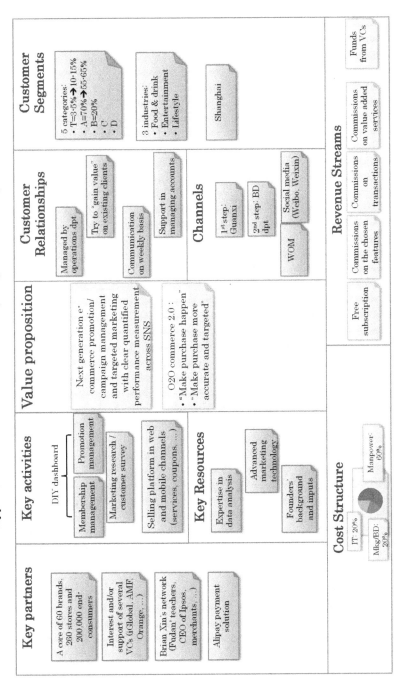

Key partners	Key activities	Value proposition	Customer Relationships	Customer Segments
A core of 60 brands, 260 stores and 200,000 end-consumers	DIY dashboard Membership management / Promotion management Marketing research / customer survey Selling platform in web and mobile channels (services, coupons, …)	Next generation e-commerce promotion/ campaign management and targeted marketing with clear quantified performance measurement across SNS O2O commerce 2.0 : • "Make purchase happen" • "Make purchase more accurate and targeted"	Managed by operations dpt Try to "gain value" on existing clients Communication on weekly basis Support in managing accounts	5 categories: • T=3-5% ➔ 10-15% • A=70% ➔ 65-65% • B=20% • C • D 3 industries: • Food & drink • Entertainment • Lifestyle Shanghai
Interest and/or support of several VC's (iGlobal, AMF, Orange, …)				
Brian Xin's network (Fudan' teachers, CEO of Ipsos, merchants, …)	Key Resources		Channels	
Alipay payment solution	Expertise in data analysis Advanced marketing technology Founders' background and inputs		1st step: Guanxi 2nd step: BD dpt WOM Social media (Weibo, Weixin)	

Cost Structure	Revenue Streams
IT: 20% Mkg/BD: 20% Manpower: 60%	Free subscription / Commissions on the chosen features / Commissions on transactions / Commissions on value added services / Funds from VCs

8 *Business Model Generation*, by Alexander Osterwalder et Yves Pigneur, 2010.

Appendix 12: A 9-Block Canvas on Merchants' Perception of Xingdian's Value Proposition.

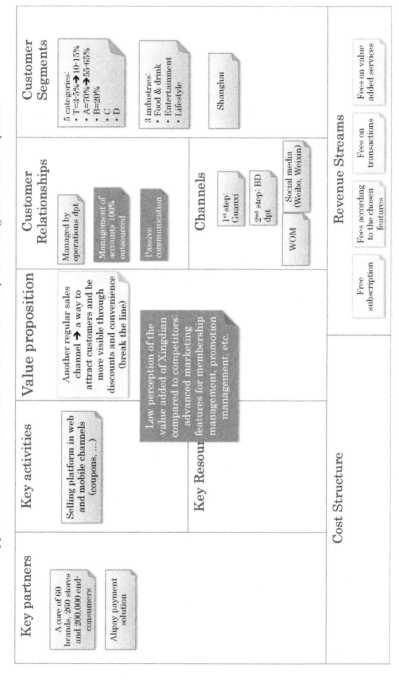

Bibliography

Atsmon Y., Dixit V., Magni M., Narasimhan L., and Wu C. McKinsey report, *2010 Annual Chinese Consumer Study, Digital Nation on the Rise: Profiting from China's Internet Revolution*, September 2010.

Chiu C., Lin D., and Silverman A. McKinsey report, *China's social-media boom*, April 2012.

CNNIC (China Internet Network Information Centre), *Statistical report on Internet development in China*, Jan 2012.

Doctoroff T. *What Chinese want? Culture Communism and the Modern Chinese Consumer*, May 2012.

Hoffman S., Lannes B., and Dai J. Bain report, *China e-commerce: Heading toward RMB 1.5 trillion, Can China earn its place as the world's largest e-commerce market?* 2012.

Osterwalder A., and Pigneur Y. *Business Model Generation*, 2010.

Walters J., Kuo Y., Jap W., and Hsu H. BCG report, *The World's next E-Commerce Super Power, Navigating China's Unique Online-Shopping Ecosystem*, November 2011.

Chapter 6

Mozat: Launching a Mobile Game in the Middle East and North Africa*

Li Yan

Department of Information Systems,
Decision Science and Statistics, ESSEC

In July 2013, after two years of running the game department of Mozat in China, Dr. Huang faced a major challenge: How to launch a new mobile game, Invader, in the Middle East and North Africa (MENA) region, independently from Shabik, a social platform that had so far been Mozat's core product. Until now, games developed by Mozat were integrated into Shabik, therefore representing a secondary role in the strategy of the 10-year-old Singapore-based mobile software company. Dr. Huang had a call with Dr. Yin, CEO and co-founder of Mozat, who gave him his views regarding how to generate more profit through the launch of an independent game. That could be the first step to diversifying the company's activities and changing its business model to boost its growth.

Becoming independent from the Shabik platform meant that Dr. Huang would be totally accountable for the success or the failure of the game. He had an engineering background, with limited experience in marketing and knowledge of the MENA region. Sitting in the meeting room of Mozat's office in China, Dr. Huang wondered how he could handle all these issues. How could a game become a success in the complex MENA region? Which countries and segments should he target first and which would be the best channels to promote it and maximise its profits? How could he leverage

---

*This case was prepared with the support of William Zoric, Julien Guery, Alexandre Guichard, Larbi Chraibi, and Côme de Las Cases, and with the collaboration of Capgemini Consulting and employees of Mozat and its partners.

Mozat's existing resources in the region? He had several options and his decisions would impact both the existence of his department and the company's future potential to grow.

Company Profile

History

Mozat was founded in 2003 by Dr. Yin and Dr. Tan, two former Chinese research scholars in Computing Science from the National University of Singapore (NUS). The young entrepreneurs had the vision that mobile devices would replace laptop Internet access and managed to convince several Asian venture capital investors to fund their project. In 2004, three years before the launch of the iPhone, Mozat started to develop a social network for mobiles, available worldwide, and it achieved unexpected success in Saudi Arabia and more generally in the MENA region. To seize the opportunity and accelerate its growth in this untapped region, Mozat allied in 2005 with Tajseed, a Saudi Arabia-based company that had strong connections with local telecom operators. Within a short time, Tajseed succeeded in closing an exclusive deal with STC, the leading telecom operator in Saudi Arabia, to launch the Shabik platform to their mobile users. The CEO of Tajseed, Faisal Saud, said:

> "*Operators were at that time 'gatekeepers'. They were key players that you had to deal with to break into the business of digital media and mobile applications. Operators enjoyed a privileged position because they had monopoly control over the market as there were no app stores then. The only way to promote an app and make it recognised was to work with them.*"

On the one hand, Mozat customised the application for STC, designed logos and convinced new operators to launch the application to their users. On the other hand, the operators were responsible for publishing the application. They were also in charge of billing activity by collecting money from subscribers and sharing the revenue with Mozat.

From 2007 to 2010, the startup experienced significant growth in the MENA market, expanding to other countries and closing deals with major telecom operators such as Vodafone in Egypt, Umniah in Jordan and VIVA in Kuwait and Bahrain. In 2010, Mozat also opened a subsidiary in Guangzhou, China, that was dedicated to the development of mobile games for the platform.

Current Situation

In recent years, the mobile communication market had undergone major transformations. With the boom in smartphones, app stores emerged and offered a new channel to app and content creators, therefore bypassing telecom operators as intermediaries. Such transformations in the market threatened the sustainability of the operator-oriented business model of Mozat. Consequently, the company had to find new ways to generate revenue and stimulate growth. They came up with three main projects. The first was to reposition the social platform in the MENA market in order to expand the user base. That project included the launch of the platform in Algeria, Iraq, and Oman. The second was the launch of a new social application called Deja that Mozat had developed alongside the commercial expansion of the social platform. The third one was the development of Invader, a new mobile game in the MENA region that would be launched independently of Mozat's social platform. The company had invested a lot of resources to develop this game, hiring iOS and Android developers as well as a team of three graphic designers. The subsidiary in China had been working on the game for more than eight months. Out of the three projects, Dr. Yin and Dr. Huang thought it was the one that could generate big profits in the short term and help the firm grow and reposition its offers in the MENA region.

Mozat's Products

In 2013, Mozat had three main lines of products (See **Exhibit 1**).

Shabik, a Social App Designed for Arab People

Shabik, the white-labelled social application for telecom operators, was Mozat's core product. It was available in English and Arabic, working on all mobile operating systems, with three main functionalities. First, it was a chat application that allowed users to engage with people around them with the same interests. Then, the application was linked to other social platforms such as Twitter or Facebook and information could be shared among different accounts. Finally, users had free access to in-house games. The social application had so far generated most of Mozat's revenues. In 2013, the Shabik platform had 16 million users worldwide with 700,000 paying users in Saudi Arabia, 450,000 in Egypt, 10,000 in Kuwait, 6,000 in Jordan, and 3,000 in Bahrain (See **Exhibit 2**).

Mozat offered the operators a fully customisable application to enhance their portfolio of products as well as increase their ARPU[1] in the process.

Deja, a Chat Application that Transforms your Photos into 'Smileys'

In the past year, Mozat had also developed a new application called *Deja* from the French expression *Déjà vu* (meaning 'already seen'). This application, available on Android and iOS, transformed users' photos into animated stickers. Users simply took a photo of themselves and a powerful algorithm would capture the unique facial features and create animated *Deja* stickers. Then, they could further customise them with a variety of eye and hair colours, face shapes, and much more to match their mood or their personality. However, the algorithm currently only worked well with Asian faces and Mozat intended to commercialise this application only in Southeast Asia initially. The long-term plan was to make the application work with Arab faces and add it to the social platform to improve its attractiveness.

Mobile Video Games

Games were the third and most challenging line of products for Mozat. Since 2010, they had been designed in Guangzhou under the responsibility of Dr. Huang, who was a former research scholar in computing science from NUS, like Dr. Yin. He had published a number of high quality academic papers and was recognised to be an expert in his field. So far, games had played a secondary role in Mozat's business as they were part of the social platform. However, they represented an alternative source of revenues through in-app transactions. Games were free but users had the possibility to buy digital items such as weapons, resources or lives in games. Mozat had experience in the field of mobile games. It had already launched several for the Shabik platform, the most successful one being *Ocean Age* 2. This game was the first one launched independently of the Shabik platform with a version in Arabic for Egypt and Saudi Arabia and another global version in English (See **Exhibit 3**).

---

[1] Annual Revenue per User.

Launch of a New Mobile Game: Invader

Concept and History

The Invader project was initiated in 2012 by Dr. Huang. This is a PvP[2] game on iPhone and Android that is similar to popular games such as Farmville (a farm simulation) and Clash of Clans (a successful strategy game), but was specifically designed for Mozat's core customer base, the MENA region. As a result, the game would be in Arabic and would take place in Ancient Egypt. The game targets young male adults who enjoy playing deep and time-consuming strategic games online with friends. Invader would be a free to play game with in-app transactions: Virtual items purchasable with real money. The game would be fully playable without spending a cent, but players would progress much faster when they purchased virtual items.

Dr. Huang came up with the idea of a brand new game when he saw the success of *Ocean Age* 2 on both feature phones and smartphones. Following the usual process of elaborating a new concept, he then asked his graphic designers to create a setting and character design that would endorse the Ancient Egypt context and appeal to Arabic players. At the same time, his game designers started to elaborate a game about battles and conquests. The game development process consisted of a lot of back and forth exchanges between Dr. Huang, the developers, the graphic designers and Dr. Yin, for each important feature. This lasted for several months and the game's commercial launch was scheduled for early 2014. The game would go through alpha and beta releases before the formal release, each iteration being improved by the previous version's feedback collected from testers.

Gameplay

Invader is a strategic game about conquering other people's cities on a large battlefield located in Ancient Egypt. The main goal is to invade as many surrounding cities as possible, attack other players to steal their resources, and keep progressing to higher levels to unlock new features.

The player starts with a small city and very limited resources. He can then start the city development by building several facilities: The town hall is the heart of the city, where warriors must be kept to defend the city

---

[2]Player *versus* Player, players fighting one another.

in case of invasions from enemies; the barrack is the warriors' 'factory', where the town population can be trained into different types of soldiers with specific skills; gold and crystal mines, from which the player would extract resources to build new facilities or create more soldiers. Other options become available after progressions, such as the customisation of a hero, the player's avatar that is a very powerful warrior with changeable weapons and appearance.

An important feature is the 'alliance', a system that allows the player to create partnerships with other players to exchange resources and back up one another in case of attack. This system is the core of Invader as it relies on the cultural trait specific to the region. As experienced in previous games, Arabic players would wholeheartedly play the game with their friends and defend them from enemy invasions, as a proof of friendship and brotherhood. A group of friends would team up and defend one another while expanding their reign.

The Strategy to Monetise the Game

As with *Ocean Age* 2, Invader is a free to play game that relies on in-app transactions for profit. Players purchase special gems with real money and the gems act as digital currency in the game. It allows players to buy various useful services, such as accelerating the process of warrior creation, having more weapons and uniforms to arm the hero, or more resources to advance in the game.

The game is designed to be playable without a single gem. But as with other free to play games such as Farmville, the progress will be significantly slowed down if no virtual items or services are purchased, adding a lot of pressure for those enthusiastic players to throw real money into the game. Several motivations would lead to the use of gems. The player might want to advance quickly in the game, as a solo gamer eager to discover more about the functionalities and to conquer even more cities. It could also be the player's wish to improve his hero's appearance, as uniforms and weapons would only be available through very hard missions or in-app transactions. There might also be pressures from friends, who would want the player to keep up with the progression of the alliance and contribute his share of resources.

This revenue model relies on gamers' addiction to the game and peer pressure from friends or alliances. If a player is reluctant to spend any money in the game, he would soon feel left behind by other players, who would have invaded his city and given him no chance to escape without purchasing strong warriors with real money.

Competition and Differentiating Factors of the Game

Some international and local companies published very similar games in the MENA region, competing directly with Invader. The most successful ones were Clash of Clans, Game of War and ممالك الأبطال ('Throne on Fire').

Clash of Clans was the first downloaded game in several MENA countries such as Saudi Arabia. It was designed by top iOS publisher SuperCell as "an epic combat strategy game". The game had almost the same features as Invader, the main differences being its graphic design and the absence of an Arabic version.

Throne on Fire was developed by Vekee Games Inc. It was by far the most similar game to Invader. Throne on Fire was "an online strategy game set in the fantasy world of medieval". Developed especially for the MENA market, it took place during crusades and it had a version in Arabic.

Other games such as Candy Crush and Angry Birds also competed for customers' time spent on mobile. Those games had been pushed by well-designed marketing campaigns. Therefore, Faisal Saud, CEO of Tajseed, wondered:

> "*Is there still a demand for a game such as Invader? Do people still want heavy games? The success of Candy Crush could mean that people are looking for simple things.*"

When asked how Invader was different from its very close competitors Clash of Clans, Game of War and Throne on Fire, Dr. Huang was very firm:

> "*Our game is different in that it is the only game where the player deliberately attacks another one, one that he may know in real life. It is particularly fun not to attack a stranger or the computer but your classmates or your colleagues at work. We think having the possibility to choose who to attack, create alliances and wage wars on other people will keep the players addicted and make them choose our game instead of the others.*"

Indeed, Invader had the differentiating feature to let the player find his friends (in real life) on the world map to attack them or to form alliances, whereas in other games, the player was only offered a random opponent or could only attack a computer-generated enemy. Having real people battling and trying to conquer territories would add more fun to the game compared to the purely computer-manipulated systems. Moreover, Mozat had implemented an in-game chat to enhance players' ability to communicate within their alliances. But no one knew if the end-users would be sensitive to these differences. The distribution and the communication strategies would be more decisive in the success of Invader.

Market Overview of MENA

The MENA region covers a territory extending from Morocco to Iran, including the majority of both the Middle Eastern and Maghreb countries (See **Exhibit 4**). In 2013, it had an estimated population of 370 million people, the largest countries being Egypt, Iran, Algeria and Saudi Arabia. There are two groups of countries in MENA. On the one hand, Gulf countries benefited from vast reserves of petroleum (60% of the world's reserves) and natural gas (45% of the world's reserves). On the other hand, countries such as Egypt, Libya, Algeria, or Tunisia suffered from high unemployment rates political instability and lack of resources. The region is much more economically and culturally diverse than it might appear. The Arab and Muslim world is indeed very unequal and complex.

Games in the MENA Region

The MENA region has been reported by many experts to be the leading emerging market for videogames. About 60% of the 370 million people in the Arab world are younger than 25, with about 70 million Internet users and over 300%[3] growth in this number in the last five years. What is more special about the MENA region is that most people there had their first experience of the Internet through a mobile phone instead of a laptop or a desktop PC. As a result, consumers are used to surfing the web and playing games on their mobile devices.

Mobile game development in MENA was often a strenuous battle. The video game industry in the area is still very immature, as shown by the lack of game publishers, a local game-developing community or financial investors. Global leading mobile apps such as Whatsapp or Skype have been banned from some of the key countries, making room for specifically

---

[3]Numbers from United Arab Emirates (UAE)-based entrepreneurship research portal Sindibad Business.

designed mobile apps and games for the Arabic market, with adapted content and language.

End users in the region are eager to play all sorts of games, and in the past years sports, games such as FIFA, Top 11 and racing games such as F1 have been the most successful genres. Card games and historical adventure games are also popular as long as they differentiate themselves by having storylines or artistic elements that look distinctly Arabic.

However, users are more and more sensitive to community-driven games that require active and real-time participation to deliver an enjoyable experience. Multiplayer and online titles have become increasingly popular in the Arab World and are part of the everyday life of young people. Being in a society where it is not so common to go out to a café and socialise, young people are seeking new ways to connect. This quest for communication and socialisation explains the growing interest in community games. Peak Games, a leading game developer and publisher in the region, has understood this inherent need to communicate among the Arab users and has consequently introduced card games, tabletop games and board games. Users are more inclined to spend money on social aspects such as private rooms and virtual gifts than to purchase in-game items. Therefore, the strategy of incorporating social features in games has proven to be very successful.

Cultural Sensitivity

The cultural and political diversity of the MENA region makes it a very difficult market to target. A methodological framework could hardly describe all the challenges game developers have to face in this region. Game designers need to be careful as the social and cultural guidelines are not consistent across countries in the Arab world.

However there is a clear set of common concerns most developers in the Arab world have to address. It includes self-representation and respect of religion and culture. Some basic values such as collectivism, honour and hospitality represent key components of Arab culture. Understanding these concepts, particularly the emphasis on modesty and honour, is essential for assessing contemporary Arab game production. Some developers have tried to do so by incorporating ethical and moral values into the characteristics of their heroes. Other designers have perceived games as a medium for communicating positive values and provoking cultural dialogue.

Cultural sensitivity in games is a very important concern to succeed in the MENA market. One does not need to be an expert in Islamic culture to know that sex, nudity, gambling, drugs, and alcohol are subjects to avoid. But sometimes, reality can be more complex, and game developers need to be very careful when approaching topics such as traditions and customs, family, workplace ethics, politics, and war as they represent sensitive topics that could easily be distorted in a game environment. Games such as *Grand Theft Auto: San Andreas* and *Darksiders* have been banned in several Arab countries due to sexually explicit and violent content. Other games such as *God of War* have been banned because they were not in line with Arab traditions and religion. More specifically, those games have been criticised for misrepresenting Islam. Their content is seen as detrimental to the image of God because God had been associated with war in the title.

To fight against misrepresentations of Islam and Arab people in games, an official game rating authority called the Entertainment Software Rating Association (ESRA) was established in 2010 in the United Arab Emirates (UAE) to evaluate and rate games based on their content and their compatibility with the culture, society and values of Islam. The rating was intended to ensure that games did not violate any Islamic traditions, according to the President of this association. Consequently, game designers have no choice but to embrace Islamic values and cultural norms if they intend to market their games in the Arab world.

Localising the Game, a Critical Step to Succeed in the MENA Market

Localisation is undoubtedly a key success factor for a game as it enhances the match between the game's features and the local culture. The success of a game depends on the delicate and precise consideration of the prevalent regional norms and values. The MENA market has always been a difficult market to penetrate as shown by many failures of international game developers and publishers that did not manage to adapt their games to the local culture and language.

There are significant opportunities in the MENA region for companies such as Mozat who could fill this void. And the only way to do it is to adapt the behaviour, language, music, and dialects to give the game an Arab touch. Peak Games' co-founder, Rina Onur, highlighted this point by saying:

> *"People want to see their national days, their special dishes reflected in these games. People who look like they're from the region, not just blonde with a cowboy hat."*

For instance, rather than celebrating Christmas or Easter, which have little relevance in the Muslim countries, the games could feature events such as Ramadan or Eid al-Adha.

Another way developers could seize the untapped opportunity is to draw inspiration from the history and tales of the region. According to Rhonda Zaharna, an expert in the MENA region and Islamic societies:

> *"The MENA region had one of the greatest reservoirs of storytelling in the whole world. All of the three main religions, and a number of massive books of mythology all came from that part of the world."*

The pre-Islamic and early Islamic period has contributed a lot to shaping the cultural heritage of the region. Legends and storytelling are part of the everyday life of Arab people and have built an exciting world of adventure, imagination and fantasy. Oral tradition is deeply rooted in Arab culture and poetry. It was passed on from generation to generation mainly because the narrator could embody the characters and engage in a true relationship with the audience: He could not only convey more emotions but manipulate the language to create verbal imagery.

However, localisation was not enough to succeed and publishers also had to build a strategy to retain users. Their activities went far beyond sales and marketing. As a consequence, investing in local support services and business development was critical in this market to create a loyal community and ensure sustainability.

Key Performance Indicators in the Mobile Game Industry

The success of a mobile game is measured by several key performance indicators, the most important one being the Average Revenue per User (ARPU). This data is easy to collect for operators but it is rarely disclosed or available for specific market segments. Besides, the ARPU includes both the monthly subscription fee and revenues from all the other value-added services (VAS) such as social platforms or games. A high ARPU does not always mean that users are eager to pay for games. As an average, it does not reflect the purchasing behaviour in some niche segments. For instance, Morocco and Iran have low ARPU in the MENA region (See **Exhibit 5**). However, these numbers are not representative of millions of people from the middle and upper class in these countries that could purchase expensive digital items. Other indicators need to be used together with ARPU to evaluate the mobile game industry.

When entering a new market in the game industry, it is not only important to analyse people's willingness to pay, but also to know the accessibility and stickiness of games. The overall smartphone penetration rate (See **Exhibit 6**) is good in the MENA region and has experienced double-digit growth for the last decade. The mobile game industry has grown alongside that of smartphones. Countries with a high smartphone penetration rate are generally those with high ARPU for mobile games.

Internet coverage (See **Exhibit 7**) is also very important when considering launching a mobile game: 3G networks are available in most of the MENA countries (apart from Iraq, where it is blocked by the government, and Palestine, Oman, and Iran); Gulf countries (Kuwait, Qatar, the UAE, and Saudi Arabia) already have 4G networks.

A single indicator is not enough to make a decision in the complex MENA market. Data about some countries could be very attractive whereas the real situation is not. Faisal Saud, CEO of Tajseed, noticed this about Egypt:

> *"It is a very interesting market because of its huge size. But the ARPU is very low, and the smartphone penetration rate is not so good either. You can only count on a potential market size of 20 million users over 90 million inhabitants."*

Another difficulty in launching a mobile game in MENA countries is that although the mobile game market has grown very fast in this region, the process has been unequal and countries have very different preferences (See **Exhibit 8** and **Exhibit 9**). When he looked at app store rankings, Dr. Huang realised there were only two games in the top-20 downloaded apps in Oman and Qatar whereas there were eight in Bahrain and 11 in Algeria (See **Exhibit 7**).

Dr. Huang was wondering which markets to target first. If his first priority was to generate profit quickly, should he put more emphasis on ARPU, the number of mobile users, the smartphone penetration rate or the attractiveness of mobile games in the specific country?

Key Distribution Partners

As the representative of Mozat, the game developing company, Dr. Huang was considering how to collaborate with other key partners in the

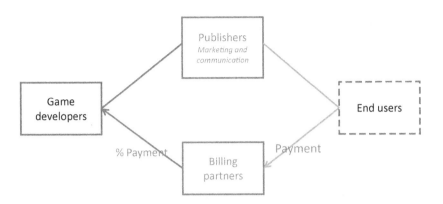

Figure 1   Key Players in the Mobile Gaming Industry.

mobile gaming industry in order to launch Invader in MENA countries (See Figure 1).

Publishers

In the game industry, it is the publisher who introduces the game to the market and takes care of its distribution and promotion. Sometimes game developers can publish their own games, but since a successful launch requires access to a large number of shops, media and channels so as to reach critical mass, the task is often delegated to publishers who are dedicated to this activity.

Despite the huge potential in the MENA mobile gaming market, very few international game companies have made this region their top priority. As a result, they simply publish their games in MENA countries without much effort to adapt the content to the local users. But the increasing popularity of smartphone and app stores has changed the market by introducing the new option of self-publishing a game and having access to a large user base.

Apart from international players, some local game companies have tried to address the growing demand from local users for games that reflect their daily life, traditions and culture, instead of playing Western-driven designs that would not necessarily fit Arab players' needs. This trend has led to the creation of several local game studios and publishing companies that take pride in designing games by and for Arabic players. However, their development is still at an early stage.

Mozat is one of those actors that has identified the untapped demand for mobile games in the MENA region. So far, it has addressed the issue of publishing games in an original way. It has partnered with telecom operators in the Middle East region to distribute its games. With their large customer base and ability to communicate with end-users directly through SMS, operators have great strength in these markets and have managed to raise awareness of Mozat's products with ease. For example, *Ocean Age 2* has more than 75,000 active monthly users.

With the rise of smartphones and app stores, operators are losing control of mobile game publishing and are being bypassed as the channel in this process. Therefore, Mozat has to adapt its strategy in partnership. Dr. Yin, Dr. Huang and Faisal Saud from Tajseed wondered if they could first publish Invader through app stores or partner with local publishers, with the goal of being a self-publisher in the long term. Indeed, Tajseed thought it had already acquired enough market knowledge and expertise to fully self-publish and market Invader.

Billing Partners

The billing partner is another key success factor for Invader as it would determine whether Mozat could get a high net payout from the game. The choice of the billing partner is particularly important in the MENA region where customers do not trust online payments and are not used to e-commerce.

So far, Mozat has been using Fortumo, an independent mobile payment solution, to take care of billing in its games. The solution was integrated into the game (*Ocean Age* 2) and when users bought online items, they simply had to confirm their phone number and Fortumo would check a list of partners (telecom operators) to see where to send the payment request. Operators confirmed the transactions and users received the goods. The users were charged on their monthly mobile bills and Mozat was paid at the end of the month. The strength of Fortumo is that payments go through the operators that the users trust. The weaknesses are that it guarantees a very low payout (about 40%) to Mozat. The rest of the revenue is shared by Fortumo and the operators, and that the solution is not available in several MENA countries such as Algeria, Iraq, Iran, Jordan and Lebanon. There are other independent mobile payment solutions such as PaybyMe and Centili covering other countries and proposing a better net payout to Mozat. If Dr. Huang decided to continue working with operators for billing, he could choose another solution.

However, telecom operators are not the only possible billing partners. With the growth in smartphone use, people have become more willing to pay on mobile devices, particularly young people. App stores (Apple Store, Google Play, and Windows Store) also offer payment solutions and give 70% of the revenue to developers. The net payout for Mozat would be higher with them. But app stores request users share their bank details and the Apple Store refuses alternative billing options such as direct carrier billing. As a result, iOS users would have no other choices to make payments.

Dr. Huang knew that no billing partners would fit all users' habits and that some countries or market segments would need several mobile payment solutions to maximise Mozat's net payout.

Communication Insights

New Media versus Old Media

Consumers' behaviour is evolving in the MENA region and people, especially teenagers, are becoming more and more sensitive to digital marketing campaigns. In countries such as Saudi Arabia, the UAE, Kuwait, and Qatar and even for some market segments in Morocco, Tunisia, and Egypt, social media has become an efficient way to promote mobile apps. Besides, the market segment targeted by Invader (young people with high ARPU) is highly connected and very receptive to mobile ads.

In the Gulf region, figures could be impressive.

- YouTube:

With an average monthly salary of between US $360 and US $3,600, an average age of 33 and 60% of them male, MENA YouTube users match Invader's main market segment. Moreover, the website has achieved great success in the region. In Saudi Arabia YouTube is currently the second most popular site (third in the UAE) based on a combination measure of average daily visitors and page views. It has a penetration rate of almost 85% in Saudi Arabia and 35% of people use YouTube daily.

- Facebook:

There are currently around 56 million active monthly Facebook users in the MENA region of which 28 million are daily users; 33 million are mobile users of which 15 million use it daily. In Saudi Arabia, a third of the 6 million Facebook users access it strictly through their mobiles. The main language used on Facebook in Saudi Arabia is Arabic, accounting for 90% of the content.

In the UAE, three out of five Internet users have a Facebook account. Facebook users in the UAE generate 2.7 billion page views each month, 69% of them are male, and they spend an average of 25 minutes on every visit.

• Twitter:

Arabic is the fastest growing language on Twitter. Saudi Arabia accounted for 30% of tweets in the MENA region. In 2012, there were 50 million tweets per month. The largest age group of Twitter users is 25 to 34 years-old followed by 18 to 24 years-old.

Mobile game developers have already used new media to promote their products. It is very common to create trailers with a simple but appealing story about the game to attract customers and to create Facebook fan pages dedicated to the game in English and Arabic, or a page with a direct link to the game in app stores.

Leverage Mozat's Resources and Customer Base

Mozat already has a customer base in Saudi Arabia, the UAE, Kuwait, and Qatar, thanks to Shabik and *Ocean Age* 2. Dr. Huang wanted to benefit from these users to test Invader and create a first wave of word of mouth. Some of his ideas included putting banners in other Mozat applications, offering special packages during the first week to reward the first batch of users, or giving more gems to the customers if they used several Mozat applications. He could also send direct emails or text messages to existing users. There were many bridges to build between the company's current products and Invader.

Concerns about the Communication Plan

Dr. Huang's main concern was how to create buzz around Invader's launch in order to push it into the top 25 in the app store rankings. The first week would be crucial for the future success of Invader as the number of people downloading it would determine where it would be published in app stores. Dr. Huang was aware that Mozat did not have as much experience in digital marketing as big publishers such as Supercell (publisher of Clash of Clans) and other competitors. He was not considering financial resources as an issue, as long as the campaign would have a visible impact on sales. About the marketing budget, the CEO of Tajseed explained:

> *"It will be more like doing some experiments on a small scale first and measuring their precise impact. The goal is to know exactly what is the result of spending $1 in TV ads, $1 in online marketing. The marketing budget will be set according to the observed results. It is a result-driven marketing plan. We will, for example, design two or three versions of banner ads. To figure out which one performs best, we will see the click-through rate and conversion rate of each banner. And after that, we will allocate the budget to the best design."*

Tajseed has tested this process for previous games by putting several TV ads with different numbers to dial to download the games. Thus, they could track how the customers learned about the game, and then focus on the most effective, improving cost efficiency.

Clash of Clans witnessed incredible success in Japan after Supercell decided to team up with GungHo, the Japanese developer of the successful game Puzzles & Dragons. The cross promotion allowed Puzzle & Dragons players who logged in Clash of Clans to get six Clash of Clans-inspired monsters to fight in the game. Each of the two games added features of its alliance into its own game. This alliance enabled Clash of Clans to rise from the 98th to the 11th in iPhone app rankings in Japan in only one month. But could Mozat convince such a big player to collaborate with Invader?

Before the launch of Invader, Dr. Huang needed to determine the partners with whom Mozat would publish Invader in the MENA region, which billing solutions to adopt, which features of the game were to be highlighted in the marketing communication, whether the messages should be different from one market to another, and what the best channels to reach the target users would be. And it was clear that he had to make the decisions quickly as Mozat was approaching the scheduled date to launch Invader.

Appendix

Exhibit 1: Mozat Products: Shabik, Deja, Invader and *Ocean Age* 2.

Screenshot from Shabik (social network)   *Deja (Chat application)*
Screenshot from Ocean Age (game)   *Invader (new game)*

Exhibit 2: Shabik's Subscriber Numbers with Collaborating Operators in MENA.

Country	Operator	Subscribers
Kingdom of Saudi Arabia	STC	700,000
Kuwait	VIVA	10,000
Bahrain	VIVA	3,000
Iraq	Zain	Yet to launch
Egypt	Vodafone	450,000
Algeria	Djezzy	Yet to launch
Jordan	Umniah	6,000

Exhibit 3: Data about *Ocean Age* 2 for Saudi Arabia, September, 2013.

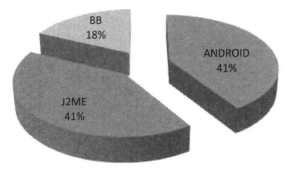

Operating System used by Mozat's current games users

- **Age range**: 15-45

- **Gender**: 90% are male, 10% are female

- 50% of the players are students

Exhibit 4

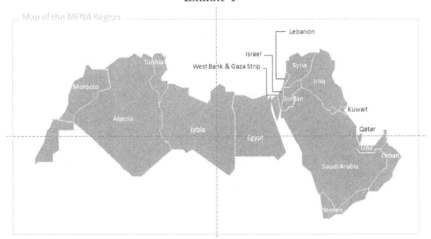

Exhibit 5: Economic and Demographic Data about the MENA Area (by Country).

Countries	Population	Under 15(%)	GDP (Nominal-billion) (USD)	GDP per capita (USD)	ARPU (End 2009) (USD)
Algeria	37,900,000	26.6	208	5,483	7
Bahrain	1,234,571	20.5	26	21,147	32
Egypt	84,550,000	31.0	265	3,131	6
Iran	77,176,930	N/A	549	7,112	9
Iraq	31,129,225	42.6	150	4,825	12
Israel	8,051,200	27.4	273	33,875	
Jordan	6,508,887	36.1	29	4,491	14
Kuwait	2,695,316	26.6	173	64,274	47
Lebanon	4,822,000	23.7	39	8,096	40
Libya	5,670,688	30.9	80	14,053	
Morocco	32,878,400	27.3	107	3,257	11
Oman	3,869,873	27.1	76	19,759	22
Qatar	2,035,136	14.4	174	85,423	35
Saudi Arabia	29,195,895	29.8	727	24,911	27
Syria	22,530,746	N/A	60	2,661	16
Tunisia	10,777,500	23.1	46	4,232	13
United Arab Emirates	8,264,070	16.8	359	43,434	36
West Bank & Gaza	4,293,313	0.4	10	2,329	19
Yemen	23,833,000	43.8	37	1,540	7

Exhibit 6: Smartphone Penetration in MENA.

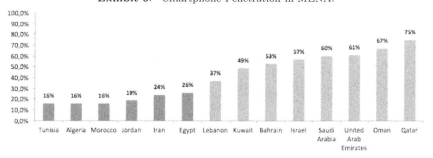

Exhibit 7: Data about the Internet and Gaming in the MENA Area (by Country).

Countries	Internet Users	Internet Annual Growth (5 yrs) (%)	Internet Penetration (%)	3G Network	Game in Top 20
Algeria	5,230,000	+8.36	13.8	December 2013	11
Bahrain	961,228	+40.03	77.9	Yes	8
Egypt	29,809,724	+29.71	35.3	Yes	7
Iran	42,000,000	+16.25	54.4	Limited	—
Iraq	2,211,860	+68.41	7.1	Yes (but not available)	—
Israel	5,313,530	+0.24	66.0	Yes	11
Jordan	2,481,940	+25.51	38.1	Yes	5
Kuwait	1,963,565	+21.53	72.9	Yes	6
Lebanon	2,152,950	+22.70	44.6	Yes	9
Libya	323,000	—	5.7	Yes	—
Morocco	15,656,192	+27.76	47.6	Yes	—
Oman	2,101,302	+62.68	54.3	Yes	2
Qatar	1,682,271	+56.84	82.7	Yes	0
Saudi Arabia	13,000,000	+22.57	44.5	Yes	5
Syria	5,069,418	+12.45	22.5	Limited	—
Tunisia	4,466,196	+22.51	41.4	Yes	9
United Arab Emirates	5,859,118	+18.09	70.9	Yes	4
West Bank & Gaza	1,512,273	+62.03	35.2	No	—
Yemen	3,691,000	+115.27	15.5	Limited	5

Exhibit 8:   Data about Strategy Games Downloaded in Several Countries (June 12, 2013).

Saudi Arabia, Algeria and UAE:

Grossing	Grossing	Grossing
Clash of Clans Supercell	Kingdoms of Camelot: Battle f... ▲7 Kabam	Clash of Clans Supercell
Game of War - Fire Age Machine Zone, Inc	Spartan Wars: Elite Edition ▲1 Tap4Fun	Game of War - Fire Age ▲2 Machine Zone, Inc
Airport City ▲7 Game Insight, LLC	Clash of Clans ▲1 Supercell	Battle Islands 505 Games (US), Inc.
ممالك الأبطال ▼1 Vexae Games Inc	Valor™ ▲1 Quark Games, Inc.	Spartan Wars: Empire of Hon... ▼2 Tap4Fun
لاء الحرب 2 Babil Games	World at Arms - Wage war fo... ▲1 Gameloft	Friendly Fire! Red Robot Labs Inc.
Lords & Knights - Medieval St... XYRALITY GmbH	Samurai vs Zombies Defense 2 ▲1 Glu Games Inc.	War of Nations™ ▲1 GREE, Inc.
Spartan Wars: Empire of Hon... ▲110 Tap4Fun	Battle Nations ▲1 Z2Live, Inc.	Knights & Dragons: Dark King... ▼1 GREE, Inc.

Egypt, Oman and Tunisia:

Grossing	Grossing	Grossing
Clash of Clans Supercell	Clash of Clans Supercell	Spartan Wars: Elite Edition Tap4Fun
Spartan Wars: Elite Edition ▲4 Tap4Fun	Fairway Solitaire by Big Fish (... Big Fish Games Inc	لاء الحرب 2 (new) Babil Games
The Hobbit: Kingdoms of Midd... ▲42 Kabam	Kingdoms at War A Thinking Ape, Inc.	Lies Of Astaroth ▼1 iFree Studio Limited
Game of War - Fire Age Machine Zone, Inc	لاء الحرب 2 Babil Games	Clash of Clans ▼1 Supercell
Kingdom Age Funzio, Inc	Plants vs. Zombies PopCap	Galaxy Life™: Pocket Advent... ▼1 Ubisoft
Kingdoms of Camelot: Battle f... ▼4 Kabam	Tong-itsXtreme (new) Automated Solutions Enabler I	Underworld Empire ▼1 Phoenix Age, Inc.
Airport City ▲24 Game Insight, LLC	Hotel Dash ▼1 PlayFirst, Inc.	Airport City ▼1 Game Insight, LLC

Exhibit 9: Data about Games Downloaded in Several Countries (June 12, 2013). Saudi Arabia, Algeria and UAE:

Grossing	Grossing	Grossing
Clash of Clans — Supercell	Star Warfare:Alien Invasion ▲80 — Freyr Games	Clash of Clans — Supercell
Candy Crush Saga — King.com Limited	Poker by Zynga ▼1 — Zynga Inc.	Candy Crush Saga — King.com Limited
Top Eleven - Be a football ma... — Nordeus	Candy Crush Saga ▲2 — King.com Limited	Game of War - Fire Age ▲6 — Machine Zone, Inc.
Hay Day — Supercell	IMPOSSIBLE ROAD (new) — Kevin Ng	Hay Day ▼1 — Supercell
Game of War - Fire Age — Machine Zone, Inc	Airplane! ▼3 — Quantum Design Group	Poker by Zynga — Zynga Inc.
Airport City — Game Insight, LLC	Zombie Tsunami ▼3 — Mobigame	Top Eleven - Be a football ma... — Nordeus
Road Riot for Tango ▲2 — TangoMe, Inc.	Air Traffic Controller 4.0 Lite -... ▲1 — C3 Software	8 Ball Pool™ ▲4 — Miniclip.com

Egypt, Oman and Tunisia:

Grossing	Grossing	Grossing
Candy Crush Saga — King.com Limited	Clash of Clans — Supercell	Spartan Wars: Elite Edition — Tap4Fun
Clash of Clans — Supercell	Candy Crush Saga — King.com Limited	Candy Crush Saga ▲6 — King.com Limited
Texas Poker ▲6 — KAMAGAMES LTD	Road Riot for Tango — TangoMe, Inc.	قناة العرب 2 (new) — Babil Games
Diamond Dash ▲27 — wooga	Dragon City Mobile — Social Point	Real Racing 3 ▼2 — Electronic Arts
Kingdom Age ▲7 — Funzio, Inc	Castle Story™ — TeamLava	Top Eleven - Be a football ma... ▼1 — Nordeus
GT Racing 2: The Real Car Ex... ▼3 — Gameloft	Fairway Solitaire by Big Fish (... — Big Fish Games, Inc	Lies Of Astaroth ▼3 — iFree Studio Limited
Game of War - Fire Age ▲3 — Machine Zone, Inc		Hay Day ▼2 — Supercell

Chapter 7

Priya Entertainments: From Scripts to Screens in East India*

Arijit Chatterjee
Management Department, ESSEC

In March 2013, when the income statements of his nine exhibition halls started coming in, Arijit Dutta, Managing Director of Priya Entertainments, felt that the time has come for a few hard decisions. Since 1990, when Dutta took over the family business, Priya Entertainments has grown substantially from owning and operating a single-screen cinema in Kolkata to becoming a significant regional player in the film industry of the eastern Indian state of West Bengal. In the last five years Dutta has opened five new cinema halls, including two multiplexes. However, the profits of several cinema halls are meagre considering the whole range of operations that keep them running. Except for a few halls, profit margins are not very high. Occupancy rates are too low to recover the high establishment costs in time. On the other hand, the domestic film industry grew by 23% in 2011–2012. The Bengali film industry has also been showing signs of a revival and steady growth. The number of movies produced tripled betwen 2006 and 2012. Arijit Dutta understands the urgent need to find innovative solutions to save his cinema exhibition business. Closing down a few halls is an option but he is reluctant to take such a drastic measure before trying to increase revenues, or reduce costs, or focus on the large untapped population in rural Bengal.

*This case was prepared with the support of Alexandre Juvin, Pierre Labat, Claire Pinot de Villechenon, and Lila Sumino, and with the collaboration of Capgemini Consulting and the employees of Priya Entertainments and its partners.

The Indian Film Industry

History

In 1896, a year after their first private screening of motion pictures, the Lumière brothers came to Bombay with their cinématographe. In the following years, short documentaries and recordings of plays were made by Hiralal Sen, Harish Bhatavdekar and Ramchandra Torne. The first full length Indian feature film, *Raja Harishchandra*, was directed and produced by Dhundiraj Phalke in 1913. In the early years of Indian cinema, pioneers such as Jamshedji Madan, Raghupati Naidu, Rajnarayan Dube, R. L. Khemka, and Dwarakadas Sampat launched their production houses and cinema theatres all over India. Ardeshir Irani directed the first Indian talkie *Alam Ara* in 1931. Starting in the late 1940s and in the 1960s, Indian directors began making critically acclaimed movies that won awards at international film festivals. Among the directors who made movies in this genre are Satyajit Ray and Ritwick Ghatak. Directors who made movies for a larger audience included Guru Dutt, Raj Kapoor and Bimal Roy.

Beginning in the seventies, we see Indian films mixing song and dance, action and melodrama, comedy and tragedy, and casting popular stars in one single movie with great commercial success. This formula, which would later define the identity of Indian films, also came to be known as the Bollywood (a portmanteau of Bombay and Hollywood) movie. Indian cinema borrowed freely from ancient Indian epics, Sanskrit drama, folk theatres, music genres, and techniques from Hollywood. In the year 2000, film-making in India was given the status of an industry. Film-related activities could now attract 100% foreign direct investment. With new avenues for financing film-making now available, older investment channels became redundant. International joint ventures such as DreamWorks–Reliance and Disney–UTV Motion Pictures became common. With institutional finance becoming more accessible, the various activities in the film production process are now managed professionally. New training institutes, well-managed studio services, and sound recording studios have cropped up all over the country.

Size and Reach

India leads the world in movie production with more than 1,000 movies per year (for cross-country comparison, see **Exhibit 1**). India also accounts for almost half of the cinema tickets sold in the world with a peak of four billion entries in 2006.[1] In the United States, for example, 1.5 billion tickets were sold in the same year. However, there is a lot of headroom to grow if productions per capita are considered. Growth prospects are also huge considering the number of screens per capita: India has 12 screens per one million inhabitants, whereas the corresponding figure for the United States is 117 screens[2] (**Exhibit 2**).

Indian films and film stars have a huge fan following at home and abroad, not only among the Indian diaspora in the USA, Europe, Australia and New Zealand, but also among the local populations of South Asia, South East Asia, West Asia, and North Africa. Madhu Kishwar notes: "In Afghanistan, after the fall of the Taliban, one of the first acts of celebration noticed was the sight of people queuing up outside cinema halls to see Bombay films".[3] If star performers such as Raj Kapoor were popular icons in post-war Russia, Amitabh Bachchan continues to be admired in West Asia and beyond, Rajnikanth has achieved cult status in Japan, and Shah Rukh Khan has his die-hard fans in today's Germany.

In 2011, after two years of decreasing revenues, the Indian film industry reported year-on-year growth of 11%. 2012 was an even better year. Revenues grew by 21%, generating close to US $1.9 billion. It mainly came from cinema tickets sales (83%), followed by cable and satellite rights (11%) and ancillary revenues[4] (5%) while 8% of theatrical revenues came from abroad. Home video revenues, however, have decreased mainly due to piracy and the growing power of new media. A few years ago, Hollywood films had 5% ticket sales but that has grown in recent times to about 8.5% because of globalisation, availability of dubbed formats, the growth of the English speaking population, and multiplexes. Indian film industry revenues are expected to reach US $3.3 billion by 2017 (a CAGR of 11.5%) largely outpacing the worldwide film industry growth.

Main Players

The biggest Indian player is Eros International with US $165 million revenue in 2011[5] and an IPO of US $80 million. Eros is in the business

---

[1] UNESCO Institute for Statistics, January 2013.
[2] Deloitte, *Media & Entertainment in India.*
[3] http://www.indiatogether.org/manushi/issue139/idea.htm.
[4] Ancillary revenues include the internet, mobile and new media revenues.
[5] Eros International Plc, *Preliminary Financial Results for the 12 months ended March 31,2011.*

of Bollywood movie production and distribution. Eros is also expanding in music publishing and TV broadcasting. Apart from focusing on a domestic market that is booming, Eros is also expanding in international markets and Indian communities worldwide. In 2011, 34% of total sales were international. National players, such as Inox, Reliance, and PVR, usually integrate their distribution and exhibition functions. Many are expanding from their historical Hindi movie market to markets of other regional language films. Regional players, such as Priya Entertainments, are smaller companies that primarily cater to a regional language market. They are also more flexible and reactive to the market. For instance, they can negotiate movies they will be screening on a case-by-case basis while larger competitors need to comply with their nationwide programs.

Different Languages and Territories, Regional Cinemas

With more than 18 official languages (**Exhibit 3**), one cannot speak about an Indian cinema. There are as many as 15 different Indian cinemas. Among those, the biggest are Hindi (Bollywood) with 45% of the market, Tamil with 17%, Telugu with 15%, Malayalam reaching 10%, and Bengali cinema with 1%.[6] Those cinemas are closely dependent on their geographical territories and, as a consequence, distribution in India is split between six domestic territories (plus one territory labelled as overseas). **Exhibit 4** shows the number of movies produced per year in the Bengali, Hindi, and Tamil film industries. The market shares do not reflect the number of people speaking the language or the quality of the movies as measured by the number of awards won. Tamil cinema, for example, commands 17% of market share, even though only 7% of Indians speak Tamil and this cinema has received fewer prizes than Bengali movies.

The Value Chain

The different aspects of the business in the film industry are best understood by the production–distribution–exhibition value chain. The producer finances and organises the logistics of the entire film project. The producer then licenses the theater screening rights of the film to a distributor in one or more territories in the market on various terms. Finally, the exhibitor

---

[6]ICRA Management Consulting Services report for the India Brand Equity Foundation.

buys the prints from the distributors on various terms and runs the shows in cinema halls in a territory.

The producer assigns the rights in favour of distributors for certain considerations. Typically, the producer keeps the rights of his movie for non-cinema revenues. The distributor plays a key role in mediating a deal between the producer and the exhibitor and is often at maximum risk from both the end parties. The relationship between the producer and the distributor ranges from a minimum guarantee model (where the risk is borne by the producer) to an outright sale model (where the risk is borne by the distributor). The different deals mainly depend on the fame of the producers and the potential of the movie. For a new movie, with unknown directors, actors and producers, the movie will usually be sold on an outright sale model. For an anticipated blockbuster, the producer will therefore rather give a commission to the distributor (from 5–15% according to the Bengali distributors) than sell him the film.

The distributor licences the theatrical rights of the films to the exhibitor. In the theatre hire model, the exhibitor collects the entire box office takings, net of entertainment tax. Risk, in this case, is borne by the distributor. The exhibitor retains a fixed amount and hands the balance to the distributor. Many single screens follow the renting system. In the fixed hire model, the distributor receives a fixed amount per week from the exhibitor, irrespective of the film's performance at the box office. Risk is borne by the exhibitor. In the revenue share model, the box office takings, net of entertainment tax, are shared between the distributor and exhibitor according to a pre-agreed ratio. This is the most commonly practiced deal in recent times, especially in multiplexes. The risk of box office performance of the film is shared between the two.

The Bengali Film Industry

Situated in the eastern region of India, West Bengal is the fourth most populous state in India. The official language is Bengali. Kolkata, the capital of West Bengal, was the former capital of India and is considered as the 'cultural capital' of the country. The Bengali film industry is an influential regional film industry in India. It is particularly known for its art films.

History of the Bengali Film Industry

In 1897, films were shown for the first time in Kolkata. It only took a couple of years for Bengali film sequences shot with bioscopes to get introduced in regular theatres. Jamshedji Madan, a Parsi entrepreneur, laid the foundations of the Bengali film industry in the late 1890s. Madan invested in the entire value chain of film-making and film-watching. In the 1920s, The Madan Company had a virtual monopoly in the cinema of Bengal. The first full length Bengali feature film, *Billwamangal*, was made in 1919 and the first talkie in 1931. In the same year, B.N. Sircar established New Theatres studio that went on to create a new benchmark in the Bengali film industry. Sircar faithfully adapted well-known literary works, produced Hindi, Urdu, and Punjabi versions of his Bengali films, and achieved an all-India presence.

War-time investment in films provided a major boost for the Bombay film industry. Production budgets soared five times along with the payments that were made to 'star' actors. Meanwhile, the partition of India in 1947 destroyed the market of Bengali movies as East Pakistan came under international trade laws. Yet, the 1950s marked the success of the parallel Bengali cinema that progressively gained more and more recognition in India and all around the world in the 1960s and 1970s. Work of renowned film directors such as Satyajit Ray, Ritwik Ghatak or Mrinal Sen fall into this category. A wider impact was that of Bengali love-stories. These romantic dramas with the star pair of Uttam Kumar and Suchitra Sen gained wide acceptance among rural and urban audiences.[7]

The Bengali film industry went through a prolonged slump in the 1980s and 1990s. Parallel cinema gave way to films for the masses. Movies were mostly copies of Bollywood commercials, but with tiny budgets. Cinema halls preferred to screen Hindi movies and households took to viewing television at home. No one watched Bengali movies outside of Bengal. During this time film-makers like Anjan Chowdhury made formula films for the masses. Often these films depicted the ordeals of the domestic servant or an honest police officer fighting for the poor.

Bengali Industry Today

In the middle of the 2000s, Bengali cinema experienced what can be called resurgence. New directors came on the scene with their sensible yet commercially successful blockbusters. Examples include Anjan Datta's *Bong Connection*, Anik Datta's *Bhooter Bhobishyot*, or Srijit Mukherji's *Baishe Srabon*. New cinema technicians and new producers willing to

---

[7]Sharmistha Gooptu, *Bengali Cinema: An Other Nation*, Roli Books, 2010.

experiment also played their part. Parambrata Chatterjee, a well-known actor, thinks that in the earlier days Bengali film directors only considered film-making as a form of art:

"I do think they were slightly moved away from the real picture... they were less aware. I would say they were less concerned about the commercial aspect of cinema. I think our generation today, people like Anik, people like Srijit, people like Moinak, people like me, people like Birsa, people like Raj Chakrabarty... all of us... we are very conscious of the economics. We do not want to make films which will be watched by a few *connoisseurs*. You will have to be on the case of giving your producers back the money that they spend. I think the so-called commercial and art house divide has been bridged."

After 2010, the Central Board of Film Certification registered around 110 Bengali films made each year, a number that is still growing. Five years ago, around 40 movies were made in one year (**Exhibit 4**). This trend illustrates the so-called resurgence of Bengali cinema compared to other regional film industries that are not developing as fast. Bengali cinema now accounts for 9% of overall Indian certified films, twice its contribution of 4% in 2006. Mahendra Soni of Shree Venkatesh Films attributes this success to "credible technicians, able directors, visionary producers, and a commendable pool of actors ready to experiment".

However, more than the quantity of films produced, Bengali cinema has always been known as a regional Indian cinema in terms of quality, having won the Best Feature Film of the year 22 times (1953–2012) and the Best Director of the year 17 times (1967–2012), since the time these awards were constituted.[8]

The global revenue of the Bengali film industry was valued at about US $28 million.[9] Of this, contribution of cable and satellite is estimated to be about US $6.5 million in 2010. When it comes to the average budget of a Bengali movie, figures vary between US $10,000 and $350,000.[10] Marketing costs are much less than a typical Bollywood movie, where the production cost has reached US $1.3 million on average.[11] Regional movies in India are seldom dubbed or subtitled. As a result, the audience of Bengali films

---

[8]http://en.wikipedia.org/wiki/National_Film_Awards.
[9]http://www.financialexpress.com/news/regional-riches/733355/0.
[10]Deloitte report: A Symphony of Art 2012.
[11]Website http://bollywoodcountry.com.

is limited to the Bengali speaking population comprising about 90 million people.[12]

Bengali films made in India can also rely on the millions of people who reside outside of India but speak Bengali (**Exhibit 5**). However, the Bangladesh government forbids the import of Bengali films made in India into Bangladesh. The 150 million Bengali-speaking people of Bangladesh remain out of the purview of the Bengali film Industry. Arijit Dutta notes,

> "Their films are not allowed here; our films are not allowed there. It would have been good for both the industries. Their films would have done well in our C, D, and E centres... our films would have done well in their A, B centres... but they want a reserve forest. I had spoken to Member of Parliament Ansaruddin Sams when we were at the North American Bengali Conference in Los Angeles. He had agreed. Present Bangladesh government had also removed the ban, but the amount of backlash they got the Bangladeshi film industry... they had to withdraw it within one day. But their movies will be profitable in our C, D, E centres. They don't understand that. They don't understand if you play tennis with a better player your game will improve."

Type of Movies

Movies made in the Bengali film industry can be broadly classified into two main genres. The first category of films can be called *masala* movies. They are generally action-comedy films, which resemble Bollywood movies, but made with a smaller budget. These films show non-realistic stories, where one hero fights tens of enemies, the lead pair dances on the streets, and comedians tell explicit jokes. The average length of the film is two-and-a-half to three hours. Like Bollywood movies, elaborate song and dance sequences may appear between two action scenes. The success of these films is generally linked to the reputation of the actors and the music in the films. Parambrata Chatterjee notes,

> "I have nothing against mainstream films. People often tell me that you are the poster boy of Bengali alternative films, what Dev or Jeet are for mainstream films you are for alternative films. I don't mind that. It does give me a very loyal fan base but often I find it very hard to make people understand that I do not have anything against mainstream films. I do not have anything against songs in films. I like picturisation, elaborate

---

[12]http://www.census2011.co.in/census/state/west+bengal.html.

action sequences. I like songs, elaborately done songs... but they have to be original, they cannot be copies."

The other genre can be labelled as urban art films. Closer to foreign cinema in content, they depict realistic plots with good content and suspense. The length is the same but less time is dedicated to songs. Dance sequences are rare, if any, and songs weave into the story itself. Success is generally driven by the talent of the director and the cast, but also by the quality of the plot itself. The average audience for that kind of film is urban, primarily in Kolkata and its suburbs. Parambrata Chatterjee notes that a very wide section of the audience "still go into the theatre thinking that they might take home something more than just the popcorn and just some thrills on the screen". Yet, one can sense exasperation in the remarks of Anik Dutta, director of the hugely successful *Bhooter Bhobisyot*. Dutta thinks that there exists in Kolkata, especially in some elite academic circles, a culture of worshipping the obscure and the esoteric. Some of his friends, he says, looked down upon him because he directed a popular movie. Some bask in inverted snobbery and take pride in their box office flops.

"There exists a huge schism between the urban and the rural," says Arijit Dutta. "No urban pictures run in the districts. Any film that probably has a little bit of urban sensitivity in it does not run in the villages. We still don't know why. They do not even run in tier 2 cities such as Durgapur or Asansol or Siliguri. We have given up on it." Referring to a recent release, he points out that while it is running full houses in the single screens and multiplexes in Kolkata, there were only ten people in a Siliguri auditorium on a Sunday. Referring to this urban–rural divide, Parambrata Chatterjee notes that there must be a market for all kinds of movies:

"Think about the international scenario... you make a film like *Casino Royale* or *Skyfall* or *Spiderman* that releases in some 50,000 theatres all across the globe. You also make a film like *Moonrise Kingdom* and it is released in 300 theatres all across the globe. That also makes money because it is made with 10 rupees and is made to recover 15, whereas Spiderman is made with 100 rupees so that they can earn back 200. There has to be a market for different kinds of things. I will not deny the urban−rural divide. I don't see any harm in that honestly because again I do not expect everyone in the US to go and watch a *Moonrise Kingdom*... he would rather go and watch the Spiderman 3, so we see this everywhere."

Decades ago, however, some genres of Bengali movies used to do well in the city as well as in the districts. Arijit Dutta notes,

> "With the excess of colour, the dancing, the overseas shootings, excessive drama, perhaps the tastes have changed in the districts. Families do not go to see films probably because of the lack of quality hardware in the theatres in the villages."

The Exhibition Crisis in the Districts

Urban areas

Cinema halls within Kolkata city are traditional single screens. Multiplexes are increasing rapidly in the city but are also being built in the suburban areas as business and residential zones are developing in the areas surrounding Kolkata. Those areas attract investors since the costs are still low. Promoters seek to build shopping malls in future residential areas before their competitors. Multiplexes are inside those shopping malls: Entertainment business is needed to attract more customers. In return, multiplexes benefit from the crowd coming to the mall.

A traditional single screen in Kolkata has an auditorium with 800 seats whereas multiplexes can be composed of, on average, four auditoriums with 200 seats in each. The number of films showed in a day is much higher in multiplexes. Urban customers are the main targets of sleek art movies with social messages. In urban cinema halls, 60% of films exhibited are Bengali movies, very few of them being commercial. This number is lower, around 20%, in suburban areas as competition from Hindi and Hollywood movies is higher. Bengali art movies still appeal to families coming altogether during night slots or weekends. Among a literate and educated audience, the success of the movie highly depends on critics in newspapers or cinema magazines.

Urban customers can afford higher ticket prices than in the districts. Prices range from INR 70[13] in a single screen, and from INR120 to INR 270 in multiplexes. The ticket rate depends on the type of film, the time slot, the day of the week and the category of seat. Ticket prices for Bengali films are lower because of lower entertainment tax (2% *vs.* 30% for the other movies). In Priya Cinema's Bioscope multiplex in Rajarhat (a fast growing new city in the east of Kolkata), for instance, ticket prices vary

---

[13]In 2012, US $1 was INR 54.

from INR 130 to INR 150 on weekdays (there are two categories of seats) for Bollywood and Hollywood movies, whereas they cost INR 100 to INR 120 for Bengali movies.

Rural areas

19 districts compose West Bengal and 68% of its population is rural.[14] While the service industry is the largest contributor to the gross domestic product of the state, agriculture and industry are the leading activities in rural areas. Theatres in those areas are mainly single screens with a capacity of 700 to 1,000 seats. The infrastructure can vary from one single screen to another. Some cinema halls can be very old with scratched or broken seats and little maintenance. Others are similar to cinema halls in urban areas with air-conditioning and push-back seats.

Exhibitors do not always own the theatres. They often rent an existing cinema hall *via* Public–Private Partnership (PPP) contracts with local institutions. Those infrastructures owned by municipalities are mainly community centres that contain not only cinema halls but also conference and exhibition rooms. Thus, it is possible to have an additional stake in other businesses such as cultural events and conferences. Up to 15 or 20% of the revenues can come from conference rooms, meeting rooms and other facilities.[15]

Single screens in rural areas are mainly in agriculture-based districts surrounded by villages where cinema is nearly the only leisure that people have outside of their home. People may come to town from 10 km away to watch a movie. It is not possible to show a film too late in the evening because people would not be able to go back home, as few of them own a car and the rest rely on public transportation. There are usually three shows per day: 12:30, 15:30 and the last show of the day starts around 18:00 hours.

Hindi and Bengali commercial movies are the most successful in rural single screens. Bengali commercial movies account for 80% of movies shown. Hindi movies account for 15% and Hollywood movies (5%) are often dubbed in Hindi. Customers look for entertaining content and their idols on the screen. Compared to urban cinema halls, the atmosphere is full of whistle and applause during the film.

---

[14]Census of Population 2011.
[15]Data from Bolpur cultural center of Priya Entertainments.

Due to the low income of rural customers, it is not possible to price the tickets the same way as in an urban area. The prices range from INR 35 to INR 40, usually unchanged through the week. The price can be lower in cinema halls without air-conditioning. Dutta remarks, "This is a reason of low profitability of single screens in districts." However, raising prices seems difficult in such areas where income is already low and price sensitivity makes a big difference. Single screens in districts have the advantage of being the primary leisure of the local population. Nevertheless, they face declining profits. The causes of this paradoxical situation include high competition and declining interest in the content of the films. The manager of a single screen in Memari, a town in Bardhaman district of West Bengal, said,

> "In the districts, even commercial Bengali films have reduced their audience. Maybe there are too many theatres. Before a commercial Bengali film used to run in 50 screens, now it runs in 150. The audience is consequently split between different screens. Maybe we need a change of the positioning of commercial Bengali films. It cannot be less commercial but the presentation has to change. Cultural events are more or less successful in the districts."

There are initiatives coming from cinema clubs and associations that organise film festivals in the districts on various themes. The objective is to gain people's interest in art movies. For example, Priya Entertainments manages a cultural centre in Bolpur, a town in Birbhum district. Film festivals in Bolpur are particularly successful among students of the nearby Visva Bharati University.

Priya Entertainments

History of the Company

Founded in 1959 by Arijit Dutta's grandfather, Priya Entertainments is a three-generation family business. It all began with Priya Cinema, the flagship single screen of the company, located in south Kolkata. The company soon extended its activity to production and distribution under the entities of Purnima Pictures and Piyali Films respectively. Meanwhile, it began managing other exhibition centres in the districts of West Bengal. In the 1990s, both the distribution and exhibition activities were gathered under the banner of Priya Entertainments Private Limited (PEPL). Purnima Pictures has not produced a film since the 1980s. PEPL manages six single screens in the districts and two multiplexes under the brand name of Bioscope (See **Exhibit 6**).

Today, Priya Entertainments is a significant regional actor in the industry. Its flagship single-screen, Priya Cinema, has gained a strong reputation and is the best reference for Bengali cinema in Kolkata. Whenever a distributor wants to have a Bengali film exhibited, he wants it to be released in Priya Cinema. Moreover, the premieres of the most important Bengali art films often happen there. As Mr. Sunith Singh, from the distributor AUM Moviez recognises it, "Priya Cinema is part of the Bengali culture." This reputation gives Arijit Dutta strong negotiating power as a key exhibitor in West Bengal when dealing with distributors. Dutta has developed exceptional relationships with several important directors, actors, producers and distributors. Moreover, Priya Entertainments manages the largest number of single screens in West Bengal.

Type of Management

One of the competitive advantages that Priya Entertainments has over its national competitors, Inox, Reliance, or PVR is that, as a regional chain with lower scale, it can benefit from hands-on management. This advantage is all the more significant in the exhibition activity. PEPL can afford to hire fewer employees for maintenance because it does not have to abide by the standards of the national chains. Managers of local theatres can directly refer to the head office.

Mr. Dutta personally pays regular visits to the different cinema halls. All major decisions are made by him. For instance, distributors must negotiate directly with Mr. Dutta if they want the cinema halls of Priya Entertainments to exhibit films. Personal bonding in the industry is very important. Dutta recognises that he does not exhibit the biggest Hindi films because he is on bad terms with their distributor:

> "I have not exhibited his movies for the last 14 years. Even if I lose some money it doesn't matter. If I lose 10, I know he will lose 50 because I own Priya Cinema, two multiplexes, and in some places, I am the only one who has a cinema."

Dutta notes that the film industry is one of those industries where deals are seldom written on paper: "If someone comes and confirms a film which is to be run three weeks down the line, once I have said yes, even if a bigger picture comes, our commitment stands to the smaller film."

Arijit Dutta is a familiar face in the Bengali Film industry. He has more than 16,000 followers on Facebook. Celebrity gatherings at Priya's terrace are a regular affair and Dutta is known for his flamboyant lifestyle.

Focus on the Exhibition Activity

Priya Entertainments' exhibition activity can be segmented into three clusters: The flagship Priya Cinema, the two Bioscope multiplexes, and the single screens in the districts.

Priya Cinema

Priya Cinema is the flagship movie theatre of the company. It has a certain stature in Bengali culture. People come to see Bengali films here, the young and the old, because Priya Cinema has not changed. It is cozy and homely, and still managed by the same family.

Priya Cinema is situated in south Kolkata. It has a capacity of 783 seats in one auditorium, with three categories of seats. The auditorium releases on an average three films a week and five shows a day. The old system is still running at Priya, for instance, no bill is generated for food and beverages, there is no computer system (different from the multiplexes), and the film tickets are printed with an old, slow machine. It is likely to remain the same, as part of the experience at Priya. As for the ticket rates, they are between INR 50 and INR 110, which is a little higher than in regular single screens.

On average, 60% of the films released are Bengali, mainly the urban genre; 30% are Hindi, and 10% are Hollywood blockbusters. In order to have their movies exhibited at Priya Cinema, distributors must pay a rental fee, which is negotiated for every film with Mr. Dutta. The rental fee is low for Bollywood and Hollywood movies. However, Arijit Dutta can negotiate very high rent for Bengali films, making Priya cinema the most profitable of the movie exhibition centres. In fact, 70% of Priya Cinema's revenues come from the rental paid by distributors, and 30% from advertising, branding, concessions and food and beverages.

Bioscope multiplexes

In 2010, Priya Entertainments opened its first multiplex: Bioscope Axis Mall in New Town, Rajarhat, an IT and computer engineering hub in the neighbourhood of Kolkata, which is planned to be a fast-growing new city.

In April 2012, a second Bioscope opened in Durgapur, one of the fastest growing tier 2 cities in West Bengal, located about 160 km away from Kolkata. A third multiplex is currently being constructed in Sonarpur, and will be the first suburban multiplex in Bengal. These multiplexes are opened in malls: The mall promoter makes the bigger part of the investment, and PEPL provides the seats, as well as the projection and sound equipment (for instance, in Durgapur, PEPL's investment was US $243,000). Once the mall is built, PEPL pays the promoter a licence fee as rent, plus a fixed percentage of its net revenues in the multiplex. The licence agreement is usually for 10 years and is renewable.

The capacity of the Bioscope multiplexes is around 800 seats split into four auditoriums. The ticket rates range from INR 130–180 at Rajarhat *vs.* INR 90–120 in Durgapur. There is a flat rate of INR 70 for morning shows and Bengali films are less expensive, ranging from INR 90–120. These prices are a little cheaper than the national multiplexes because Bioscope's standards are a notch lower than those of Inox, Reliance or PVR.

Movies released in Bioscope are more diversified than the movies shown in Priya Cinema. On average, 55% are Hindi films, 25% are Bengali films (both of the commercial and urban genre), 12.5% are Hollywood films and 7.5% are Telugu films.

In Bioscope multiplexes, food and beverage gets a much higher share of the revenue than in single screens. However, net margins are not stabilised yet for both multiplexes because the one in Durgapur is just six months old, and because the Rajarhat zone has not developed as fast as expected, even if it should become a significant residential area soon. Both multiplexes occasionally rent their auditoriums or other facilities to host cultural or corporate events.

Single screens in the districts

In the districts, PEPL manages six single screens in partnership with public institutions. Most of them are approximately 10 years old, but look even older. As Ashis Chakraborty, Head of Operations at Priya Entertainments, says, "In the districts, we don't always upgrade the equipment to the latest standards." However, PEPL cinema halls are said to be slightly more comfortable than the other single screens in the districts. For example, most of them are air-conditioned. **Exhibit 7** shows the location of the cinema halls operated by Priya Entertainments.

The films released in PEPL's single screens are mostly commercial Bengali movies. The only cinema hall that releases urban Bengali films is the one PEPL manages in Bolpur, which is doing particularly well because it is located next to Visva Bharati University, an institute of national importance. With an average of 40% occupation rate, those single screens have trouble covering their general expenditures that are mostly fixed costs split between salaries (30%), electricity (25%), maintenance and repairs (15%) and security and housekeeping (30%, often outsourced to another company). Profits are meagre in the districts. **Exhibit 8** shows income statements of the various movie theatres. Dhrubadeb Chatterjee, Head of Finance at Priya Entertainments, notes:

> "The cinema habit is going down in the districts, people having less time to go out and owning TVs at home; if over the past 5 years, our cinema revenue has grown, it is because we enhanced the rates."

Dealing with the Exhibition Crisis in the Districts for Priya Entertainments

The alternatives for PEPL's single screens in the districts

Arijit Dutta is facing a serious dilemma about his exhibition activity in the districts: What should he do with his less profitable single screens?

The first thing that comes to his mind is the need to increase revenues in those cinema halls. He could try to get more revenues from the ticket sales. However, the contracts of PEPL with the distributors are on a rental basis, just as they are for Priya Cinema: Single screens do not directly earn anything from the tickets, but they get a weekly rent from the distributors to exhibit their film. The rent is fixed in previous negotiations between the distributor and Mr. Dutta. It will be higher in the halls that are more successful. Increasing the number of tickets sold would then increase the negotiating power of the exhibitor for further deals with distributors.

Another lever could be to try to get more money from other sources of income such as hosting cultural events, renting the conference room, advertising or branding. These activities today represent about 12% of the cinema halls' revenue, but this share could increase. For instance, Gitanjali at Bolpur, PEPL's most profitable single screen, earns more money from the rent of its conference rooms for corporate or cultural events. Dipanjan

Basak, Assistant Manager of Sales and Marketing at Priya Entertainments, notes:

"Our manager at Bolpur has good relations with the companies around. We have fixed clients who keep organising their annual conference at Bolpur cinema hall."

Eventually, PEPL could also try to get more money from food and beverage as this only counts for approximately 5% of the revenues in the districts. The proportion can be much higher in the multiplexes. However, increasing F&B prices in the districts seems difficult, as people are extremely price-sensitive in rural areas.

Most of the costs of the cinema halls in the districts are fixed. Their general expenditures can be split into salaries (30%), electricity (25%), maintenance and repairs (15%) and security and housekeeping (30%). Agreements with the municipalities require Priya Entertainments to pay a monthly rent to the local institution. Power supply is the only variable cost, as a huge part of electricity costs can be attributed to the use of air-conditioning. This cost can be reduced in the winter. PEPL hires 10 to 15 employees per cinema, and outsources security and housekeeping services to another company. **Exhibit 9** compares three movie theatres by their facilities, customers, movies and revenue.

Eventually, if these two options — increasing revenues or cutting costs — do not fare well, Dutta has to consider closing the theatres. He has been reluctant to take that step.

Attracting more people from untapped audiences

Well-connected urban customers are easy to reach *via* email and phone. Tickets can be booked online on Priya's website or *via* service providers. The manager of Bioscope, Rajarhat notes:

"People are willing to pay a little more to make sure that their tickets are booked online. It would be difficult to do the same thing in the districts as 12 rupees extra over a ticket price at 30 to 40 rupees is too much."

In rural areas literacy rates, as well as internet connectivity, is lower. The cell phone is widely used, but 30 to 40% of users cannot use text messages. Advertising is usually done through posters and microphones. When there is a new release, an advertisement car with posters is sent to surrounding villages. It is therefore door-to-door communication to entice people to come to the next show. It also deeply relies on word-of-mouth: For good movies, the spread of good opinion can have a huge positive impact on its box-office.

Young people aged 16 to 25, account for a major portion of customers coming to theatres. Fewer women come to see movies as they are not used to going out without a male escort during the evenings.

The competition with piracy and TV

Although the film industry is one of the main employers in West Bengal, the industry is under threat from TV channels as well as that of piracy, particularly in the districts.

The television industry is developing with double-digit growth in West Bengal, where the overall TV business already amounts to US $260 million in 2011[16] (ten times the figures of the cinema industry). Bearing testimony to the rise of the Bengali TV industry, the incidence of Bengali channels colliding with Hindi and foreign cable channels increased from five in 2000 to 15 in 2011.

Almost every family house in the districts is equipped with a TV. This free entertainment is often preferred to Priya Entertainments' cinemas, because of both the cost of a ticket and that of transportation to reach the cinema hall. Among those programmes, households are getting particularly addicted to several Bengali and Hindi TV soaps, instead of being sensitive to new movie releases. Arabinda Ghosh, chief of marketing and strategic development at Priya Entertainments, notes:

> "My wife is really addicted to those TV series. She prefers me to come back home at 10 pm instead of 8 pm so that she can watch them quietly."

There are plenty of TV shows and series that can satisfy this audience. The manager of the single screen at Memari notes:

> "Television is the main competitor. Customers are looking for entertainment and television is comfortable; they can watch it on a daily basis. TV is the biggest threat as they provide Bengali and Hindi series."

In addition to the competition from TV soaps, Priya Entertainments' exhibition centres in the districts also suffer from TV channels broadcasting

---

[16] Deloitte report: A symphony of Art, 2012.

the same films within a short time. Indeed, rights for TV are often sold by producers only two or three months after the cinema release, not to mention the fact that a few regional cable channels do not shy away from illegally showing the films before obtaining the rights. This phenomenon of course reduces the time exhibitors have to make revenues for a film, but they know the producer does not have the choice because of the industry's second main enemy: Piracy.

Tackling piracy has become a real puzzle for the Indian film industry, but here again it is the business in the districts that suffers most from illegal ways of watching a film. In India, unlicenced copies of films are said to deprive the industry of 14% of its revenues, which amounts to about US $180 million.[17] Unlike urban areas, where online downloading is on the rise, piracy in the districts almost exclusively comes in the format of pirated DVDs one can buy in the streets. With the digitalisation of the industry, pirated DVDs can now be found of the same quality as the film's original copy.

Facing the issue of piracy, the only main player of the industry able to save the cinema is admittedly the government. However, both nationally and in Bengal, the government has done little to tackle piracy. In spite of a law against film copyright violation (a fine of US $800 to $3,200) and a prison term of six months to three years[18]), pirated DVDs are sold sometimes just in front of theatres without anyone feeling threatened. Until the government offers its help with punishment and awareness programmes, there is no questioning the fact that the best thing Dutta has to do to counter piracy is to get as many people as possible coming to his cinemas, before illegal copies invade the market. This leaves him a window of three to four weeks of shows for a single movie.

Arijit Dutta is visibly angry when he talks about piracy:

"It's *dacoity* [banditry]. Anyone pirating must be put into jail and the case forgotten for 10 years because you are stealing someone else's property. Video halls are buying them... even in the city people are buying them instead of buying a ticket for 60 rupees. For 10 people that's 600; you go buy a pirated copy for 50. The government has no political will to control piracy, that's the problem. But not only is the government losing revenue, they are also killing the industry. If one starts thinking of the whole society... these people are not poor... the pirates

---

[17]Northbridge Capital Asia report, 2011.
[18]1957 Copyright Act and following Amendment of 1984.

are not poor. They are earning more than the industry is earning. And that money is being channelled to the black market, terrorism, all sorts of anti-social activities. Government doesn't seem to realise that."

Parambrata Chatterjee recalls an incident when he went to the Sundarbans:

"Seven days after the release, I was traveling in the Sundarbans with my Dutch girlfriend. In a remote island, I saw a video screening going on for 10 or 20 rupees, something like that. They are watching a pirated copy. If we cannot bring cinema to this section of the audience at an affordable price, this is bound to happen. Let's hire a big van, have a screen on it. It is easy to get people attracted as long as there are moving images, noise, sound, music... if we move from village to village and organise screenings, people will pay and watch."

Dutta notes that there is little or no piracy in South India because of the culture of fan clubs:

"The fans will kill the person. Police doesn't even need to. The fans will break the shop, the video halls if there's any... Police need not do anything, nobody needs to do anything."

As early as 1949, political parties in Tamil Nadu decide to use films as a propaganda tool. This quirk of history proved to be a boon for the film industry. Five out of the seven chief ministers in the state are from the film industry. Public policy supported film-making and film-watching. Fan clubs of cinema stars and the political machinery of these cinema stars developed a widely distributed downstream market for the movies. The fact that the state of Tamil Nadu achieved 98% rural electrification by 1975 helped boost the distribution of movies in the rural hinterland. In 1975, only 26% of the villages of West Bengal had electricity; 25 years later, 25% of the villages of West Bengal were without electricity.

Trying to solve the content issue

Gautam Jain, Director of Real Reel Pvt. Ltd., notes that there is an urgent need for market research to discover the changing tastes of audiences in the districts:

"With greater exposure to other media, the district population may have developed an appetite for newer genres and slicker entertainment products, which the current Bengali commercial films and television may not be fully satiating. The Bengali industry will have to understand and cater to these newer needs to ensure future success."

The classic segmentation that states art movies are for urban areas and that commercial movies are for the rural districts is slowly fading away. Indeed, even if art movies still do not succeed in the districts, commercial movies also have to comply with growing difficulties since rural audiences are getting bored with that kind of films. They find that the plot is lacking originality and they are continuously watching the same story, but with different actors. On the other hand, art movies and foreign films lack the *masala*: Action, song and dance, leaving few options for the cinema halls.

Finding new content is becoming paramount for exhibitors. Moreover, as most competitors feel making money in the district is impossible, it lets a huge untapped market and the first mover has a huge edge. The Bengali film industry is not an isolated island and as a result of globalisation, the audience is constantly evolving as well. "People are getting exposed to a huge amount of global fodder." Parambrata notes:

> "Somebody sitting in, for instance, Birbhum, is still getting to watch a Airtel DTH or Tata Sky, HBO, Star Movies. Forget about world movies, I am talking about American films. Of course they are watching *Superman* and *Spiderman* and all these blockbusters, but at the same time they are catching glimpses of films like *Serendipity*. They also know that this is possible. Why don't our films, the film made in my native language, why are we not trying to at least go... try to crawl up there... to reach those standards? The demand comes from the audience actually. We see that more with the refusal of older formulas. One great thing about the Bengali film scenario today is: One cannot depend on formulas right now. The audience is constantly challenging you. Constantly".

Dutta was aware of the big changes that the industry is facing today. The Bengali diaspora market has started to pick up. A company called Databazaar has made Bengali movies accessible to the North American audience with a revenue model for the producers. Large theatre chains are thinking about valueplexes and miniplexes that will offer movies to the rural audience at very low prices. In this scenario, change is risky, but not changing is even riskier. Should he close his cinema halls that are not profitable enough and focus on the money-making ones? Should he keep them and try to make them profitable? Can he provide a low cost and good experience to the huge rural market? He called his top managers and put this topic on the agenda for discussion.

Exhibits

Exhibit 1: Number of Feature Films Produced.

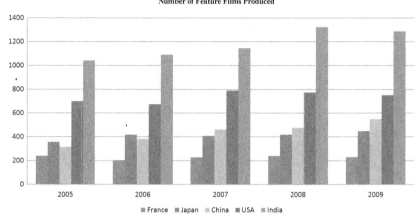

Source: UNESCO Institute for Statistics, January 2012.

Exhibit 2: Screens per Million Inhabitants.

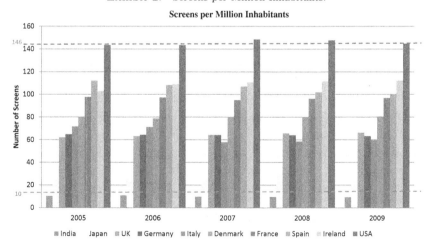

Source: UNESCO Institute for Statistics, January 2012.

Exhibit 3:   Languages of India (Speakers in Millions).

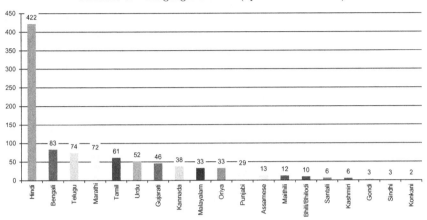

Exhibit 4:   Movies Produced per Year.

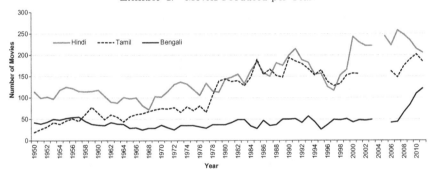

Exhibit 5:   2008 Data.

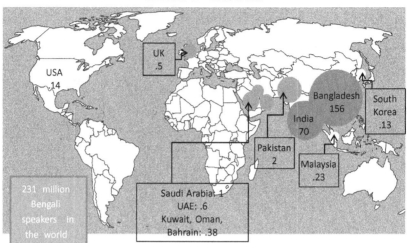

Exhibit 6:   Priya Entertainments' Organisational Structure.

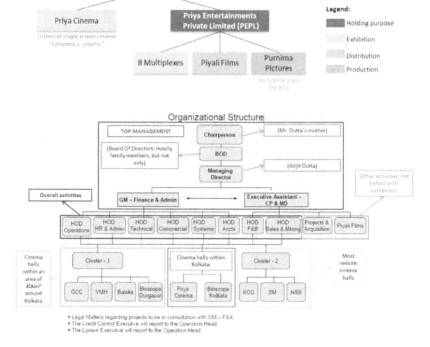

Source: Priya Entertainments' internal documents.

Exhibit 7: Cinema Halls Operated by Priya Entertainments.

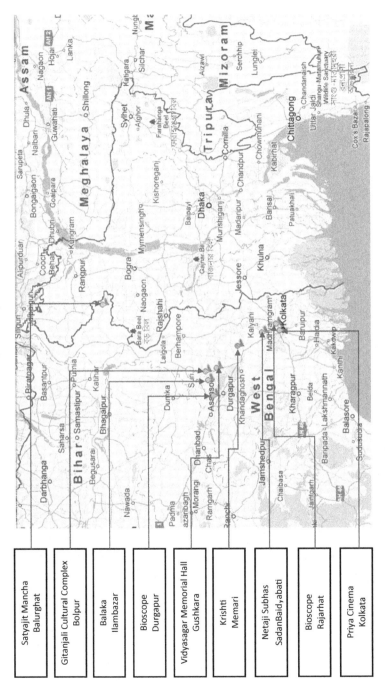

Satyajit Mancha
Balurghat

Gitanjali Cultural Complex
Bolpur

Balaka
Ilambazar

Bioscope
Durgapur

Vidyasagar Memorial Hall
Gushkara

Krishti
Memari

Netaji Subhas
SadanBaidyabati

Bioscope
Rajarhat

Priya Cinema
Kolkata

Exhibit 8: Income Statements of Exhibition Halls.[18]

	Priya Cinema Kolkata 1958 2012–2013	PEPL 2012–2013	Bioscope Rajarhat 2010 2012–2013	Bioscope Durgapur 2012 2012–2013	Gitanjali Bolpur 2000 2012–2013	Krishti Memari 2005 2012–2013	VMH Gushkara 2006 2012–2013	SM Balurghat 2009 2012–2013	Balaka Ilambazar 2010 2012–2013	NSS Baidyabati 2011 2012–2013
Founded in										
Revenue from Operations										
Auditorium[1]	26,366,655	30,084,101	8,977,698	7,470,660	5,041,401	3,128,133	1,644,443	1,608,455	1,323,161	890,150
Other Facilities[2]	1,725,941	8,535,040	2,339,353	1,546,366	357,299	2,482,498	241,265	1,347,886	102,854	117,519
	28,092,596	38,619,141	11,317,051	9,017,026	5,398,700	5,610,631	1,885,708	2,956,341	1,426,015	1,007,669
Less: Cost of operation										
Purchases[3]	460,097	4,268,309	989,702	902,825	—	1,156,579	134,690	909,779	82,594	92,140
Establishment cost[4]	1,793,496	4,816,272	879,998	526,137	617,074	951,021	471,707	761,579	379,991	228,765
Operating overhead	6,297,983	21,330,494	7,101,312	8,465,750	2,660,626	1,619,462	402,479	360,938	381,509	338,418
Other operating overhead	1,672,503	7,863,918	1,912,890	1,634,453	1,575,839	1,257,383	265,799	637,219	227,319	353,016
	10,224,079	38,278,993	10,883,902	11,529,165	4,853,539	4,984,445	1,274,675	2,669,515	1,071,413	1,012,339
Operating profit	17,868,517	340,148	433,149	(2,512,139)	545,161	626,186	611,033	286,826	354,602	(4,670)
Less: Depreciation	730,260	1,310,919	652,668	—	42,144	330,792	91,620	182,268	57,324	67,171
	17,138,257	(970,771)	(219,519)	(2,512,139)	503,017	295,394	519,413	104,558	297,278	(71,841)
Add: Other income[5]	7,803,871	1,649,534	600,417	808,095	1,050	51,650	57,362	53,295	35,095	42,570
Net profit	24,942,128	678,763	380,898	(1,704,044)	504,067	347,044	576,775	157,853	332,373	(29,271)

[1] Ticket sales and auditorium rent for special programmes.
[2] Other facilities include restaurant, guest houses, conference rooms, meeting rooms, marriage halls, food and beverages.
[3] Purchases are mostly for food and beverages.
[4] Establishment costs include seats, carpeting, interiors, projection system, sound system, screens etc.
[5] Other income includes: interest income, signages, renting other additional spaces, car parking/cycle stand fees, weighing machines, commissions received, and recovery of common service (internal adjustments).

Exhibit 9: Comparison of Three Cinema Halls.

	Gitanjali Cultural Centre, Bolpur	Krishti Cultural Centre, Memari	Bioscope, Durgapur
Facilities	750 seat auditorium; conference room (50 seats); seminar room (50 seats); Open air theatre; in-door & outdoor cafeteria & cyber café; handicrafts showroom; art gallery.	800 seat auditorium; conference room (150 seats); guest house (3–4 A/C rooms); restaurant; marriage hall, banquet hall.	Three auditoriums (812 seats total); stage; 300 seater conference room.
Customers	This center is located near Visvabharati University, founded by Rabindranath Tagore. Apart from the residents of Bolpur, the regular customers are the students. Priya nurtures an active film society screening on average 40 movies a year. The foreign movies released are subtitled in English, aiming at a somewhat educated population of cinema that knows English. Priya Entertainments provides the auditorium for free. Screening of a movie is often followed by a discussion (film appreciation course). Foreigners and some students of the university also like Bollywood movies.	80% are 16–25 years old. Elderly people are only 2–3%. This is an agriculture based region with a population of three lakhs. Low income area, no industries except for cold storages for potatoes. This town is surrounded by 15 villages. People can come from about 10 Kms away. 60% of the visitors come to town only for the movie. Customers are looking for entertainment, not social messages. Word-of-mouth really helps. Affordability is the key. Television is the main competitor. Customers are looking for entertainment and they can watch television (soaps) daily from the comfort of home. Television is also a bigger way to promote movies. Local cable channels can rent a commercial movie for 1,000 rupees a month. There are no nice places to hang around nearby. Another hall has about 1,000 seats but the experience is poor.	60% of customers are students; lot of Telugu students. Houseful shows for Telugu, especially in online tickets. Two rows are reserved for internet bookings. Screening from Friday to Sunday. Telugu students are not rich, but they are cinema-crazy people. The actors for them are like Gods. Priya maintains a database of phone numbers. They request for a slot at 4–5 pm because of four hours bus journey. Competitor: INOX ticket prices were higher. They were forced to decrease their rates when Bioscope opened. INOX does not show Telugu movies. People tend to be loyal to INOX because the theatre chain is present for a long time.

Movies	2–3 films are screened in a month in three slots: 12:30, 15:30, and 18:15 hours. If there are good releases, 3 different films can be shown and screenings are not restricted to Bengali or Hindi movies. Sometimes film festivals are themed on a famous director/period/country, for instance, Italian films of the 1960s. Bengali Commercials and Bollywood movies are also released. People like to have options. Commercial films sustain the business, and good movies are for the university crowd.	Bengali Commercial: 80%; Hollywood (Dubbed in Hindi): 5%; Bollywood: 15%. Slots:12:30 hours (students + young couples); 3:30 hours (students + young couples); 18:15 hours(Family) People are behaving better, so it is easier to operate. Lots of families are coming now; they are better behaved and more educated. New releases are on Fridays; three shows a day; mostly the same film running; same film for one week mostly. Sometimes a fourth show is added for big movies, but not regularly.	Four new movies are released in a week. Sometimes five to six. Type of film released: Hollywood, Bengali, Hindi and Telugu. Telugu community is scattered throughout Durgapur. 60% Hindi films, 30% Bengali (50% commercial, 50% urban), 5% Hollywood, 5% Telugu. The rates are same, but Hollywood and Hindi movies are higher than Bengali. Telugu movies are 130 rupees flat.
Revenue	80% of revenues from ticket sales; 15–20% of revenues from conference room, meeting room, and other facilities. Rs. 1 lakh per year rent + 50 % of ticket sales to SSD. Huge AC units generate a cost of Rs. 2lakhs/month for electricity. Two cultural events in a year; Baul music and tribal dances are the specialty of this area. In the month of December, and during the Holi festival, people come from all over the world. Open-air cinema has informal kind of seats for adda/chat with friends. Little revenues but no costs. Groups can perform for Rs. 1,500. They keep the rest. Conference rooms used twice a month; Cost/6 hours: small Rs. 3,000; big Rs. 8,000.	80% of revenues come from ticket sales (Rs. 35–40/ticket). 12% of revenues come from branding, conference hall, advertisements, guest house, and cultural events (three/year); 5% from F&B. Recently, the hall ran 13 houseful shows for a Bengali commercial movie: *Challenge 2*. Occupancy rate was about 85%. For non-famous actors, the occupancy rate is about 20%. On an average, it is 40%. The guest house targets companies' employees who need to stay. This increases the restaurant's revenues (3–4%). The non-AC restaurant's margins dropped from 20% to 12% because of inflation. Cinema is profitable without restaurant.	Revenues: advertisement (10%) (shops and posters), F&B (65%: revenue sharing 50–50 with the mall), ticket (25%). 65% of profits from ticket sales. Mall gets 18% license fee. Occupancy rate: weekends 39%, weekdays 17%. Ticket price: weekdays (90–100); weekends (100–120). The new plan is discounts on morning show for every kind of movies (Bangla, Bollywood, Hollywood). More profitable on weekdays and if the film has been running for a long time. Food & beverage revenue is shared with the mall owners. 50–50 sharing for popcorn. F&B: 45% goes to the company.

Part C

Introduction

Global Brands Addressing Local Challenges

Headquartered in France, global consulting firm **Capgemini** today has nearly 145,000 employees across 40 countries. However, in 2011, the company faced a challenge that will be familiar to many multinationals operating in Asia: How to recruit and retain the right people for the organisation.

In India, the company's human resources (HR) department was coping with increasing staff turnover. Finally emerging from the global financial crisis, businesses in the US and Europe were starting to recover and the demand for IT services was growing. India is an important centre for the off-shoring of IT services, so having the right people in place to deliver them was crucial to Capgemini's success in the market.

The case elucidates some of the reasons behind high employee turnover rates and deals with the issues of implementing a new HR strategy adapted to an emerging economy like India. It highlights the problems associated with retaining human capital and focuses on the importance of developing people's skills and competencies in order to increase employee satisfaction in a fiercely competitive and fast growing industry.

Also in 2011, another French company faced a different kind of challenge in India. In the case of car maker **Renault**, the company had recently begun to manufacture and sell cars under its own brand in India. It had ambitions to grow its market share and was considering the best strategy to achieve this. The plan was to first establish the brand through Renault's premium models and then use this brand recognition to give its smaller cars a mass market appeal.

The marketer leading the charge needed to take his knowledge and experience of brand communication in France and apply it to the specificities of the Indian automotive market. Part of this process involved benchmarking other industries' practices in terms of communication in India. The case describes a number of innovative marketing campaigns and explains why they have been successful in India. By bringing together these complementary sources of knowledge, Renault's marketer provided himself with the tools to design a powerful communication strategy to meet the ambitious target that had been set.

The third case in this section also concerns **Renault**, but this time the setting is China. Following the success of the SUV model Koleos in China, Renault has been trying to increase its brand awareness to reinforce its position in the market. The marketing team was preparing to launch two new models in the sedan segment, Fluence and Latitude, but faced a number of challenges.

Koleos was well suited to the Chinese market, given the popularity of SUVs and the fact that the competition in that segment remained weak. But Renault's marketers were faced with the fact that there was more awareness of the Koleos model than of Renault itself. Further, there was a disconnect between the marketing efforts of car dealerships at a local level and the central marketing strategy, so the team was looking for a way to achieve consistency. As a relatively small player with budget constraints, Renault needed to come up with an innovative and low-cost communication plan to compete with the automotive giants operating in China.

All three cases in this section provide insights into the challenges and opportunities faced by global brands as they make their way in emerging markets. In different ways, they each highlight the fact that leveraging knowledge of cultural specificities can lead to the most innovative solutions.

Chapter 8

Capgemini India: Making Employee Retention a Priority*

Cedomir Nestorovic
Management Department, ESSEC

In November 2011, Ashish Mahal, from the Talent Management team, was preparing for a meeting with his manager Prateek Pradesh, the Human Resources Director of Capgemini Information Technology and Outsourcing Services India to present his strategic plan to improve employee retention in the company. Ashish is operating in the context of the post-financial crisis period that reveals new trends in the IT business as clients in the US and Europe recover and demand is growing. Integrating the HR strategy with business needs in high skills is a priority. The HR Director, having read an article about the retention of high-potential employees and the talent management strategies of competitors, gives a few general recommendations to Ashish:

> *"You are a former HR consultant and after almost two years, you still have a fresh look at the company. For your mission, I advise you to keep in mind that HR practitioners like us must play a proactive role in the software industry. As business partners, we need to be aware of business strategies, and the opportunities and threats facing the organisation. As strategists, we need to achieve integration and fit into an organisation's business strategy. As interventionists, we need to adopt an all-embracing approach to understanding organisational issues, and their effect on people. Finally, as innovators, we should introduce new processes and procedures, which we believe will increase organisational effectiveness. I believe this will help you in your reflection."*

*This case was prepared with the support of Marilia Bossard, Aurélien Boyer, Alizée Brière, and Meryem El Alami, and with the collaboration of Capgemini India.

Given these recommendations, Ashish decides to make a broad reflection on retention levers, according to the Indian specificities of the IT industry. He wants to think of all aspects of the employee value proposition. Another constraint is the scalability of any idea he may have, given the size of the company, which employs around 35,000 professionals all over India. The Mumbai location where he is based represents only 19% of the total workforce of Capgemini India. In this context, Ashish starts brainstorming. He struggles to answer some key questions. What are the levers that can help an international IT company like Capgemini to retain its employees? How can the HR strategy meet the business needs and trends? What are the key attributes that would make high potential employees stay at Capgemini, beyond salary? Ashish has different documents at his disposal to come up with new and innovative ideas that can impress his boss and improve employee retention.

Cagpemini's Internationalisation: Engine of Growth

Ashish's plan for an HR strategy in India is the latest step in a process of 'Indianisation' of Capgemini's strategy that had begun a decade earlier. The growth dynamics of Capgemini based on acquisitions and increased by internal growth — principally in terms of human capital — drove its rapid expansion. Growing first in Europe, then Latin America and Asia, by 2011 Capgemini India accounted for over 28% of the total Group headcount.

Group Birth and Expansion

Capgemini traces its roots to the French city of Grenoble, where Serge Kampf founded Sogeti in 1967. By 1975, the acquisition of two large IT services companies, CAP and Gemini Computer Systems, had established the company as European leader, present in 21 countries. Capgemini built its success on internal growth and acquisitions. Today, it is one of the top five IT services and consulting companies worldwide. Capgemini is structured in several business units: North America, Central and Southern Europe, Northern Europe, and Asia–Pacific. As the global IT market evolved, Capgemini prioritised four business lines: Consulting, outsourcing, technology, and local professional services. It also identified three strategic priorities: To make outsourcing a primary development track, to create and develop production capacities in low-wage countries and to engage more local professional services (**Exhibit 1**).

The Competition

Capgemini's competitors can be divided into three groups: Global, offshore, and regional players.

- Global players include the two information technology giants, IBM and HP. Their presence in other, closely related, hardware and software technology markets enables them to capitalise on their client relationships in a larger market. The pure IT service players, Accenture and CSC, Capgemini's most direct competitors come next.
- The offshore and regional players (mainly Indian in origin) are the emerging IT services and, the biggest among them, such as TCS, Infosys, Wipro, Cognizant, and HCL, can claim to compete against the global players.

In order to face up to the competition, all the players, particularly global companies such as Capgemini, have strongly stepped up their presence in India, adjusting their delivery models so as to allow their offshore teams to participate in and, subsequently, to increase their involvement in the development of clients' projects. In this way, they have been able to restore their margins and lower their prices, so keeping a competitive edge. The offshore players, on the other hand, have responded by strengthening their local presence to develop client proximity.

The Group Strategy

The Group intends to continue growing its overseas workforce. At the end of the first quarter of 2011 overseas employees represented around 39% of the Group's total workforce and are targeted to hit 50% in two to three years' time (see Exhibit 2 for figures on IT services growth markets). Key advantages are competitive pricing, the capacity to develop more projects to take advantage of the economic upturn, and also innovation with the development of Centres of Excellence, whether in horizontal areas (for example, software testing and Business Information Management) or vertical (such as Energy and Telecoms). Offshore not only provides an additional production capacity and the arrival of a true industrialisation of services, but it has also become, over the course of several years, a lever for qualitative growth, thanks to the development of centres devoted to innovation.

The Journey of Capgemini India

In 2000, Capgemini acquires Ernst & Young's Consulting Division globally and establishes the presence of Capgemini in India. Even at first glance, the journey of Capgemini India shows an upsurge. In 2001, Capgemini India opens its first development centre in Mumbai, with 250 engineers. In 2011, after 10 years of acquisitions, expansions, and achievements in diverse areas, the employee base of Capgemini India exceeds 35,000. The company is based in seven cities in the country: Pune, Hyderabad, Mumbai, Kolkata, Chennai, Delhi, and Bangalore. One of the key strengths of Capgemini is its technology prowess. Capgemini India offers the full spectrum of services from Consulting to Technology and Outsourcing Services from India including Business and Technology Consulting, Custom Software Development, ERP and System Integration, Application Management, Infrastructure Management, and Business Process Outsourcing (BPO).

"People matter, results count"[1]

Capgemini's production capacity is mainly driven by the people it employs, and the company attaches great importance to developing and maintaining its human capital. The inability to recruit, train or retain employees with the technical skills required to satisfy its client project commitments could impact the Group's financial results. As of December 2010, Capgemini India accounted for 28% of the Group headcount with 30,859 employees (+39% of the workforce compared with 2009). Organic growth accounted for 8,600 additional employees (**Exhibit 3**). Capgemini India needs to retain and strengthen its manpower. The company reaffirmed its commitment to its seven core values: Honesty, boldness, trust, freedom, team spirit, modesty, and fun. The competitors recorded significant levels of growth (+24% for TCS revenue compared with 2009, +20% for Infosys) which stressed the competition in the Indian IT labour market.

'Incredible India' and IT Industry Dynamics

After ten years of business in India, Capgemini still deals with the specific challenges of the Indian IT sector. Post-financial crisis, the IT business is seeing a surge in demand as clients in the US and Europe recover. In parallel, the balance of 2011 highlighted that the HR department has to

---

[1] Capgemini slogan.

cope with increasing employee turnover and Capgemini needs an effective HR strategy and policies for retaining employees in 2012. Integrating the HR strategy with business needs and aligning with market trends in the IT sector are priorities for success.

The Revolving Door of Employees at Multinational Companies

India is a major centre for offshoring of IT services where Capgemini IT Services, as a multinational company, faces increased HR challenges in the Indian growing market compared to national competitors. East Asian countries have been successful in capturing a large share of the global sourcing of IT hardware, and India has emerged as a major centre for offshoring of IT services, principally for a few select markets like the US and Europe. The Indian IT and BPO industries have played a major role in placing India on the international map and transforming the country into a global player for providing world class technology solutions and business services. The industry is mainly governed by IT software and facilities, for instance, System Integration, Software experiments, Custom Application Development and Maintenance (CADM), network services and IT Solutions. Over the years, India has been the most favourable outsourcing hub for firms on the lookout to offshore their IT operations. The factors behind India being a preferred destination are its reasonably priced labour, favourable business ambiance and availability of expert workforce. But, in the Indian market, professionals' attitudes are changing as India becomes an expert's hub. A growing proportion of the local workforce feels more attracted by domestic employers than by Western multinationals. This shift finds its justification in the Great Recession that decreased multinational companies' reputation and attractiveness. Indian professionals do not believe they are likely to get exciting career opportunities in companies where expatriates generally occupy senior positions. They would lose motivation for global mobility opportunities as the growth rate is more promising in their home country than in Western economies. In parallel, Indian companies like Infosys or TCS grow more and more successful, modern and attractive to Indian professionals. The professionals who go to work for a foreign multinational company have the potential for quick promotions but most do not stay at the company as long as they had intended.

The Global Explosion in Market Opportunities and the Shortage of Manpower in Numbers and Skills

One of the most important challenges facing Indian IT companies concerns the HR aspect. In a tight job market, many organisations experience precipitous and simultaneous demands for the same kinds of professionals. However, the related issues are varied: Recruitment of a world-class workforce and their retention, compensation and career planning, technological obsolescence and employee turnover. Furthermore, given its phenomenal growth, the Indian IT–BPO industry needs to move up the value chain to successfully deliver higher value, complex business critical services that are not transactional and require deep domain expertise. That is why integrating the HR strategy with business strategy is becoming a new trend. HR practices must be aligned with the success of business plans which, to a great extent, depend on HR policies for recruitment, retention, motivation and reward. The other major areas of concern for HR personnel in this context are management of change, matching resources to future business requirements, organisational effectiveness, and employee development. Retention and motivation of personnel are major HR concerns today as the average tenure for an IT professional is less than three years. IT companies are striving to understand which organisational job and reward factors contribute to attracting the best talent. Rapid and unpredictable technological changes and the increased emphasis on quality of services are compelling software businesses to recruit adaptable and competent employees who combine technical knowledge with conceptualisation and communication skills, capacity for analytical and logical thinking, leadership and team building, creativity and innovation.

IT Specificity: Strong Demand for Career Practices and Learning/Training Policies

The skill level of IT professionals is one area that presents a considerable challenge for the Indian IT industry. IT companies need to facilitate employees' retention and skills upgrading through re-training policies. The common idea that the key leverage to retention is salary must be revised. Money may be a prime motivator for starters, but for those into their third or fourth jobs, other aspects may be more important. The use of new technologies, the support of learning and training, and a challenging environment ranks higher than competitive pay structures as effective retention practices. Learning and development opportunities are created by IT companies as the rate of technological change is high and may even be higher than the time required to acquire competence in one area. Software professionals themselves expect that their employers provide them with all the training they need in order to perform not only in their current role, but also in related ones that they may subsequently hold within the organisation. Employees want to gain new knowledge, which will be used by their organisation. On the basis of the new learning they want to work in higher segments of the software value chain and climb the career ladder. However, constant upgrading of employee skills poses another challenge for HR personnel. With the advent of a work situation where more and more companies have to concede that their valued employees are leaving them, career path management is becoming absolutely necessary. The focus of this new paradigm should not only be to attract, motivate and retain key 'knowledge workers', but also on how to reinvent careers when the loyalty of the employees is to their exciting learning opportunities rather than to the organisation itself. Today's high-tech employees desire a continuous upgrading of skills, and want work to be exciting and entertaining, a trend that requires designing work systems that fulfil such expectations. As employees gain greater expertise and control over their careers, they reinvest their gain back into their work.

Blueprints for a New Strategic Plan in 2012

In order to find a strategy that would suit the company needs, Ashish tries to investigate all available documents within the organisation, but also on the internet to find out about competitors' strategies and HR trends in the IT sector. Based on his observations, he tries to come up with recommendations for his manager.

Employees at Capgemini IT and Outsourcing Services

Capgemini professionals have deep domain knowledge as they execute multiple projects from comprehensive solution design and implementation to technology services spanning offerings across SAP, Oracle, Microsoft, Java and practices such as Testing and Business Intelligence. With the growing offshore business, employees increasingly need to communicate in different languages with clients from all around the world, who have diverse cultural backgrounds. Due to time differences with foreign clients, some consultants work during the night shift. They are trained on specific domains and technologies but they are building capabilities in quality management, behavioural, managerial and leadership skills. In India, consultants are also industry experts who are completely devoted to solving problems and making advancements within their respective industries, assuring the best contemporary solutions within each industry segment. Technology professionals can be specialised in one of the following sectors:

- Government and Public Sector.
- Energy, Utilities, and Chemicals.
- Manufacturing, Retail, and Distribution.
- Telecom, Media, and Entertainment.
- Financial Services.

Employees also have tools, methodologies and best practices based on years of experience in all major industries to cope with the unique requirements and unique challenges of each industry in India.

An Interesting Survey

Ashish reads the testimony of current employees at Capgemini. The study, prepared in July 2011, is about employees' satisfaction, needs and expectations in the company (**Exhibit 4**). The employees' interviews give Ashish a better idea of the attributes that would retain IT professionals in the company. He observes that most employees do not consider compensation as their first priority. The following extracts attract his attention.

What are the attributes of an ideal company for you?

Employee A: "My ideal company would be highly professional, with ethics to be followed, with opportunities for the employees as well as mentoring for the employee. I have a lot of friends who work in IT from my engineering school and I keep in touch with them to get insights on employers in my specialisation."

Employee B: "An ideal company should actually look out for the employees concerns; they should first trust the employees and their skills. For example, if I am given a job of managing something so then they should trust us and what we have done; obviously guidance will be there but I think there should be an open environment for honesty and respect. Employees should be given opportunity to speak of their concerns and their ideas and obviously they would bring business and help employees in terms of career growth. They would provide more opportunities for on-site and client interfacing. The second one would be attending SAP forums, technical and educational forums which are made at the global levels, that is an opportunity that they can give and they can leverage the existing talent which is there."

Employee C: *"I would say work—life balance because I am a very private person and I really give time to my family. I don't want to be working above my hours so I have time for my family, my children and that is the most important thing for me, especially when they are sick."*

What are your professional expectations for the next two to three years?

Employee D: *"I would like to move to some senior position, like manager position, also handle teams, because in the past I have handled teams so now I want to move up the ladder and become a manager. I want challenging management opportunities. That is why I would like to have good opportunities in terms of learning perspectives as well as career evolution like the opportunities of client facing in a consulting firm is quite high, the management trusts employees and they are open for feedback, bonus and honesty that is really comfortable."*

Employee E: *"I expect very challenging projects, good work—life balance, good learning opportunities of how the industry is doing and how to be in line as a consultant in terms of knowledge and experience."*

Competitors and Their Employees

Then Ashish investigates on the Internet in order to benchmark competitors' initiatives. He realises that companies like Infosys, Wipro, or TCS have different solutions to provide benefits to employees. The best practices that have lowered competitors' attrition rates have been listed by Ashish. The solutions concern all aspects of employees' life and work in the company. Infosys has a Talent Management tool called 'Talent Edge'. The platform helps to integrate talent management solutions. It manages processes across HR functions including recruitment, administration, talent management, payroll, compensation and benefit administration, learning management, succession planning, and career planning. The process assesses and ranks workers, records job preferences, creates career paths, develops long-term goals, assigns mentors, identifies competencies, devises training plans, and creates development plans. It also enables managers to identify courses and enroll their team members. Enterprise Learner provides schedules to instructors and facilitates grading. Wipro has followed the same trends by modernising its training facilities. The archaic system now gives way to 'Virtual Campus', a web-based learning initiative that integrates multimedia, instructor-led and real-time learning techniques into a facilitated, collaborative learning environment. Wipro has other innovative solutions to improve employees' retention. Wipro offers a state-of-the-art gymnasium and recreational facility called 'The Arena'. Recreation facilities like basketball, tennis, indoor games and mini gym can be accessed free of charge. Finally, 'Voice of Wipro' constitutes an employee perception survey in which employees are invited to design the change they want. For HCL Infosystems the priority is to create communication channels between the management and employees. That is why they introduced leadership development programmes based on the philosophy "recruit the best, retain the best, and reward the best": It is a training and development framework that includes certifications and self-assessment opportunities.

HR Experts' Advice on the Retention Challenge

Ashish decides to call Sharukhan, one of his former colleagues from the Research & Development team, to get valuable information from an HR consultant. Sharukhan mentions one solution that can help to cope with the retention challenge because it meets employees' needs. He introduces Ashish to the concept of 'executive coaching' that is being born or re-born in India:

Ashish: What is the role of a coach? How does it contribute to business productivity? When is coaching useful or required?

Sharukhan: The role of a coach is to facilitate and help a person to learn, develop and enhance performance. I believe it is a significant part of the 30% in my '40–30–20–10' rule on learning and development, where the 30% refers to learning through a developmental relationship. The 40% of learning happens through specifically designed challenges in work assignments; 20% through life experiences and 10% is through training courseware and conventional training. In recent times, there is increasing acceptance of the significance of this developmental relationship, as a powerful process to unlock the potential of individuals.

Ashish: How mature is the concept of executive coaching in India?

Sharukhan: Historically, India has always been very close to the concept of coaching as the metaphor of 'guru–shishya parampara' is something that we in India have had as a very unique practice. In embracing more modern methods suitable for 'collective' learning, we had lost it a bit in recent times. We are rediscovering this heritage! The current concept of executive coaching is still in a very nascent stage in the corporate world. However, the good news is that both corporates and individuals are starting to recognise its impact and relevance as a method of facilitating, learning, development and performance.

Ashish: What is the future of coaching in India?

Sharukhan: Coaching, in the near future, will become increasingly prominent as a practice. I envisage that organisations will invest lot of time and resources in nurturing coaches internally as well as fostering a culture of learning through increased coaching relationships. Coaching has the power to energise and build tremendous momentum in an organisation."

Framing the Proposal

It is in this context that Ashish Mahal is framing his proposal based on the needs of Capgemini's employees and his plans to exploit the opportunities he sees. His main concern is to introduce new solutions, processes, and procedures that will motivate employees to stay at Capgemini. He has committed to focus on innovation and hopes his proposal will satisfy Prateek as much as it meets employees' expectations.

Exhibits

Exhibit 1: Breakdown of Revenue by Business.

Local Professional Services
16%

Consulting
6%

Outsourcing
36%

Systems Integration
42%

Source: Financial report 2010.

Exhibit 2:   Strong-Growth Countries.

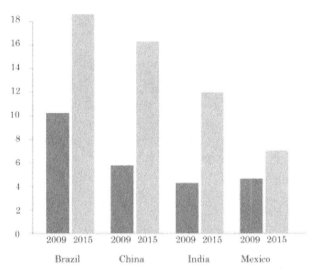

Source: Financial report 2010.

Exhibit 3:   The Top 10 Countries by Headcount.

THE TOP 10 COUNTRIES BY HEADCOUNT *	31/12/2009	31/12/2010	Variation	
			Number	%
1 India	22.178	30,859	+ 8,681	+ 39%
2 France	19,771	19,927	+ 156	+ 0.8%
3 Netherlands	9,474	9,037	- 437	- 4.6%
4 United Kingdom	7,777	8,443	+ 666	+ 8.6%
5 United States	6.438	7,089	+ 651	+ 10.1%
6 Brazil	394	6,795	+ 6,401	(+++)
7 Spain	4,582	4,391	- 191	- 4.2%
8 Poland	3,762	4,010	+ 248	+ 6.6%
9 Germany	3,307	3,198	- 109	- 3.3%
10 Sweden	2,100	2,315	+ 215	+ 10.2%
TOTAL OF TOP TEN	79,783	96,064	+ 16,281	+ 20.4%
Other countries	10,733	12,634	+ 1,901	+ 17.7%
GROUP TOTAL	90,516	108,698	+ 18,182	+ 20.1%

* The calculation of numbers of employees in any one country excludes offshore staff carrying out operations destined for that country.

Source: Financial Report Capgemini Group 2010.

Exhibit 4: Questionnaire.

Capgemini Employees interview

1- Profile of the Employee

In which Business Unit do you work?

What is your role in this BU?

What is your level?

How long have you been working in Capgemini?

What is your background? (studies, professional experience, etc)

2- Employee before entering Capgemini

Why did you choose Capgemini?

What perception did you have of Capgemini before entering the company?

Were you proud to announce your family/friends you were going to work for Capgemini?

○ I strongly agree ○ I somewhat agree ○ I somewhat disagree ○ I strongly disagree

3- Employee overall Expectations

What do you expect from your job?

What are the most important attributes of your ideal company? (choose 3 of them)

☐ Job security ☐ Growth opportunities ☐ Work-life balance ☐ Positive Work environment ☐ High wages

☐ Training & development opportunities ☐ Strong Brand Image ☐ Overseas opportunities ☐ Transparent Appraisal System

4- Career Practices

Are you satisfied with your career evolution in the firm up to now?

○ I strongly agree ○ I somewhat agree ○ I somewhat disagree ○ I strongly disagree

Why?

Does it correspond to the expectations you had before entering the company?

○ I strongly agree ○ I somewhat agree ○ I somewhat disagree ○ I strongly disagree

What are your expectations in terms of evolution in the company in the next 2-3 years? (in an ideal world)

Do you think you have exciting growth opportunities in this company?

○ I strongly agree ○ I somewhat agree ○ I somewhat disagree ○ I strongly disagree

Why?

Are you satisfied with the performance assessment process?

○ I strongly agree ○ I somewhat agree ○ I somewhat disagree ○ I strongly disagree

Why?

Do you think it is fair?

○ I strongly agree ○ I somewhat agree ○ I somewhat disagree ○ I strongly disagree

Why?

Do you think it is transparent?

○ I strongly agree ○ I somewhat agree ○ I somewhat disagree ○ I strongly disagree

Why?

Do you think it is useful?

○ I strongly agree ○ I somewhat agree ○ I somewhat disagree ○ I strongly disagree

Why?

Would you appreciate to talk about your career evolution not only with your manager but also with another person?

○ I strongly agree ○ I somewhat agree ○ I somewhat disagree ○ I strongly disagree

Why?

Are you aware of all the processes concerning L&D, career evolution, performance assessments, feedbacks?

○ I strongly agree ○ I somewhat agree ○ I somewhat disagree ○ I strongly disagree

Why?

Is your manager aware of all the processes concerning L&D, career evolution, performance assessments, feedbacks?

○ I strongly agree ○ I somewhat agree ○ I somewhat disagree ○ I strongly disagree

Why?

5- Learning & Development Practices

Is there a minimum number of training hours you are expect to attend in a year?

○ Yes ○ No

Do you attend at least 40 hours of training in a year?

○ Yes ○ No

Why?

Does the training catalogue correspond to your expectations?

○ I somewhat agree ○ I somewhat disagree ○ I strongly disagree

Why? (Is it diversified enough?)

Do you think the training sessions you attended were useful for:

The kind of work you do

○ I strongly agree ○ I somewhat agree ○ I somewhat disagree ○ I strongly disagree

Your career evolution

○ I strongly agree ○ I somewhat agree ○ I somewhat disagree ○ I strongly disagree

Your personal development

○ I strongly agree ○ I somewhat agree ○ I somewhat disagree ○ I strongly disagree

Do you think that training programs help you to:

Develop your technical skills

○ I strongly agree ○ I somewhat agree ○ I somewhat disagree ○ I strongly disagree

Improve your overall performance

○ I strongly agree ○ I somewhat agree ○ I somewhat disagree ○ I strongly disagree

Deal with your weaknesses

○ I strongly agree ○ I somewhat agree ○ I somewhat disagree ○ I strongly disagree

Feel more motivated

○ I strongly agree ○ I somewhat agree ○ I somewhat disagree ○ I strongly disagree

Build new relationships with your colleagues

○ I strongly agree ○ I somewhat agree ○ I somewhat disagree ○ I strongly disagree

Do you prefer e-learning sessions or modules in classrooms?

○ e-learning ○ modules in classrooms

Why? (Is it because you like meeting people or because you like be taught by an instructor?)

How long in advance would you like to have the schedule of trainings available?

○ 1 month ○ 3 months ○ 6 months ○ 1 year

Why?

7- Conclusion

What are the key elements that makes you stay at Capgemini regardless of the salary?

Chapter 9

Renault India: Benchmarking against other Industries for Marketing Success[*]

Li Yan

Department of Information Systems,
Decision Science and Statistics, ESSEC

As he was preparing for his final presentation on Renault's communication strategy in India in late November 2011, Roger Laroux de Secourt[1] thought about the challenges ahead for the French brand in India. Renault wanted to be one of the five major foreign carmakers in India and occupy 2.7% of the passenger car market by the end of 2012, from a 0.3% market share in July 2011. Achieving this objective would require Renault to have a full range of cars. Renault had launched two cars in 2011, and prepared to launch three more models by the end of 2012. In terms of positioning, Renault wanted to establish itself as a premium car brand, while at the same time launching car models to cater for the mass market too. This would be an extremely challenging task, hence special communications tools were required. Roger, who had been designing successful communication strategies for the brand in France, was confident that what he was going to propose would be innovative and efficient for the brand in India. He had spent almost two months in India developing communication tools for Renault there. Now it was time to present them and to convince Renault India's executive board that they would be critical for the brand's future in India. Before the meeting, Roger decided to review all the points.

---

[*]This case was prepared with the support of Gatti Etienne, Lenhardt Jerome, and Sfez Isabelle, and with the collaboration of Capgemini Consulting and the employees of Renault India and France.
[1]Pseudonym: For illustration purpose only.

Renault's History and Strategy

Renault has a long history in car manufacturing. Founded in 1898 by French engineer Louis Renault, the company distinguished itself from the beginning with technological innovations and success in car racing. Indeed, from the first modern gearbox in the early 20th century to the first turbocharger in the 1970s, many key innovations established Renault as a pioneer in the car industry. As for racing victories, great successes achieved in the early 20th century in European road car rallies (such as the Paris–Bordeaux race in 1901) were followed by 10 Formula 1 championship titles from the 1970s, and the 2011 Red Bull car powered by a Renault engine.

The company experienced different stages as it was transformed into a government owned company in the aftermath of World War II, and was again turned into a private company in 1996. Meanwhile, many iconic, popular and affordable cars were produced, such as the Renault 4 and the Renault 5. In terms of sales growth, Renault experienced ups and downs. While the 1960s saw a great rise in the number of cars sold, two oil supply shocks in the 1970s brought the car industry, including Renault, into deep financial crisis. The financial health of Renault recovered in 1987, which allowed the company to finance external integration to a greater extent. In 1999, Renault and Nissan began an alliance and became the fourth largest car manufacturer worldwide in 2010. Other synergies were created with Dacia and Samsung motors.

Carlos Ghosn, the Chief Executive Officer of the Renault–Nissan Alliance, announced in 2011 a comprehensive five-year strategic plan: Renault 2016, which aimed to generate growth and free cash flow. These objectives will be achieved through the launch of a broader range of innovative cars designed for traditional and new markets, a reinforcement of Renault's brand image, and a stronger management of the cost structure. Indeed, new fast-growing markets have become essential for Renault to counterbalance the low sales growth in traditional markets. The BRIC countries (Brazil, Russia, India and China) had thus become strategic for the development of the group. **Exhibit 1** shows the significance of international sales in total group sales.

Renault in India

Renault entered the Indian market in 2005, by establishing a Joint Venture (JV) with the Indian automotive group Mahindra & Mahindra. The Logan, a mid-segment sedan (in fact a car completely designed by Dacia, but produced in India), entered the market in 2007. The launch of the Logan was not a success as its sales figures, especially compared to its local competitors, remained low. Despite this failure, Renault was determined to increase its market share in India. In 2009, a Renault design studio was launched in Mumbai, signalling the willingness of the brand to understand and integrate regional cultures and styles to its own design language.

The Logan Model

The Logan sedan was developed jointly by Renault and Dacia and was first launched in Romania in autumn 2004. It was built as a simple and practical car, able to sustain a tough treatment and very inexpensive to buy and maintain. It achieved great sales volumes in Romania and notable success in France when it was introduced in 2006 and labelled as a low-cost product (sales volumes were up 53% on an average between 2005 and 2009, up to 533,000 per year in 2009). In India, the car was assembled by Mahindra & Mahindra and started to be sold in 2007. A low quality check and a poor after sales service, combined with the fact that it was largely sold to taxi companies who appreciated its robustness and reliability, explained the poor image and impacted its sales with just over 44,000 cars (only 2% of global production) sold in India until the termination of its production in 2010.

In 2010, Renault decided to end the JV with Mahindra & Mahindra in order to start producing and selling cars under the Renault brand. The goal was to have a full line-up of cars, ranging from the small compact hatchback (A2 segment) to a full premium 4 × 4 (SUV segment), with five different models in total, at the end of 2012. In terms of market share, the target was set at 2.7% (100,000 cars) of the entire passenger car market in India by the end of 2014, a big step up from the 0.3% market share in mid-2011. A production plant in the outskirts of Chennai, designed to produce both Renault and Nissan cars, was inaugurated the same year, with a capacity to produce 400,000 cars per year. A strong focus on the dealership network was also crucial to signal to Indian consumers Renault's clear intention of increasing its presence. Renault planned to increase its network from 14 outlets in mid-2011 to 100 at the end of 2012. In May 2011, the first model, Fluence, was launched, followed by Koleos in September. The third model, Pulse, was presented in October 2011 during the Formula 1 race in Delhi, before being formally introduced to the market in early 2012. Such a frenzied launch schedule showed Renault's eagerness to succeed in India. But as the brand itself was new, and its association with the failure of the Logan was still lingering, a complete makeover of the brand image was essential to support this new range of cars. **Exhibit 3** gives picture of the brand associations in mid-2011.

Renault's brand strategy was first to establish the brand as premium with the first set of cars launched by mid-2011 (Fluence and Koleos), and to extend this image to smaller and less expensive models later. Indeed, Fluence was a mid-sized sedan, priced from INR 1.3 million (US $21,000) competing with Volkswagen Jetta, Honda Civic and Chevrolet Cruze. Meanwhile, Koleos was an SUV, priced from INR 2.2 million (US $36,000) and competing with high-end cars such as the BMW X1 and the Honda CR-V. The consumer target was 30 to 40-year-old men, with a high disposable income, who wanted a high quality and high value product. Although sales of both Fluence and Koleos experienced high growth, the volumes remained low. High sales volumes were the target of the third model, Pulse, which was to enter the small car A2 segment by early 2012, to compete with models such as Hyundai i10 and Maruti Suzuki Swift. **Exhibit 2** shows the predominance of the A2 segment in passenger cars in India. The A2 segment was extremely competitive in India. Brand image would be a key to success there. But becoming a premium brand was not enough to differentiate Renault from its competitors. Renault needed to communicate something else, something consistent throughout the whole range of cars. This is the big question that haunted Renault India's marketing department. Help was needed.

Enter Roger Laroux de Secourt

As this period was critical for Renault's future in India, some managers at Renault's headquarters in Boulogne Billancourt suggested that a task force based in France could help develop an innovative, premium communication plan. Others advocated the idea that a communication specialist should be sent to India to help them on-site. As time was limited, the latter idea gained most support and was finally chosen. Soon many names were considered as candidates to be sent to India, but one name stood out from the rest: Roger Laroux de Secourt.

Roger Laroux de Secourt, 32, was the Communication Manager of Renault in France, and was known by almost everybody at Renault for his innovative way of thinking. He was the one to stress the importance of promoting the idea of innovation to bolster Renault's image in its domestic market. He was responsible for finding the 2010 motto: *Changeons de vie, changeons d'automobile* (meaning 'change life, change car').

Roger had progressed well in his career at Renault's headquarters. Freshly graduated from ESSEC business school in 2003, he entered the group as Assistant Communication Manager for the Megane car. It did not take him long to be given more responsibility as the assistant communication manager for the whole range of cars in 2007. In 2009, he succeeded in installing Renault's clean energy programme as a key communication element for the entire group. This coup resulted in Roger becoming the youngest communication manager in France, at the age of 30.

He was the right man to help Renault succeed in India. What's more, he had always wanted to discover this country. The decision was made. Roger was going to spend two months in India studying the market and the communication opportunities for Renault.

The Indian Market: India's Strong Growth is Favourable for the Indian Automotive Industry

Over the past five years, the Indian economy had grown at an average rate of 9%. India's economy was the ninth largest in the world by nominal GDP (**Exhibits 5 and 6**) and the fourth largest in terms of purchasing power parity. This growth trend was expected to continue.

India's demographic growth, characterised by 50% of its population under 25, together with an increasing speed of urbanisation, was favourable for the car industry. The same went for the increasing savings and incomes of Indian households: 13 million households have an annual income of US $10,000 to $50,000.[2] This segment was expected to triple by 2012 to reach 40 million households. At the same time, income for average, middle-class households was also on the rise.

Even though in October 2011, India's passenger vehicle market ranked as the world's seventh largest, the car penetration rate of the Indian market remained low. (India is among the lowest in the world's top 10 auto markets.) Thus, there was huge potential in this market, especially when the increasing affordability of cars for Indian customers was considered.

---

[2] *Reviving the Growth Engine — India's Automotive Industry is on a Fast Track*, Booz and Company report.

India's Automotive Market Overview

The overall passenger vehicle market in India was expected to grow from 1.7 million units in 2008 to 2.4 million units by 2013. According to a Booz & Company report, by 2012, annual car sales worldwide would increase by about 11 million units per year, with India accounting for 20% of the increase. At that point, India would become the world leader in small-car market growth.

India was the second largest two-wheeler market in the world in terms of sales volumes after China. In 2010, more than 75% of motor vehicles were two-wheelers because of their low price. Over the two years prior to Roger's arrival, the Indian two-wheeler industry had shown a strong volume growth. Indeed, in 2009–2010, it had grown by 25% and in 2010–2011 by 27%, reaching 13.3 million units. Such popularity was due to low price, high fuel mileage and the ability to drive easily in dense traffic. But still, the two-wheeler household penetration rate was much lower in India (36% in 2010) than in other emerging markets such as Thailand, Brazil, and Indonesia.

Although penetration remained low, the four-wheel passenger vehicle market had grown impressively with the growing middle class, and small cars dominated (**Exhibit 7**). In 2010, India was the largest small car market in the world. The success of this segment was due to its competitive advantage and its cost effectiveness that matched Indian consumers' needs. The low prices of those cars would, in the future, help quadruple the number of potential new car buyers, making it very attractive for car manufacturers. Then India was likely to emerge as a small car production hub.

Renault's Competitors: India's Passenger Vehicle Market is dominated by a Few Players

In 2011, most global car manufacturers that were targeting the Indian market had strong local strategies. They wanted to establish India as one of their sourcing hubs. To adapt themselves to the Indian market and meet Indians' preferences, they were developing models specifically for the Indian market.

Several major players dominated the passenger vehicle market in India. Maruti Suzuki, Hyundai Motors and Tata Motors were the three main actors, accounting for 80% of total sales volumes of passenger vehicles in 2010 (**Exhibit 8**).

Most foreign car makers had focused on the premium car segment and had, with the exception of Hyundai, avoided the highly competitive small car segment, still dominated by a few players, such as Maruti Suzuki and Tata. But this was deemed ready to evolve, considering the significant opportunities offered by this segment.

Renault's Communication Strategy

Through the year 2011, Renault had launched two cars: Fluence (code name: L38), a sedan offering high specifications, premium positioning and value for money; and Koleos (code name: H45), a flagship SUV offering high specifications with a premium positioning. These launches had been designed with the purpose of building Renault's image and to position the brand as premium. However, being premium was different from being luxury. Renault did not want to be a luxury automotive brand competing with the likes of Mercedes, BMW or Audi. Premium brands aspired to be prestigious, but Renault's marketing strategy was to target mass market and to leverage volume, rather than expensive and exclusive products. From this perspective, Fluence and Koleos were a strong foundation in terms of communication for future growth and were essential to prepare for the launch of the following models: Pulse (code name: B58), a dynamic hatchback, and Duster (code name: H79), an affordable SUV. Renault wanted to develop high expectations among Indian consumers regarding its products. Thus its promise was:

"Inspires You to Expect More Out of Life"

The brand vision was to be a people-centric, global company that every customer feels proud of. Its values were: People friendly, innovation, aspirational, and trustworthy. The product promise to Renault customers was to upgrade the travel experience, while delivering superior performance and comfort to all. Dynamic, modern and elegant design made the cars reflect consumers' aspirations and instilled a pride of ownership.

Koleos' ideal customer was male, aged 35 to 45, with one or two children, who was successful in his profession (a wealthy businessman or senior corporate manager) and who had a hedonistic state of mind. This customer wanted to express his individuality in a collectivist society and was looking for a machine that offered him performance and prestige at the same time as reflecting his free spirit.

Fluence's ideal customer was male, aged 30 to 40, with one or two children, an early achiever who was extremely successful. He was energetic and valued his quality of life and his family. He was well-read with refined taste. His vehicle was a reflection of his success and character.

Considering all these elements, Roger was wondering who would be the ideal customer for the Pulse given the price (US $4,500) and the segment (A2 compact hatchback). One of the specificities that Roger noticed about premium in India was that, unlike the Western way to consider premium as an enjoyment for the customer, Indians tended to define premium through other's perceptions. Thus success and achievement were the key values to give a premium perception to an automotive brand in India. The issue was that the entire automotive industry, from the local cheaper brands to the high-end foreign manufacturers, communicated premium with different tones (See **Exhibit 9** for examples of print advertising). For instance, the commercial for Cruz by Chevrolet depicted a group of men hanging out with a car looking cocky and aggressive. In this advertisement, the car was a traditional masculine status-oriented attribute. Chevrolet leveraged the social recognition and need for accomplishment of the upper middle-class. At the same time, Volkswagen's Jetta advertising did not show the typical customer but preferred to show with humour the confidence people have in the quality of the brand. Volkswagen wanted to leverage its international recognition and its high quality by presenting its cars as an incarnation of the customer's modern attitude and status.

In 2011, Renault produced and broadcast only one TV advertising campaign for the launch of Fluence. This commercial depicted a young couple in a luxury environment, proud to be different from the tradition. The signature was "Status Redefined". The brand was associated with a different idea of luxury, with the main theme a sense of achievement through peer recognition.

In terms of budget allocation, Renault's strategy was clearly oriented toward advertising in newspaper and outdoor with 58.46% and 20.23% respectively of the total communication budget dedicated to these media. Due to the high cost of advertising on TV, it was not a key media in Renault's strategy. The most costly campaign across all media was the "Bonjour India" brand campaign in daily newspapers from May to June 2011. This campaign (See **Exhibit 12**) depicted Renault concept cars in front of famous monuments of India. Several people within the company, as well as outside the company, had complained about this particular campaign and its lack of understanding of the specificities of the Indian consumer. Indeed, many dealers received phone calls from potential customers for the prototype presented in the print advertisement. Some experts in communication and advertising in India criticised an artificial 'Indianisation' through the clichéd background as well as the mismatch with Indian advertising expectations.

Roger took notice of these comments but after reading a study on premium influencing media by AT Kearney (See **Exhibit 10**), he started to wonder if the media planning and the communication strategy were consistent with a premium positioning.

Indians particularly tended to value more real experiences such as in-store and mall displays where they could interact physically with brand representatives. Based on that fact and given the tremendous importance for premium and luxury brands of the customer relationship and the in-store experience, Renault had developed a national sales experience process across all its dealerships. This process relied on well-groomed and trained staff. However, the sales materials were not consistent across all the dealerships. Roger was very surprised to see, as he visited a dealership in Delhi, that the sales force was using black and white printed copies extracted from the Renault India website. Moreover, the design of the dealership in terms of colours and the quality of the furniture were not really premium, especially in comparison with the Renault dealerships he had experienced in China. There was also a lack of advertising on-site as well as a lack of display about the brand, its history and Formula 1.

In spite of a communication strategy to position Renault as a premium brand, still few customers associated status and trust with the Renault brand. This fact was a major issue to tackle because, as Roger noticed about the Indian market, status was a key component to create an aspirational brand and trust was a must-have for consumers who feared that one day their car would collapse.

The Opportunities: Best Practices from Other Industries

Roger, following the advice of the Director of Marketing of Renault India, decided to screen the best practices of brand communication in India from other industries, in order to gain useful insights on how to communicate the Renault brand. This research brought him the following best cases:

LG: A Key Differentiator Strategy

LG positioned itself in India as 'good for your health'. Its communication strategy was focused on health, whereas its competitors only highlighted technology. The 2008 LG Golden Eye ad campaign, broadcast on TV and radio, combined the core functional attributes of the product with the health benefit of having a TV that takes care of your eyes. This campaign was the result of a survey by LG which showed that the health issues associated with prolonged TV-watching were critical for Indian consumers. Hence LG needed to address this consumer concern and aspiration for a better product. The effect of the campaign proved to be beneficial for LG, as the perception in the post-campaign surveys revealed increased brand awareness (+50%) and a new association of the brand with good health.

Samsung: The Store Experience

Samsung in India had paid specific attention to providing a holistic store experience. All the products were shown in such a fashion that customers could wander through, going from the TV section to the computer area, and finally strolling through the fridge section. Such a display allowed the brand to showcase its technology and indicated to consumers that all their needs were taken care of. Moreover, it provided the entire brand experience: Samsung blue and white colours were everywhere and the modern finish of the furniture offered a high-tech, advanced feel. From the survey conducted by Roger in malls, it appeared that Samsung was the only brand whose in-store experiences were consistently cited as a successful communication channel by Indian consumers.

AVIVA: Value Customers

In November 2010, the insurance company AVIVA launched an innovative campaign named "You are the Big Picture" which aimed to raise funds for education in India.[3] AVIVA's customers and employees were asked to upload their pictures on AVIVA's Facebook page, which would then be projected on to a landmark building in Delhi. AVIVA would donate US $3 for each picture uploaded. The idea caught on and more than 50,000 customers and employees uploaded their pictures. In terms of brand recognition, AVIVA benefited strongly from the campaign, as customers really felt proud to be an AVIVA client.

---

[3] Aviva's detailed campaign is visible on: http://www.avivaindia.com/en/MediaCenter/PressRelease/NA_1_1-11-2010.aspx.

"Aviva's campaign demonstrates that a company needs to show it values Indian customers. In today' s India, this interaction with customers can be activated through social media but needs to be followed by a real event. This is crucial."

— Ms. Sunyana, communication expert, Delhi

Pureit: Engage with Customers

Pureit is a water purifier brand, part of Hindustan Unilever group. In January 2010, Pureit launched a communication campaign that aimed at capturing new clients through existing clients. To do so, Pureit asked 200 customers to invite five or more friends who were not Pureit customers. They were contacted by text message to come to their friends' home to test Pureit products. The new testers, if impressed with the products, would allow their friends, the existing Pureit customers, to give their phone numbers to the company to arrange a meeting. If the sale was successful, the existing customer would receive a free Pureit product. This campaign relied on the fact that people trust their entourage and value their opinions, especially in India. Indeed, the survey conducted by Roger showed that peers' opinion was one of the key attributes looked for in a product, a car in that instance.[4] This campaign proved very successful, not only in terms of raw sales (it exceeded its sales target), but also in that it allowed Pureit to gain a vast amount of potential customer information.

After having accumulated these practices, Roger decided to see how they might apply to Renault's strategy in India. He needed to see how a mix of these cases could help Renault really connect to Indian consumers. AVIVA's initiative could work by putting the customers at the center of communication content. Samsung's practice showed that Indian customers were particularly responsive to a brand that was able to deliver a strong and coherent store experience. The LG case underlined that to differentiate was critical, if it really appealed to the uniqueness of the Indian market, while Pureit's idea relied even more on a consumer behaviour that is idiosyncratic to India. How Roger could apply these learnings to Renault's communication was the key question. Maybe using the following specificities of the Indian automotive market could help in that matter.

---

[4]The survey conducted on 210 individuals in India showed that peer advice was the first attribute looked for in a car, with 26% of respondents.

Formula 1

Formula 1 was new in India. The first Grand Prix took place in November 2011 in Delhi. But awareness of the sport had been increasing although it remained "very low compared to cricket in India", in the words of Formula 1 mogul, Bernie Ecclestone.[5] This was true when compared to the total population. When compared only in the high end of the Indian income pyramid, Formula 1 awareness was much higher. In the survey conducted by Roger in malls, all respondents (belonging to the middle-to-high income class) knew about Formula 1 and its coming to India. Moreover, the most well-known attribute of the Renault brand was its Formula 1 activity. **Exhibit 3** shows the significance of Formula 1 for the brand. While other foreign car manufacturers had no specific asset to associate with their brand, Renault had a key differentiator in Formula 1.

Furthermore, Renault could use Formula 1 in India because it appealed to its whole customer target. It appealed to the young customers targeted by Pulse who appreciate the dynamism of the sport. And it also appealed to the more mature customers who cherish the heritage of the brand in racing technology and its transfer to road cars. But issues remained concerning the viability of Formula 1 in terms of communication. As indicated by Mr Balasubramaniam, Director of Marketing for Renault India: "Formula 1 is very episodic as only one race occurs in India every year." A whole communication strategy could not be based on such short-lived hype. It could, however, be part of a broader strategy.

Social Media in India

Social media had seen a rapid expansion in India. The total number of users by the end of 2011 was over 60 million, while Facebook ranked first and counted more than 42 million unique visits per month (topping traditional giant Orkut's 11 million monthly visits). Moreover, mobile platforms accounted for 60% of total social media usage, reflecting the Internet usage trend in India and worldwide. What was interesting and specific to India was the way users interacted in these media. According to Professor Anke Schwittay of Auckland University, Indian customers were really keen on engaging with others, on publishing personal information

---

[5]M. Jeelani, (11/2011) When Rubber meets the Road. Caravan magazine: http://www.caravanmagazine.in/Story.aspx?Storyid=1165&StoryStyle=FullStory.

and getting information.[6] This shows in the way they approached brands on social media. Indian consumers leveraged social media to get information about a brand and to make a purchase.

According to a September 2011 survey by Nielsen, 40 million Indians were using social reviews when making purchase decisions. What's more, 67% of Indians who were on the web used online reviews to help them make purchases, while 60% of Indians who were social media users were open to being approached by brands.[7] In terms of influencers in the automotive market, one forum (teambhp) and one magazine website (zigwheels) dominated the market, as indicated in **Exhibit 4**. These influencers' perception of a brand is thus critical for brand advocacy. All these elements showed the importance of integrating social media into a communication strategy in India. Indian customers really put value on and trust peer advice. Understanding this trust could prove highly beneficial for Renault.

TV and Print Media in the Automotive Industry

TV and Print were the two first media in terms of automotive consumer recognition. In the survey conducted by Roger, more than half remembered advertisements that were on TV, while more than 25% remembered those in print media (See **Exhibit 9**). Moreover, most Indians surveyed acknowledged the fact that emotion could only be conveyed through a TV film, whereas print was useful to support the message conveyed on TV.

Therefore, given the importance of the emotional link between Indian consumers and brands, TV seemed to be crucial in order for Renault to reach the most consumers. However, TV advertisements remained a very periodic means of communication. Print was essential to ensure long-term message delivery. TV and print were therefore two essential and complementary means to conduct a successful communication campaign in India.

After gathering all this information, Roger felt the weight of the task upon him. Many elements needed to be taken into consideration to help Renault deliver a successful communication strategy in India. The

---

[6]A. Schwittay (5/2011) New Media practices in India: Bridging past and future, markets and development. *International Journal of communications*, http://ijoc.org.
[7]Nielsen New Media survey (09/2011) http://blog.nielsen.com/nielsenwire/global/connecting-and-engaging-with-digital-indian-consumers/.

perception of premium in India, and how it differed from the Western perspective, needed to be thoroughly understood in order to appeal to Indian consumers. Renault's perception in India was crucial to outline key advantages and ways to improve. Then, in terms of opportunities, the rise of social media, coupled with Formula 1's burgeoning awareness in India could be considered, as well as previous examples of innovative communication in other industries.

Roger had his work cut out.

Appendix

Exhibit 1:   Renault Sales Growth per Geography between 2006 and 2010.

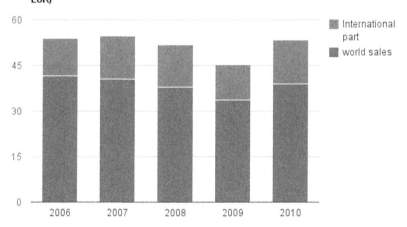

Source: Atlas Renault 2011.

Exhibit 2: Proportion of A2 Segment in Total Passenger Car Sales in India in 2010.

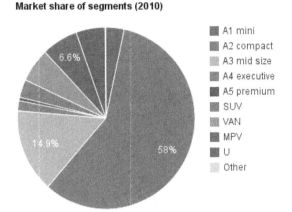

Source: Society of India Automotive Manufacturers.

Exhibit 3: Renault Key Attribute Rankings from 1–5 Aggregated From the Survey Conducted on 230 Individuals in India in 2011.

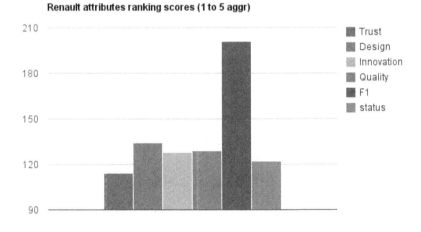

Exhibit 4:   Major Automotive Social Media Market Shares in India in Terms of Unique Visitors in 2010.

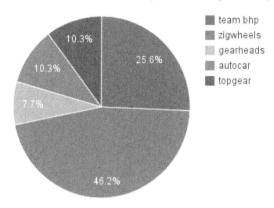

Exhibit 5:   Indian Annual GDP Growth from 2005 Until 2010.

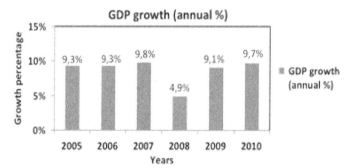

Source: World Bank Database.

Exhibit 6: Indian Annual GDP per Capita Growth from 2005 until 2010.

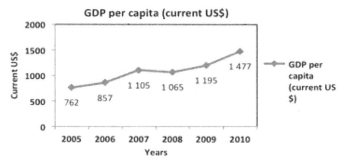

Source: World Bank Database.

Exhibit 7: Passenger Car Volumes: Segment-Wise Concentration.

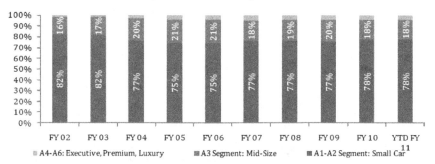

Source: SIAM, ICRA's Estimates; YTD till February 2011.

Exhibit 8: Trend in Market Share of Leading OEMs in the Domestic Passenger Vehicle Market.

OEMs	FY 02	FY 03	FY 04	FY 05	FY 06	FY 07	FY 08	FY 09	FY 10	YTD* FY 11
Maruti Suzuki	50.4%	46.7%	46.7%	45.9%	46.1%	46.1%	45.9%	46.5%	44.7%	44.9%
Hyundai Motors	13.0%	14.6%	14.4%	13.4%	13.9%	14.1%	14.0%	15.7%	16.2%	14.4%
Tata Motors	13.2%	14.7%	15.5%	16.9%	16.5%	16.4%	14.7%	14.9%	14.7%	14.0%
M&M	6.6%	7.4%	7.6%	7.5%	7.4%	6.5%	8.4%	7.7%	8.0%	7.2%
General Motors	1.3%	1.2%	2.0%	2.7%	2.7%	2.8%	4.3%	4.0%	4.5%	4.3%
Ford	2.2%	2.2%	2.4%	2.6%	2.5%	3.0%	2.2%	1.8%	1.9%	3.9%
Toyota Motors	3.7%	4.3%	4.7%	4.1%	4.1%	3.7%	3.6%	3.0%	3.3%	3.1%
Honda Motors	1.6%	1.9%	2.4%	3.5%	3.7%	4.4%	4.1%	3.4%	3.2%	2.5%

Source: SIAM, ICRA's (*Till February 2011).

Exhibit 9: Print Advertising Display in Newspapers, Magazines, and Hoardings (Chevrolet Cruze, Volkswagen Jetta, Renault Fluence).

The all-new Jetta. You'll do anything to drive it.

 DRIVE THE CHANGE

Exhibit 10: AT Kearney 2009 Research Report on Luxury Industry in Emerging Countries: Key Purchase Influencers for Premium Goods in India.

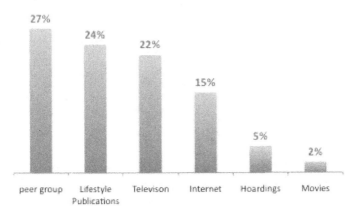

Exhibit 11: Renault Attributes Ranked from 1–5 by Interviewed Customers: Score is aggregated.

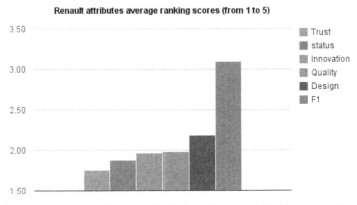

Source: Study on 210 Persons Conducted in Malls in Chennai, Delhi, Mumbai, and Bangalore.

Exhibit 12: "Bonjour India" Print Advertising Campaign (Hoardings).

Exhibit 13: Picture of a Renault Dealership in India (Delhi).

Exhibit 14: Picture of a Renault Dealership in China (Shanghai).

Chapter 10

Renault China: The Challenge of Increasing Brand Awareness[*]

Li Yan
Department of Information Systems,
Decision Science and Statistics, ESSEC

In 2009, Renault's sales started to improve in the Chinese market, thanks to Koleos, its SUV model. This model achieved huge success and became extremely popular among Chinese car buyers, partially due to a general passion for SUV models in this market. Koleos enabled Renault to multiply its sales by six between 2008 and 2009 with promising projections for the year 2010. In order to leverage the impact created by the success of Koleos, Pierre Chang,[1] director of Renault Asia and Africa regions, made the decision on September 5, 2010, to launch two new models, Latitude and Fluence, by mid-2011. He was aware of Renault's weakness in China: Poor brand awareness. In a recent market survey, the French car maker realised that the Koleos model was far better known to Chinese customers than the Renault brand itself. This was a severe challenge for the team to face, since brand attractiveness is one of the most important criteria when choosing a car. Mr Chang planned a first meeting to discuss this issue with the Chinese marketing team five days later.

The Meeting

The marketing team was headed by Philippe Li,[1] marketing director of Renault China, along with the financial director of the China unit,

---

[*]This case was prepared with the support of Margaux Tiberghien, Pierre-Antoine Brun, and Charles Decock, and with the collaboration of Capgemini Consulting and the employees of Renault China and France.
[1]Pseudonyms: For illustration purposes only.

Alexander Zhang.[1] Both were present for this meeting. Joseph Ming,[1] the product planning manager opened the meeting:

> *"Thank you all for attending this essential meeting. As you may have known, the Renault family will be enlarged with two new models: Latitude and Fluence. After the success of Koleos, our strategy is to reinforce Renault's position as a French CBU[2] brand in the Chinese Market. Latitude is a sedan model designed for the Chinese market. It is an elegant, comfortable and well-designed model targeting businessmen. Fluence is a sporty model, comfortable and refined, designed to support our brand rebirth in China."*

After an hour-long explanation of the target, competition and features of the two models, the marketing team already had the impression that launching Latitude and Fluence would not be as easy as Koleos. Koleos was the right model to launch at the right time as the SUV was extremely popular in China and there were very few competitors in that segment at that time. To increase Renault brand awareness would be crucial for the success of the new launches.

> *"Well, sales volume is increasing for this year; however, it is still quite low and we need to be careful with our budget. You have to design a low-cost communication strategy."*

These concerns from Alexander Zhang highlighted the challenges for the marketing team: Communicating the brand to the Chinese customers in a cost-efficient and innovative way. Mr Chang reminded the marketing team:

> *"Of course, as we discussed in July, Chinese customers talk about Koleos without knowing the Renault brand. We have to leverage Koleos to strengthen Renault brand awareness and to establish our position as a reliable car brand in the Chinese market before launching Latitude and Fluence. I trust you, Mr Li, and your team. I am sure you will find a good strategy to enhance Renault brand awareness."*

Renault's Strategy

Before designing a new communication strategy, Mr Li decided to gather his team to sum up Renault's current strategy in China, which is organised into four points.

---

[2]Completely Built Unit. Renault produces all its cars outside of China and imports them.

- *Casual Luxury*: The Renault brand is positioned as a 'casual luxury' brand. Renault offers distinctive design and innovative technology with high quality at an affordable price along with premium service. This strategy aims to communicate the same image through vendors and media to deliver a consistent message to customers (See **Exhibit 1**).
- *R-Redi*: Renault-Retail Environment Design Initiatives (R-Redi) aims to rebuild the distribution network to provide a better image of Renault and a new interpretation of hospitality, peace of mind, convenience and long-term customer relationship *via* the dealership.
- *TOE*: Renault Total Ownership Experience (TOE) echoes the R-Redi strategy of hospitality, peace of mind, convenience and long-term customer relationships *via* the dealership by providing a three-year (or 100,000 km) warranty, three years' (or 60,000 km) free maintenance and 24 hour free road assistance.
- *Product Rejuvenation*: The strategy is to develop a local after-sales product enhancement programme and to develop a hybrid distribution business model.

In order to design the new communication strategy, Mr Li asked his marketing intelligence department, which is responsible for market analysis and benchmarking, to draw an overview of Renault's current situation in China and its environment.

Renault's Current Situation in China

The history of Renault in China is quite short. It is the only major foreign brand with no joint venture to sell cars in China. Renault tried to launch a joint venture in the early 1990s with Sanjiang to produce the Renault Trafic in China. The Chinese car market was exploding then and all the foreign car manufacturers wanted to secure a share of it. However, instead of seeing exponential growth, Sanjiang–Renault stagnated because of its inexperience in the car market. Only a few hundred cars were sold in China and this joint venture terminated its production in 2002.

Renault's sales in China are negligible considering the size of the market. Even though its sales experienced a big increase, Renault sold only 5,321 cars in 2009 in a market with a total annual volume of 11.5 million cars sold. Renault is late compared to other Western brands such as Volkswagen, which arrived in the market in the 1980s.

Low consumer perception

Chinese people consider Renault as an old brand with a low service level. Renault buyers tend to be people who are influenced by French culture due to their educational background or their work experience. For instance, many Chinese Renault customers have already travelled or studied in France or work for French companies. Those customers have high expectations in terms of customer service. The TOE service strategy is the answer to their expectations. For Mr Li, this part of Renault's strategy should be emphasised within the new communication strategy.

Low awareness of French car brands

In China, brand is extremely important as it ensures the quality and prestige of the car in the mind of the consumer. A brand with high awareness and good reputation is a required criterion for buyers when choosing a car. In many cases, the country of origin influences the brand perception. For instance, German car brands hold the leading positions by far in the Chinese car market, as they are synonymous with high quality, security, reliability, and performance. On the contrary, the perception of brands from France is more related to attributes such as elegance, romance, freedom and love. This explains why French fashion, cosmetics and wine products are so attractive for Chinese consumers. However, such perceptions of French brands do not contribute to the awareness of a car brand for which more 'masculine' attributes are often considered.

Low exposure of mass media communication

China is a mass market but deeply segmented due to huge differences in consumption patterns among the different regions and cities. Targeting the whole country as a single market is ineffective, therefore car-makers focus on certain parts of the country or certain types of cities to ensure they maximise their profit. As a result, intense communication exposure is made by big car brands in tier 1 and tier 2 cities, where the demand for cars is highly concentrated. For Mr Li, the size and strength of these companies make it extremely hard for Renault to compete in the same areas, knowing the gap between their available budgets. With a low budget and low exposure in mass communication, the French brand is hardly noticeable in this country.

Chinese Customers' Specificities

To design an efficient communication strategy, Renault's marketing team needs to identify Chinese consumers' specificities and adapt Renault's communication message to its target.

Chinese values

In Chinese society, taking care of family is one's top priority in life. Being family-oriented is a key Chinese value. As a consequence of this, family plays an important role in the car purchasing decision. Even if the man of the family makes the final decision to buy the car, he would always ask for advice from his wife, his children and sometimes his parents.

Another important value of Chinese society is *mianzi/lian*, meaning 'saving face' (keeping one's honour, reputation and pride). This central value of Chinese culture influences social behaviour and leads to the obligation to succeed. Owning a prestigious car is a symbol of success, which is important for *mianzi*.

Guanxi, which is translated as 'social network' or 'social relationship', is another factor strongly influencing relationships among people in China. Belonging to a community is positively connoted in China.

Car purchasing process

The purchasing process is highly formalised and efficient. Before purchasing a car, Chinese consumers tend to inform themselves about the car brand, model, specifications and price through research done on the Internet or through friends or relatives. Word-of-mouth is the main source of information during the car purchasing process. Then, they go to different showrooms to compare several specific models from different brands and get familiar with the dealers. A relationship is essential for the purchasing decision, this step is strategic for the car dealer to build trust with customers. Third, they will try the car and finally make the purchase. Usually they would visit a car dealer two or three times before making the final decision.

The process is far shorter compared with that in Western countries since most Chinese customers have more or less formed an idea about which model they are willing to buy before entering the shop. Therefore, the information step is central. For that reason, evangelisation by existing customers and online communication of brand information are crucial for Renault's strategy.

Geographic disparity and consumer profiles

Chinese customers' behaviour is very different according to their geographical locations. The coastal population and tier 1 and tier 2 city inhabitants enjoy higher income, have better access to Western brands and adopt high-end technologies faster. Inland and tier 3 city populations are newcomers in the consumer society. They are more sensitive to word of mouth and more likely to trust a salesperson than comments on the Internet. Their access to new means of communication is still fairly limited. Along with these differences in customer behaviour, the former are more likely to be influenced by Western culture, while the latter are more attached to traditional Chinese values.

CBU buyers

CBU buyers are three to four years younger than CKD[3] buyers. They have a good educational background and a managerial position or are small business owners. They mainly live in tier 1 and tier 2 cities. They enjoy the premium value and prestige that are embodied by a CBU car brand. Brand image is the number one reason for them to buy a CBU car.

Communication Trends in China

Another issue complementary to the marketing message is how to deliver this message. **Exhibit 3** provides an overview of means of communication available in China.

Chinese consumers value the Internet

Chinese consumers use the Internet to obtain pre-purchase information about cars. They look for information from car-dedicated websites, read news, compare models and prices, reflect on other car users' comments and

---

[3]Completely Knocked Down. CKD automobiles are imported as parts and not as one assembled unit.

feedback and participate in forum discussions. Vertical automobile websites such as Xcar and AutoHome represent the main sources of information for Chinese consumers when conducting car comparison. To get information from these websites is one of the most important steps in the purchasing process. Internet has a stronger impact in China than it does in other countries (See **Exhibit 4**). 59% of Chinese Internet users made purchasing decisions based on user-generated information online. This figure is 19% in the US.

Growth of social networking site (SNS) users

With more than 235 million SNS users, 294 million blog users and 148 million bulletin board system users in 2010, China hosts the biggest online social population. Although major international SNS services are banned in China due to censorship, local players dominate the digital media landscape with a better understanding of Chinese users' needs. The main websites are RenRen and Kaixin001, equivalent to Facebook; QQ, equivalent to MSN and Facebook; Sina Weibo and Tencent Weibo, equivalent to Twitter; and Youku, equivalent to YouTube. Entertainment, searching and sharing information about brands and gaming are the top three activities Chinese consumers participate in on social networking websites (See **Exhibit 5** for social media landscape in China).

The rise of mobile usage

In line with revenue growth, the rate of household possession of mobile phones rose steadily and significantly from 40.8% in 2003 to 84.9% in 2008. In 2010, there were more mobile Internet users in China than in any other country: 66% of Chinese Internet users access the Web *via* mobile phones, and use them for instant messaging, voice calls and emails.

Best practices in communication

In 2009, the most preferred car brand in China was BMW (See **Exhibit 6**). The brand communication of BMW has not only covered every traditional media (television, radio, magazine), but has also invested a substantial budget in social media (See **Exhibit 7**). BMW communicates through its foundation, promoting cultural, educational and charity events. This strategy provides the brand with a positive corporate image among Chinese customers. In 2008, BMW launched Mission 3 in China for the launch of its BMW 3 series model (See **Exhibit 8**). BMW developed in September 2008, a mobile application including videos, wallpapers and exclusive M3 mobile themes to promote the BMW Series 3. The company created the BMW owner club to develop community and loyalty among customers and to increase word of mouth among existing BMW customers and potential customers.

Mr Li reminded himself of an interesting case his wife shared with him. It seems that cosmetics brand Lancôme developed a very interesting community in 2006 and launched a successful campaign on Kaixin001 in 2009 (See **Exhibit 9**).

Renault's Strengths

After reflecting on all the difficulties Renault has faced in China in the past, Mr Chang would also like to highlight the strength of this brand. Renault is a powerful and prestigious brand with a long history of success in France. The Renault brand benefits from strong advantages that need to be explored and exposed to the Chinese market.

Renault is a CBU brand

Being a CBU car completely manufactured outside China is considered to be premium by the Chinese customers. In addition, among all the CBU brands in the Chinese market, Renault's price advantage is obvious. It has additional values that appeal to Chinese car owners: Renault cars are sophisticated, premium and target middle and high class customers, plus they are environmentally friendly and provide innovative technology.

Image of France is attractive

While French car brands remain largely unknown in the Chinese market, they can rely on the general attractiveness that is associated with the French way of living. With values such as family, culture, romance, freedom, and conviviality, French values resonate in China. Increasing the positioning of Renault as a French brand by strengthening the association between the Renault brand and these values, could improve Chinese customers' perception of this brand.

Renault can benefit from Koleos' success

As a demonstration of social status and lifestyle, SUV models are very popular in the Chinese market, and it is estimated that the passion for the SUV will continue. Renault can leverage Koleos' success to lead its communication strategy. Koleos' distinctive design, innovative technology and high quality at an affordable price provide Renault with a sophisticated brand image, echoing the 'casual luxury' strategy. Renault needs to find a way to let Chinese customers better understand the Renault brand through their interest in Koleos.

Renault's Current Communication Strategy

Mr Li is aware of the weakness of Renault's communication strategy in China. As a small player, budget remains low. Finding new and innovative ways to communicate is one part of his project, but his team cannot neglect the fact that some existing communication practices could be improved. **Exhibit 10** provides a breakdown of the current marketing spending.

Renault on the Internet

With 60,000 unique visitors per month, Renault's website traffic is lower than that of big car brands. Brand details are displayed on Renault's official website which include product information, brand information and history, events, news, product brochure downloads and test-drive advertisements. Along with updates on the official website, car dealers publish additional content on their micro-blogs such as news, events, and information on specific models. They also interact with customers through their own forums.

The Renault marketing team dedicates a small part of the budget to advertising on third party websites. But with the increasing popularity of this media as a communication channel, prices for banner ads on these websites are soaring.

Public relations events

The Renault marketing team currently focuses its communication strategy on promotion *via* events. For every invited journalist, if the event is taking place somewhere other than his or her home city, Renault will finance accommodation and transportation. Several types of events were organised by Renault's PR team during the past year: New model launches, media test-drives, corporate social responsibility events, celebrity sponsorships, Formula 1 and auto-shows (see **Exhibit 11** for further information). For the moment, most of the major events are related to Koleos specifically. Still, compared with big car brands, fewer journalists are invited to Renault's events, but Renault cannot afford to cover the costs of too many journalists.

Car dealers' communication responsibilities

For the launch of each model, Renault's marketing team provides car dealers with a marketing platform document containing all the information and advantages concerning the specific model and a plan of their marketing activities. They create a document to provide sales people with selling points for the model so that they can present them to the potential buyers. As direct ambassadors of the brand to consumers, car dealers hold a huge responsibility in the communication strategy. While maintaining a consistent and uniform image as Renault dealers, each of them also develops unique events to promote Renault models and the brand according to their budget and needs. Such events include cocktails, gifts for existing customers who refer new customers, weekend escapes and test-drives.

After reflecting on all these issues, Mr Chang determines the following steps for the new marketing project:

- The first step will be to improve the current communication strategy by determining which practices need to be continued and which need to be abandoned.
- The second step is to develop new and innovative communication methods in order to promote the Renault brand by taking into consideration Renault's weaknesses and strengths in China, Chinese customers' specificities, and the new communication trends in China.
- The last step is to evaluate the cost and benefits of the new communication methods. The Renault China marketing team has to keep in mind that their budget is very limited so they need to be aware how the new strategy will impact the structure of the communication budget.

Exhibit Summary

Exhibit 1: Casual Luxury Strategy of Renault.

Exhibit 2: Renault History and Perspective in China.

Exhibit 3: Means of Communication in China.

Exhibit 4: Quality and Credibility of Information Sources for Car Purchases.

Exhibit 5: Social Media Landscape in China.

Exhibit 6: Most Preferred Car Brands in China in 2009.

Exhibit 7: BMW in Social Media Websites.

Exhibit 8: BMW Mission 3.

Exhibit 9: Lancôme Social Media Strategy.

Exhibit 10: Renault China Marketing Budget Repartition in 2009.

Exhibit 11: Renault China Marketing Channels and Costs.

Exhibit 1:   Casual Luxury Strategy of Renault.

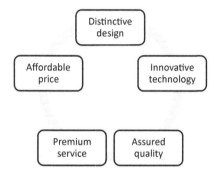

Exhibit 2: Renault History and Perspectives in China.

In the recent years, Renault has developed its international presence through alliances and acquisitions. The alliance with Nissan in 1999 was part of their strategy of development in Asian market, which represents the biggest opportunities for automobile manufacturers currently. That also explains why in 2000, they bought Samsung Motors, a Korean brand founded in 1994, to settle Renault in the Asian continent. In 1999, Renault also bought Dacia, a Romanian brand founded in 1966. With this purchase, the brand will take advantage of the hub of development in Central Europe and Eastern Europe. With the model Logan, the group targets emerging countries all over the world.

On February 9, 2006, Carlos Ghosn announced the Renault Contract 2009. This plan emphasised three main points: Quality, profitability and growth. This growth plan defined the new Renault strategy for the next four years: To become the most profitable European car brand in the world. Renault planned to be present on five continents and decrease its sales dependency on Europe to 50% by 2010.

The new alliances with Asian brands were part of this strategy to develop in Asian market, with two main objectives:

— Enter highly hermetic markets such as Japan with Nissan and South Korea with Samsung Motors, third and second Asian markets after China respectively.
— Reduce production costs by developing global synergy through increasing the number of common parts.

Exhibit 3:   Means of Communication in China.

Media	Advantages	Disadvantages

Television	• Wide coverage
	• Increase brand awareness quickly
	• High attention rates in tier 1 and tier 2 cities
		• Short duration
		• Do not target well
		• Expensive:
		  • 100K RMB for 15 seconds in a local TV channel in Ningbo
		  • 1M RMB in a national TV channel like CCTV
		  • CCTV and 10 local TV channels: 20–30 million RMB for three weeks coverage

Newspaper/ Magazine	• Target well if in lifestyle magazine or travel magazine • Traditional media important for Tier 2 and Tier 3 cities • Wide exposure to targeted audience	• Short duration of the displayed ad or article • Too many newspapers: More than 1000 in Shanghai. • Expensive
Car Magazine	• Target well at professionals with specialised car magazines	• Limited audience • Expensive

(Continued)

Exhibit 3: (*Continued*)

Media	Advantages	Disadvantages
Radio	• Large audience, especially during rush hours • High attention rate in big cities	• Only an oral message • Short duration • Audience are mostly likely to be car owners who listen to the radio while driving • Expensive
Billboards	• Large audience • Long duration: At least three months	• Do not target well • Expensive: 500 K RMB/year
Internet	• Cheap and quick to communicate • Long duration of displayed ads or articles • Large audience, easily targeted • Can provide a lot of information and interaction • Common channel to compare products	• Hard to control information • Low coverage in small cities and in the West
Mobile Internet	• Quick and cheap • Booming market for smartphones, it will be No.1 communication channel in China	• Hard to control, may have negative impact on the brand • Still low penetration in China • Seen as cheap advertising for the moment

Exhibit 4:   Quality and Credibility of Information Sources for Car Purchases.

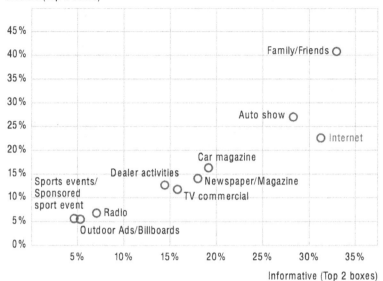

Credible (Top 2 boxes)

Informative (Top 2 boxes)

Exhibit 5: Social Media Landscape in China.

		Type	User Demographics	Active Users (millions)	Reg. Users (millions)
Qzone (Tencent)	QQ空间	Nickname SNS	Teens	190	481
RenRen	renren	Real-name SNS	Students, white-collars	95	170
Pengyou		Real-name SNS	Students, white-collars	80	131
Sina Weibo	新浪微博	Microblog	White-collars	70	90
Kaixin001		Real-name SNS	White-collars	40	95
51.com	51.com	Real-name SNS	Lesser-tier cities, rural users	40	178
Douban	douban	Real-name SNS	Urban youth	20	40
Taomee (Seer, Mole, etc.)	Taomee	Children's SNS / Games	Children, mothers	20	180
Tencent Weibo		Microblog	Lesser-tier cities	20	100
Jiayuan		Dating SNS	White-collars	11	30
Tao Jianghu (Taobao)	淘江湖	E-commerce SNS	All	10	1200 (all Taobao)
Bai Shehui (Sohu)		Real-name SNS	White-collars	5	30
Zhenai		Dating SNS	White-collars	3	26
Baihe		Dating SNS	White-collars	2	23
iPartment		Avatar / dating SNS	Urban youth	1	20

Exhibit 6: Most Preferred Car Brands in China in 2009.

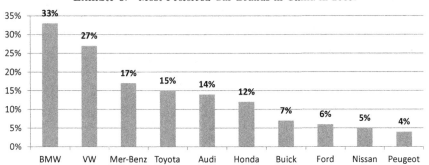

BMW	VW	Mer-Benz	Toyota	Audi	Honda	Buick	Ford	Nissan	Peugeot
33%	27%	17%	15%	14%	12%	7%	6%	5%	4%

Exhibit 7: BMW in Social Media Websites.

A three-step strategy to introduce the BMW brand on Kaixin001

Step 1: Launch:

Before the official launch of its brand page on Kaixin001 in 2010 (http://www. kaixin001.com/bmw), BMW had already rolled out some great test campaigns on Kaixin001 since Oct 2009. BMW displayed information on brand page such as BMW Car model Showcase, Fan and visitors' avatars and Brand Zone tabbed sections. The brand page was divided in several areas, displaying different types of information:

- Message board.
- Profile information.
- Pictures.
- Blog: New product launch, news report and interactive activities.
- Re-tweet (of blog entries).

Step 2: Engagement:

- X1 Smiley Face Sharing competition: Fans who shared smiley faces with 10+ friends in one day would get a chance to win unique BMW X1 prizes (**1,365 participants**).
- Image Puzzle Game: For each game, BMW provided a combination of two images; participants needed to guess the result and upload their answer image (**7,969 participants**).

Step 3: Integration in Popular Car Parking Game:

"Car Parking" is one of the most popular games on Kaixin001, which has accumulated a remarkable number of players in China:

- **45 million people** have installed the game on their Kaixin001 profile pages.
- **5.5 million people** are playing it on a daily basis.

Compared to other automobiles in the game, BMW cars are much more expensive. Thus players needs to first make a lot of virtual money in order to own a BMW car. When they finally get a BMW, players express feelings of achievement.

2008 BMW and QQ

BMW created an online contest based on Qzone for BMW new vehicle line 1.

Participants were encouraged to share pictures from their life. The images were then voted to win big prizes, including the 1 series BMW. A key part of the communication process was BMW's launch of the 1 series at the Beijing automotive show: Participants were encouraged to follow links to information about the auto show. The promotion was a good way to arouse customers' curiosity and interest. This one-month campaign gathered over 27,000 participants and generated 1,104,241 votes.

Exhibit 8: BMW Mission 3.

BMW Mission 3 is divided into three parts: Physical Limit Challenge (mission 1), Mind Developing (mission 2) and Soul Touching (mission 3). From the beginning of March to the end of June, 2008, tryouts were held at 69 BMW authorised dealerships all over China for the national tour, which stretched across the country from June 11 to July 1. Each member of the final winning team won one year's free use of a BMW 3 Series with unlimited mileage, as well as other prizes.

The national tour started in the historical southern city of Guangzhou, passed through cities including Changsha, Chongqing, Wuhan, Shanghai, and Beijing, and ended in the northern industrial center of Shenyang. The tour consisted of seven stages:

— June 11–13, Guangzhou–Changsha;
— June 14–16, Changsha–Chongqing;
— June 17–19, Chongqing–Wuhan;
— June 20–22, Wuhan–Shanghai;
— June 23–25, Shanghai–Qingdao;
— June 26–28, Qingdao–Beijing;
— June 29–July 1, Beijing–Shenyang.

Participants selected from the tryouts took part in one of the seven stages. During each three-day race, team members had to display their potential and advantages, went through a series of physical and mental challenges, and completed the three missions. The winning team of each stage gathered in Shenyang in early July. The final lucky draw saw one team win the big prize. The other winning teams of each stage also received prizes.

Exhibit 9: Lancôme Social Media Strategy.

In 2006, Lancôme built its own Chinese online community (www.rosebeauty.com.cn). On this website, consumers can get information about products and interact with brand managers and other consumers through the forum, by rating products. The site also provides beauty advice.

In 2009, Lancôme started to use SNS site Kaixin001 to drive traffic to this community with an online beauty contest that lasted 50 days; 18,038 people participated in this contest and over 1,232,459 votes were registered; Lancôme products were offered to winners.

Alongside, Lancôme created two online tests targeted at white-collar women: A skin test and a career personality test. Over 200,000 women took the test.

By leveraging SNS, Lancôme has successfully increased its brand awareness in China.

Exhibit 10: Renault China Marketing Budget Repartition in 2009.

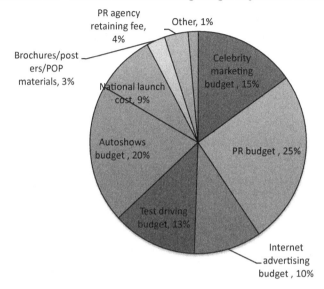

Exhibit 11: Renault China Marketing Channels and Costs.

	Description	Cost
Sport Events	• Formula 1 is good for the brand image because it is covered by all the media • Target well • Associated with high technology • Still not very popular in China	• Really expensive
Auto Show	• Positive for brand image and sales • Interaction platform between end customers and sales persons • Organised both at national level (in Beijing and Shanghai) and in local cities by car dealers	• More than 300 K RMB per show

(*Continued*)

Exhibit 11: (*Continued*)

Launch of a New Model	• Important coverage • National communication impact • Promote model and brand	• Two million RMB per launch
CSR Events	• National coverage • Attractive both for customers and media • Provide positive corporate image	• Depends on the events
Celebrity Sponsoring	• National or local coverage depending on the popularity of the celebrity • Brand image depends on the image of the celebrity • Hard to measure the effectiveness of this strategy	• E.g., for a concert sponsoring: 1.3 million RMB
Media Test Drive	• National coverage • One model promotion • Positive impact for the brand as customers and press can test the model and give their own opinions • Word-of-mouth effect	• Around 1.5 million RMB

Part D

Introduction

Social Entrepreneurship

Social entrepreurship is defined as the attempt to use business techniques to solve social problems. It is a challenge exemplified in the following cases, which focus on two non-profit organisations balancing a desire to achieve humanitarian goals with the need to deliver financial stability and sustainability.

In the first case, **PlaNet Finance** is featured once again (See Chapter 3), but this time its objective is to help vulnerable farmers in Cambodia and Vietnam. The project, called FinInc Asia, has been designed to improve financial inclusion and help tackle food insecurity in the region.

Before the arrival of PlaNet Finance, famers in Cambodia and Vietnam found that typical microfinance loans did not meet their needs. The interest payments did not match their cash flow due to the seasonality of farming, meaning that microfinance institutions faced higher risks when lending to farmers and thus were less willing to do so.

To meet this need, PlaNet Finance developed a new loan product with a repayment schedule that was tailored to the requirements of farmers. In order to implement the new loan, PlaNet Finance worked with a microfinance institution in each country; however, there was a dramatic difference in results between the two. In Cambodia, the pilot project was performing well, while in Vietnam, it suffered setbacks before even getting off the ground.

The case explores the differing attitudes to microfinance and the intervention of Western NGOs in the two countries and looks at how an organisation like PlaNet Finance can best market its products to both local microfinance institutions and the end-users. With a particular focus on agriculture, the case discusses whether there is a 'social return' component to agri-microfinance that is different and more compelling than other such investments.

Cambodia is also the setting for the second case, which focuses on a French NGO called **Pour un Sourire d'Enfant**. The organisation, which has been operating since 1995, faced stagnating donations from its traditional donor base in Europe. Therefore, it was looking at alternative sources to shore up funds. However, not all the stakeholders were in agreement about how to proceed. Instead, there were clear, competing preferences. One group of stakeholders preferred a more traditional way of raising funds by widening the net to bring in new donors. Another group favoured a more commercially oriented strategy that would build on the expertise and reputation that Pour un Sourire d'Enfant had developed over the years.

As with PlaNet Finance, the case of Pour un Sourire d'Enfant illustrates the dilemmas faced by an organisation that has reached the cusp where social motives meet commercial imperatives.

Chapter 11

PlaNet Finance: A New Microfinance Loan in Cambodia and Vietnam*

Ashwin Malshe

Marketing Department, ESSEC

In November 2012, Jay Supetran was on a visit to Vietnam and Cambodia to study the impact of a last-stage microfinance project in the agricultural sector. For the past two years he had been working as Regional Coordinator in both countries for French microfinance advisor PlaNet Finance (PF). The project, titled FinInc Asia, was aimed at improving financial inclusion and social impact regarding food security in the region. Specifically, PF was keen to tackle the lack of a relevant financial product for vulnerable farmers in Vietnam and Cambodia. PF worked closely with a few local microfinance institutions (MFIs) to design a new financial product, the 'Agri-Microfinance' (AMF) loan. The purpose of the loan and the repayment schedule were to better fit the needs of farmers. As a first step, only a few MFIs were selected by PF to conduct a pilot test for AMF under FinInc Asia. In the pilot test, the Cambodian MFI, Thaneakea Phum Cambodia (TPC) was performing well, whereas the Vietnamese MFI, Thanh Hoa Fund (THF) had barely started to develop its offering in the countryside.

Jay had been working closely with both the MFIs and knew that there were structural differences in the attitudes towards microfinance in the two countries. Yet, he was not convinced that these alone explained the vastly different performances of the two MFIs. Jay was anxious to find the source of the differential performance as project completion was less than three

*This case was prepared with the support of Antoine Cuénin, Gregoire Delamare, Valentin Lecouteux, and Suzanne Mercereau, and with the collaboration of Capgemini Consulting and the employees and partners of PlaNet Finance.

months away. If the pilot test in Vietnam was considered a failure, it would jeopardise the penetration of AMF loan products in new MFIs. It was also important to run this project to its very end, as PF's credibility was at stake. "Why are the outcomes of Cambodian and Vietnamese MFIs so different?" Jay wondered. Was it the way the MFIs worked? Or that the governments in the two countries had different policies toward microfinance? Was it a cultural difference? There were so many factors that could explain the gap. The identification of the cause for this differential performance was a key to identifying solutions for improving the uptake of AMF products leading to more food security, the primary goal of FinInc Asia project. Time was of the essence.

PlaNet Finance (PF) Group

PF describes itself as a leading international non-profit organisation with the mission to alleviate poverty through the development of microfinance, therefore increasing the unbanked and underbanked's access to financial services.[1] Since its founding in 1998, PF has evolved into a group entity, whose collective mission is to increase the access of financial services through the development of microfinance. With 1,300 employees worldwide and operations in 80 countries, the group is renowned for its expertise in four different areas of the microfinance industry:

- Rating: Evaluation and rating agency for MFIs and other financial institutions.
- Funding: Advisory services in debt management and financial vehicles, peer-to-peer lending platform and capital investment.
- Microinsurance: Development and management of microinsurance programmes.
- Consulting and research: Advisory services, technical assistance in microfinance, field-based microfinance programme financing, research and training.

PF Advisory Services

PF Advisory Services is the Group's non-governmental organisation (NGO), which supports MFIs through technical assistance and advisory services. It has three main units of expertise:

---

[1] http://www.planetfinance.org/.

- Microfinance and Consulting: This serves a wide-range of actors, especially MFIs, primarily providing them with non-financial services such as assistance on capacity-building, training, design of processes, etc. This includes consulting services for banks, financial institutions, and retailers to help them enter the microfinance market and reach 'bottom of the pyramid' clientele.
- Microfinance and Knowledge: Provides support to the microfinance sector through sharing of experience and best practices. Also, advises governments or other actors on their microfinance strategies, regulations and policies.
- Microfinance Plus: Leveraging the MFI's network and resources to tackle critical issues such as health, environment, education problems, and rural areas development; for example, leveraging the existing MFIs' infrastructure to provide training to micro entrepreneurs and especially women.

In 2011, PF Advisory Services' total annual resources were US $12 million (compared to US $350,000 in 1998). Of these, 22% came from sales of advisory services and the remaining 78% came from both private and public partners. PF Advisory Services offers private partners several ways to support its activities. For example, partners could help by providing in-kind (i.e., in the form of goods and services) staff services, donations (IT, software etc.), or direct financial support for the development of microfinance projects.

Microfinance Overview

Microfinance aims to provide financial products and services to people not qualified for those supplied by the traditional financial structure. Although microfinance products were initially designed for the urban population, now microfinance caters to more rural areas. Estimates indicate that there are more than 10,000 MFIs worldwide. It is a booming industry that has seen 30% annual growth over several years.

Microfinance has long been considered as a charitable cause aimed at giving money to poor people. However, the industry has reached a significant level of professionalism and is using the same vocabulary (loan portfolio, portfolio at risk, etc.) as the classic financial industry. The range of products offered evolved from mere microcredit in the 1970s to today's more complex ones such as insurance, fund transfers and savings plans. Further, loans have become more and more specific to client needs. Microfinance products can be for an urban shop owner, a micro entrepreneur, or in the case Jay was considering, a farmer. By focusing exclusively on maximising 'social return on investment' (SROI) in contrast to simply the financial return on investment, microfinance helps the most vulnerable people in underprivileged areas.

Microfinance, however, remains a controversial topic. With an average annual interest rate of 37% for microcredit, these loans are often considered expensive given the resources of the people who avail themselves of them. Further, it is hard to measure the real effect MFIs have on their clients. Many argue that microfinance is only tackling short-term survival needs without taking into account long-term ones like education or training.

Microfinance in Vietnam and Cambodia

Two-thirds of the world's microfinance borrowers live in Asia[2] and the number of these borrowers doubled between 2006 and 2011. Cumulatively 74 million Asian microcredit borrowers have borrowed more than US $34 billion.

In 2008, the Asia–Pacific Microcredit Summit in Bali celebrated the success of microfinance in the region. Nevertheless, there remain critical drawbacks, especially in terms of financial inclusion. The lack of adequate financial access for farmers is one of the main reasons why 240 million people in the region still lack basic food security.[3]

Vietnam

Vietnam's economically active population demands microfinance services. In 2011, cumulative microfinance loans worth US $5.5 billion were given to around nine million borrowers.[4] **Exhibit 1** shows the number of borrowers and aggregate microfinance loans between 2003 and 2011. Almost all of the microfinance activity in Vietnam is through government-backed institutions.

---

[2]Asia Microfinance Analysis and Bench-marking Report 2008. http://www.themix.org/sites/default/files/2008%20Asia%20Microfinance%20Analysis%20and%20Benchmarking%20Report.pdf.

[3]Nihal Amerasinghe. Poverty, Food Security, and Agricultural Biotechnology: Challenges and Opportunities.http://www.adb.org/Documents/Conference/Technology_Poverty_AP/adb5.pdf.

[4]http://www.mixmarket.org/mfi/country/Vietnam.

Cambodia

Cambodia has 33 registered MFIs. The local structure is relatively well-organised and some MFIs are clearly in competition with others in order to increase their portfolio size. In contrast, in Vietnam only two MFIs are registered. The ecosystem in Cambodia is more diverse and a few players are clearly serving the same targets with different products and services.

In 2011, cumulative microfinance loans worth US $1.6 billion were given to around 1.4 million borrowers.[5] **Exhibit 2** shows the number of borrowers and aggregate microfinance loans between 2003 and 2011.

The FinInc Asia Project and its Background

To reduce risk, MFIs typically fund small urban shops with regular and stable cash flows. Further, these small businesses often have collateral to offer as a guarantee for the loan. As a consequence, all potential borrowers use the same financial product for different needs.

Traditionally perceived as risky clients, farmers do not qualify for standard microfinance loan products. Before the arrival of PF, only multi-purpose or seasonal loans were offered to farmers. They could use the loan for any purpose and not only for agriculture. However, the interest payments did not match their real cash inflow as the seasonality of farming activity creates fluctuations in the inflow and outflow of cash during the year. Consequently, MFIs face higher risks when lending to farmers.

On the one hand, farmers' credit requirements are high as they need to purchase certified seeds, fertilisers, herbicides, as well as harvest and process produce. In addition, the risks threatening production are high. Pests, natural calamities, low yield, or low buying price are a few of the risks directly faced by farmers that could seriously harm their ability to reimburse loans, resulting in credit default. As a consequence, MFIs have progressively drifted away from their original social mission and instead supported activities that generate regular cash-flows. This strategic shift results in a struggle to balance MFIs' financial goals with their social goals. This widespread dearth of agricultural credit has been a major cause of the food insecurity of 240 million people in the Mekong region and in

---

[5] http://www.mixmarket.org/mfi/country/Cambodia.

the Philippines. In 2012, 15.4% of Cambodia's and 8.3% of Vietnam's populations were undernourished.[6]

PF perceives the exclusion of farmers due to their inherent riskiness as a potential threat for food security in the area. Therefore, PF is helping MFIs to develop Social Performance Management (SPM) within their organisations. SPM consists of a set of principles designed to serve needy people without changing the initial objective of microfinance. PF thus summed up their objective:

> *"In order to address the aforementioned challenges of limited financial access among the rural poor and the food insecurity problems it creates, PF proposes a three-year programme that will contribute to increased productivity among underserved small and low-income farm households through more inclusive financial services, responsible practices and synergy of efforts among microfinance networks and institutions in three Southeast Asian nations: The Philippines, Cambodia, and Vietnam. These countries have been selected because of the active role they play in the global microfinance sector. Cambodia and the Philippines are leading countries when it comes to outreach, innovation, and the application of information and communication technology. Vietnam represents not only a large and so far untapped market, but is also the gateway to other Mekong region countries where poverty is high."*

The FinInc Asia project has four main objectives:

1. Development of financial and non-financial products and services that meet the needs of low income farmers, especially specific AMF loans.
2. Integration of SPM into 45 participating MFIs *via* local microfinance networks.
3. Integration of financial literacy, consumer protection and transparency in participating MFIs.
4. MFI Network strengthening, action research, peer learning and exchange of expertise.

Jay and his team were involved in Cambodia and Vietnam, while another project manager handled the project in the Philippines. A trusting working relationship with microfinance networks takes time to achieve. This is in part because they are both implementation partners (for objectives 1, 2, and 3) but also recipients of technical assistance (objective 4).

---

[6] World Bank (http://data.worldbank.org/indicator/SN.ITK.DEFC.ZS).

As implementation partners, they need time to understand the 'partnership' rather than 'donors' approach, of which few of them are familiar.

The project implementation was over a period of 36 months in three strategic phases. Phase 1 activities included market research and studies, the development of training materials, financial product development, and pilot testing. Phase 2 encompassed the full implementation of each key result area. Finally phase 3 was designed to measure the impact created by activities in phases 1 and 2.

Despite major differences between Vietnam and Cambodia in terms of maturity in the microfinance sector, PF decided to launch the FinInc Asia project with the same schedule in both countries for ease of coordination. The effort estimated for each project's task and the availability of each resource were considered the same, when the work breakdown structure was made for Vietnam and Cambodia. Thus Jay and his team launched the project using microfinance as a tool to reduce food insecurity through better financial access.

Two Countries with Different Characteristics

Before the implementation of the FinInc Asia Project, Jay identified a few differences between the two countries. They can be classified in three main categories.

Historical

As an under-developed, post-conflict country and one of the poorest in Southeast Asia, Cambodia receives support from plenty of NGOs. They came to contribute to the country's development, which is still marked by a violent recent history and glaring poverty. The Cambodian Ministry of Interior reported that more than 1,500 NGOs[7] are registered in Cambodia. This large number makes this small country of 14 million inhabitants one of the nations with the highest concentration of NGOs in proportion to its population. Since 1992, from the beginning of the UN mission UNTAC (United Nations Transitional Authority in Cambodia), the number of NGOs has increased from 20 to the current 1,500. The absence of active political institutions and the commitment to development in Cambodia has left a

---

[7]http://www.ccc-cambodia.org/downloads/publication/Final%20Report%20NGO%20 Contribution%202010.pdf.

void that many NGOs have filled. Thus, Cambodia has a long tradition of welcoming NGOs and PF has experienced trusting relationships and total cooperation from local MFI partners to implement the FinInc Asia project.

The case of Vietnam is a bit different. Even if the number of NGOs has reached 700 and has provided Vietnam with nearly US $1.7 billion in non-refundable aid,[8] Vietnam's complex history as a formerly colonised and war-torn nation has impacted the social and business culture. For example, PF complained about lengthy and time-consuming negotiations with local MFIs. They had great difficulties in building relationships with local MFIs, which delayed project implementation. The guide 'Doing Business in Vietnam' notes that building trust in Vietnam takes more time than other countries. Specifically it states, "Business relationships in Vietnam are relatively formal and tend to take time to develop as Vietnamese like to get to know their foreign counterparts before conducting business. Vietnamese may be suspicious of those they don't know well at first, so be sure to spend the time during the first few meetings getting acquainted."[9]

Indeed, PF ensured that its project was kept top-of-mind *via* repeated meetings and thus demonstrated their commitment. Nevertheless, they faced difficulties in sharing knowledge and in implementing organisational changes in local MFIs.

Political

Three out of every five Cambodians are directly linked to agriculture. With one third of the national GDP contribution, the agricultural sector is considered crucial for the development of the country. As Cambodian officials are elected by the population, they need to get farmers' approval during election time. Therefore, government policies are aligned to benefit the farming sector. Agriculture has recently been declared as a national priority for the economic development of the country.[10]

---

[8]http://en.baomoi.com/Home/society/www.qdnd.vn/Foreign-NGOs-pledge-US151-mil-to-reduce-poverty-in-Vietnam-by-2011/82564.epi.

[9]http://www.communicaid.com/Access/pdf/library/culture/doing-business-in/Doing%20Business%20in%20Vietnam.pdf.

[10]http://www.nzte.govt.nz/explore-export-markets/market-research-by-industry/Biotechnology-and-agritechnology/Documents/Agribusiness-market-in-Cambodia-February-2011.pdf. *Exporter Guide: Agri-business in Cambodia.*

Over the last 50 years, the government has played a key role in agriculture,[11] with positive and negative consequences. In the 1960s, agricultural cooperatives were established and sponsored by the Cambodian state. From 1975 to 1979, cooperatives became forced collective labour during the Khmer Rouge government. Today, farmers' organisations can be farmer groups, associations, communities, cooperatives and federations. The goal is still to increase collective bargaining power.

In contrast, in Vietnam, agriculture only contributed 19.4% of its GDP,[12] while the manufacturing industry accounts for more than 42%.[13] Therefore, government priorities are aligned in favour of industry and services. With several State Owned Enterprises (SOEs) dealing with wood or more sophisticated goods in the south of Vietnam, the state is clearly helping the development of industry and services.[14]

Economic

While Cambodia is on a path to greater economic development, decades of war and internal conflicts have left it as one of the world's poorest countries. Poverty remains a prevailing policy issue, with 30.1% of the population under the poverty line in 2007 according to the Cambodia Socio–Economic Survey, with high prevalence in rural areas.[15] Food insecurity is also a crucial issue as one-third of Cambodia is undernourished,[16] meaning they consume less than the Minimum Daily Energy Requirement (MDER). Consequently, the Cambodian government actively supports NGOs and MFIs that are fighting poverty.

Even if hunger and poverty have existed for a significant period of time in Vietnam, the current situation is not as dramatic as it used to be. Vietnam's current poverty rate is 12% and 6.7% of the population is under the poverty

---

[11] *Farmers' Associations in Cambodia: Internal Functions and External Relations.* Faculty of Social Sciences, Chiang Mai University, Thailand, September 2008, based on Chandler, D. 2000. *A History of Cambodia.* Chiang Mai: Silkworm Books.

[12] http://www.new-ag.info/en/country/profile.php?a=471. *New Agriculturist: Country Profile*, Vietnam.

[13] *ibid.*

[14] Vietnamese State Industry and the Political Economy of Commercial Renaissance: Dragon's tooth or curate's egg, 2007.

[15] http://www.foodsec.org/fileadmin/user_upload/eufao-fsi4dm/docs/Cambodia%20CS ES%20Analysis%20Report.pdf.

[16] *ibid.*

line.[17] The significant reduction in poverty that occurred during the 1990s was the direct result of the over 7% real GDP growth that was stimulated by the *Doi Moi* suite of reforms.[18] One key element of these was the reform of agricultural land that allowed individuals and families long-term rights to use the land. Despite an attractive foreign direct investment policy and a vibrant economy, Vietnam has still an outdated institutional framework inherited from the central planning system. PF and other Microfinance actors often complain about the legal framework, or absence of it, which is slowing their development.

Feedback from the Field

Three months before the end of FinInc Asia, a team of four ESSEC students was delegated to visit the two pilot-tested MFIs. Their job was to assess the level of implementation of this microfinance project. Their findings are grouped as follows:

Regulation

Cambodia is ranked as "one of the world's best microfinance environments, enabled by its economic growth, strong regulatory regime and limited outreach of commercial banks".[19] Indeed, the existence of the Cambodia Credit Bureau (CBC), a reliable regulatory structure, is a major asset in the development of the sector. It provides information, analytical tools and prevents frauds. The level of trust all along the microfinance value chain is ensured due to this independent regulation authority.

In Vietnam, the government has the role of a direct participant in microfinance instead of that of facilitator. The MFI is clearly fragmented and needs to be strengthened. The main goal is to encourage "the adoption of internationally recognised good practices".[20] The lack of regulation represents a major barrier to trust-building among external partners. Moreover, only two licenced MFIs are currently registered in this country.

---

[17] http://www.un.org.vn/en/about-viet-nam/basic-statistics.html.
[18] http://siteresources.worldbank.org/INTVIETNAM/Resources/Vietnam-Poverty-Ana lysis.pdf.
[19] http://www.mixmarket.org/mfi/country/Cambodia/reportPremium: Microfinance Information Exchange, Market Intelligence Summary.
[20] http://www.microfinancegateway.org. *Regulating Microfinance in Vietnam: New Opportunities, Old Challenges.*

Even if other structures fill the gap, the existence of MFIs is essential to reach a level of professionalism by sharing best practices.

Human Resources

A major gap exists between Cambodia and Vietnam in terms of MFIs' human resources management. On the one hand, in Cambodia, TPC's staff is mainly composed of undergraduates from the country's universities. Credit officers studied at least two years at the university before being recruited. They had a high-level of understanding concerning loan-risk issues and a good understanding of agri-production issues.

On the other hand, in Vietnam, THF is operated by volunteers working for the Women's Union in Thanh Hoa. The staff does not possess in-depth understanding of financial risks or agri-production issues. Given that credit officers were not trained professionals, this was having an adverse impact on the operations of this MFI.

Financing

Cambodia mainly relies on private investors to fund their loan programmes. Generally speaking credit portfolios are still financed by external investors,[21] who seek a positive return on investment. MFIs need to carefully manage their resources and risk indicators to be able to reimburse those investors.

In Vietnam, many states' development agencies invest in Vietnamese programmes of microfinance without expecting any returns. When funds are more or less considered as subsidies, the MFIs have little incentive to be prudent in giving out the loans. Even if the portfolio risk remains relatively low, the usage of the fund may not be optimal.

Jay's First Solutions

As Jay has been working in Cambodia and Vietnam for the last few years, he knows the particularities of the region. He carefully considers potential solutions to help MFIs in the region.

---

[21] http://www.bwtp.org. Asia Resource Centre for Microfinance (ARCM): Cambodia Country Profile.

Global Level

Jay believes that he will need to develop personal links with officials in Vietnam. Indeed, lobbying would be very useful to influence the national regulation framework in the microfinance industry. Also, financing sources could be positively influenced by a governmental action plan. Having a stable source of cash to lend would definitely help the MFI to better plan its work. He believes the Central Bank could help the sector by giving funds to improve access to credit in the region.

A local NGO could create a cooperative to regroup all institutions that aim at helping vulnerable farmers. For this to happen, the prerequisites to become a licenced MFI would need to change. Once again the government must be pushed to foster growth in the microfinance sector. Jay is convinced it is one of the most important key success factors for the future development of microfinance in Vietnam.

Local Level

Jay is concerned that it took the project team significantly longer than originally planned to build relationships and mutual understanding among the partner microfinance networks and their member MFIs in Vietnam. A number of key activities that were originally planned in the first year could not be completed. Jay recalled that he attended a cross-cultural negotiation workshop at university and decided to investigate possible reasons for the project delay in that field.

After reading again his course on negotiator profiles by Gesteland,[22] he realised that there was a major disconnect between the Vietnamese partners and his project team. While the Vietnamese are relationship-focused,[23] the PF project team is mainly deal or transaction-focused.

Gesteland defined relationship-focused people patterns as:

- Usually reluctant to do business with strangers.
- Make initial contact indirectly: At trade shows, on official trade missions or *via* intermediaries, introductions and referrals.
- A reliance on close relationships rather than contracts to resolve disagreements.

---

[22]Gesteland, R (1999). *Patterns of Cross-Cultural Business Behavior.* Copenhagen: Copenhagen Business School Press.
[23]*ibid.*

Jay considered whether his project team failed to identify and solve every cross-cultural misunderstanding. He is now aware of local sensitivities, which will enable him to slow down and not get down to business too quickly. Now he appreciates even more that it takes plenty of time to build trust in Vietnam before talking business.

Exhibits

Exhibit 1: Microfinance Uptake in Vietnam.

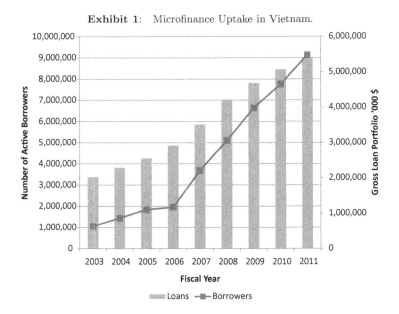

Exhibit 2:   Microfinance Uptake in Cambodia.

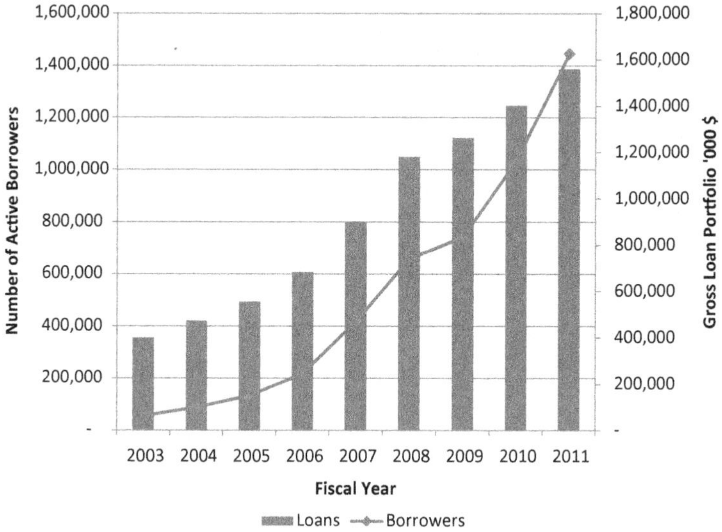

Chapter 12

Pour un Sourire d'Enfant: The Need for
a New Funding Model*

Ashwin Malshe

Marketing Department, ESSEC

In June 2013, Mr Vibol La, the director of the Pour un Sourire d'Enfant Institute (PSEI) in Phnom Penh, Cambodia, received an email from his boss, Mr Sarapich Pin, the director of the non-governmental organisation (NGO) Pour un Sourire d'Enfant (PSE). PSE is a French NGO operating in Cambodia. Founded in 1995, PSE is dedicated to helping children and youth[1] from poor families by providing them with good education and thus a chance to get their families out of poverty.[2] Its initial operations started modestly near a dump in Phnom Penh. Today PSE boasts of a vast complex of school buildings and courtyards, capable of hosting classes and activities for 6,500 children. PSEI works as PSE's vocational education arm. The email mentioned that Sarapich had just attended the PSE board of directors' annual meeting in France. Anticipating stagnating or even decreasing donations from Europe, the board had set an objective of 25% of funds to be raised in Asia by the Cambodian office through donations or self-generated revenue. This was a big challenge for PSE and PSEI. The email concluded: "Since you have been here from the beginning, I trust your judgement. I want to have your insights on what we can do. Can we meet as soon as I come back next week?"

Vibol could sense the urgency in those words. That morning, the PSE centre was abuzz with students passing through courtyards toward their

---

*This case was prepared with the support of Nicolas Prévotel, Balthazar Raguin, and Shahan Sheikholslami, and with the collaboration of Capgemini Consulting and the employees and partners of Pour un Sourire d'Enfant.

[1] Five to 24-years-old.

[2] **Exhibit 1.**

classrooms, children eating breakfast at the cafeteria under the supervision of their foster mothers, teachers starting their classes, and staff members shuffling between offices. Vibol reflected that the whole atmosphere of the centre, the very existence of PSE could be jeopardised by a shortage in donations. Vibol's PSEI was PSE's biggest area of expenditure and Sarapich wanted to discuss the climbing costs of its operations. The number of students entering vocational education was increasing year after year, whereas the cost per student was also increasing because of inflation. Additionally, the PSEI required significant investments in facilities and equipments to ensure good quality vocational training. With stagnating donations and increasing costs, PSE's mission to get children out of poverty and enable them to earn a sustainable livelihood was at stake. Although many ideas were floating throughout the organisation for managing the situation, not all were acceptable to all the stakeholders. Different stakeholders viewed risks and potential rewards differently. While the Cambodian team proposed to develop commercial activities such as corporate training, the board of directors in France emphasised the charity and fundraising side of PSE. The PSEI was in favour of a commercial solution. Therefore, ahead of the meeting with Sarapich, Vibol had to gather his best ideas and compelling arguments to reconcile commercial activities with PSE's social principles.

History of Pour un Sourire d'Enfant (PSE)

In 1993, Christian des Pallières, a young retiree on an advising mission, arrived in Phnom Penh, Cambodia and for two years worked with an NGO, SIPAR, to rebuild the primary school system and to set up Institutes for Teacher Training. Reflecting on that day in October 1995, when children led him to the Phnom Penh dumpsite, he recalls:

"The association was created when we discovered the Phnom Penh garbage dump. There, in stifling heat, among flies and rats, hundreds of barefoot children rummaged through a decomposing, stinking, worm-infested mess of refuse, in which they sank up to their knees. We were stung by what we saw: tiny children, filthy, thin, with festering wounds and exhausted gazes, and still worse, the children were eating in the stench. It was horrible to see; we stood there stung; we never imagined a place like this could exist. It made us want to cry, we felt sick, overcome with such a deep enraged feeling that was impossible for us to allow these children to continue

living in such conditions. From that moment on, our lives were going to change...[3]

A War-Torn Country[4]

At that time, Cambodia was a country left in ruins by 25 years of civil war. The new government re-established schooling as a "nation-building priority"[5]: Approximately 14,000 would-be teachers were given a very short training to teach 1 million children who had enrolled in 14,000 primary schools (often, nothing more than a straw hut). Teaching materials and books were non-existent, paper for notebooks was a continuous problem, general insecurity was omnipresent, and poverty deterred families from sending children to schools for more than a few years. In 1993, when Christian des Pallières came to Cambodia, the education system barely got out of a state of collapse, but little progress had been achieved.

The First Years of PSE

Pour un Sourire d'Enfant (meaning 'for a child's smile') started in 1995 on the Phnom Penh dumpsite with around twenty children in a *paillote* ('straw hut' in French), and focused on providing them with shelter, food, and basic health care. Christian des Pallières and his wife, Marie-France, quickly understood that they could not help all of the hundreds of children working in the dumpsite by themselves. Hence, they founded PSE with a few friends and family members and started to raise funds from private donors in France.

"From Misery to a Skilled Job": PSE's Operations

PSE could be broken down into two major organisations even though they were not separate: PSE and the PSEI, its vocational education arm. PSE as a whole was in charge of selecting children from the most impoverished families, who were working as scavengers, street vendors at night, river spinach gatherers in the poor districts of Phnom Penh, or merely at

---

[3]Presentation video on pse.asso.fr, "PSE at a glance".
[4]From the comprehensive Wikipedia pages related to contemporary Cambodian history.
[5]Sideth S. Dy, *"Strategies and Policies for Basic Education in Cambodia: Historical Perspectives"*, Institute of Comparative and International Education, Graduate School of Education, Hiroshima University.

risk from their families. It was also responsible for sending the children back to school, accompanying them until graduation, and ensuring that they entered the labour market with the necessary skills to find a proper livelihood.

However, PSE did not compete with state education in order to meet these objectives. A remedial centre for accelerated education (for the 750 children who were too old to start classes at their level of knowledge; the other 3,830 were sent to state schools) and the PSEI were the only educative activities PSE undertook. Social services and regular follow-up, aid for re-housing, family support schemes (compensation in rice, nurseries), social employment at the centre for the parents, boarding houses for the most vulnerable children, healthcare consultations and counselling, and summer camps were here to support the core objectives of PSE. By helping the parents, the association made sure the children were able to benefit from a normal education. In 2011–2012, 4,950 children benefited from PSE's programmes (expected to grow at 6,640 in 2013), impacting a total of 4,140 families, of which 90% live below the national poverty line (US $0.93 per day per family member).[6]

PSEI had been created in 2000, when the association realised that the children did not have the right qualifications to find stable employment when they graduated and that the state universities were not equipped to deliver practical skills. The PSEI started with a Hospitality Food & Beverage (F&B) school, but 10 years later, it had developed into eight different schools preparing for 29 career skills, ranging from technical careers (mechanics, construction, hairdressing) and business careers (sales, retail, office administration) to hospitality (hotel, restaurant, beauty care). In 2012, PSEI represented 33% of PSE's operational expenses. The goal was to provide the children with as much practical experience and manual work as possible. To that end, PSEI invested in professional equipment and real-life facilities. It opened a hotel and a restaurant for training in the centre and another restaurant in Phnom Penh for final year students. Lastly, it introduced internships and partnerships with companies as a core component of the curriculum and sought to increase the presence of PSEI students in companies through alternative training and corporate scholarships. In 2011–2012, around 70 teachers taught 1,350 young students (estimated 1,570 in 2013). In 2011, as a final achievement, a Memorandum

---

[6]All data on PSE children are drawn from PSE annual activity report 2011–2012.

of Understanding (MoU) with the Royal Government of Cambodia (RGC) allowed PSEI to deliver state diplomas at the end of its trainings (at grade 9, grade 12, and BBA levels).

After experiencing remarkable growth during its 20 years of operations, in 2013 PSE's total budget amounted to US $7.3 million.[7] Private sponsorships accounted for 74% of the budget. Sponsoring one child cost US $75[8] per month, but each sponsor could give a lower or higher donation to PSE. The cost for a boarding child or a student in vocational training was more, as was the cost for boarding vocational training. Sponsors often committed support over longer durations. The donor base comprised around 8,000 regular individual donors, most of whom were recruited in the close entourage of the founders and during their fund-raising tour (55 to 70 donor meetings in France and in Europe over two months). Each year, the tour recruited between 400 and 1,000 new donors.

The budget was then divided between the operational budget (67%) and the investment budget (33%).[9] The operational budget covered all costs related to PSE's programmes: Vocational training, remedial centre, help to public schools, protection and housing, etc. It included all subsequent costs: Uniforms, daily meals, and teachers' and employees' salaries. Operational costs had been rising (up by 15% in 2012) because the number of children was increasing (up by 5%), especially in the most expensive programmes such as vocational training (up by 16%) and aid for re-housing.[10] The other important part of the budget was the investment fund, which was financed either by private donors, Corporate Social Responsibility (CSR) departments of large companies, or institutional donors. Most of the time, these donations were allocated to specific projects approved by the Board of Directors and supervised by the managers. The separation between the operational and investment budgets guaranteed clarity and transparency in donations' allocation, but also intended to limit fluctuations in the operational budget. In early 2012, the founders announced their decision not to participate in the fund-raising tour for personal reasons. A few members of the board were concerned that without the founders, the effectiveness of such tours would be reduced.[11]

---

[7] PSE Annual Activity Report 2011–2012. Also see **Exhibit 2**.
[8] See **Exhibit 3**.
[9] Interview with Ouk Sovan, ex-Director of Fund-raising, October 31, 2013.
[10] PSE Annual Activity Report, 2011–2012.
[11] Interview with Martin de Roquefeuil, Board member, November 7, 2013.

The Dilemma Facing PSE on the Future Course of Action

PSE has been on course to achieving its original goal to fight poverty. However, with rising student enrolment as well as costs, the organisation was now at a critical juncture. They created comprehensive support for the children and their families within their geographical reach, while their existing facilities and infrastructure operated at near full capacity. Yet, to help more children and to create new programmes, PSE would have to make significant new investments. However, with donations from Europe stagnating and potentially declining, funding any future activities now became a serious challenge.

Broadly speaking PSE management was split between two points of view. The local management was young and displayed an entrepreneurial spirit. This led to the emergence of many projects such as the catering business, market studies, and executive training in the School of Business (SoB), training and assessment in the School of Hospitality (SoH), a new private SoH for paying students, new hotels and restaurants, and even a recycling business. Each idea capitalised not only on the great enthusiasm of the field team, but also on the reputation of PSE and its strong ties with the government and companies in Cambodia.

On the other hand, several board members and the volunteers working in France thought that, while great ideas emanated from the PSE managers, some projects were risky. They perceived consolidating the current situation as the priority. At the centre of the concerns was any potential damage to the image of PSE and the negative consequences the failure of a new project could have for the fund-raising activities. Some of them believed that an NGO such as PSE should strictly function as a charitable organisation, while others were open to setting up a small social business. Whereas everyone agreed that PSE should raise 25% of its funds directly in Asia, disagreements arose on the best way to achieve this objective. Board members argued that PSE had to refocus on the 'paillote', on giving livelihood to the "children of the poorest of the poor".[12] On the other hand, Cambodian management argued that it needed to shift its priorities to create a global impact on the Cambodian society, by extending to other categories of the population and by improving the quality of education of PSEI.[13] Vibol wanted to create a social business, but he acknowledged that

---

[12]Interview with Ghislaine Dufour and Martin de Roquefeuil.
[13]Interview with Sarapich Pin (November 4, 2013) and Vibol La (November 8, 2013).

PSE board members had valid concerns. He wondered which among all the projects that the PSE staff had envisaged were the most promising and had strong chances of success.

The Alternatives for Social Business

Vibol started by noting down all the viable alternatives available to start a revenue-generating social business. These ideas were not just a figment of the imagination of PSEI staffers. Instead, these projects were already being tested, which enabled Vibol to compare their strengths and weaknesses.

Hotel and restaurants

Founded in 2002, the SoH was one of the largest departments with 32 teachers and 440 students (up 30% from 2012). Its dean, Mr Dave Garrison, was an energetic entrepreneur who had a long-standing experience in hospitality management. He had already submitted many business propositions and was pressing Vibol to take advantage of them.

The school provided its students with practical training and true-to-life experience for eight career paths. Typically, the students spent most of their time in the application facilities (kitchen, dining room, hotel, front office, etc.), and at the time of graduation they were ready to work in the field of their specialisation. The school had many ties with hotels, restaurants, and companies in foodservice industry, which provided internships and employment opportunities to PSE students. All the teachers had prior work experience in well-respected hotels (50% in five-star hotels) and kept in contact with their former employers. The 10 largest hotels of Phnom Penh, part of the School Advisory Committee, had an active role in auditing the school's curricula and advising on the realities of the hotel industry. Finally, the Ecole Hôtelière de Lausanne, a Swiss world-leading hospitality school, had led several trainer-training and capacity-building missions in PSE.[14] The school was one of the first in Southeast Asia to be ASEAN (Association of Southeast Asian Nations) certified and authorised to deliver ASEAN standard diplomas, making it a school of international standing. The ASEAN certification comprised four levels, which ensured the quality of certified workers, while restricting their area of employment. For example, due to their superior training, level 1 workers were more likely to be hired in

---

[14]Presentation of the SoH and other PSEI schools on institut-pse.org.

a five-star hotel and were legally allowed to work in any of the ten ASEAN countries, while level 2 workers were restricted to working in Cambodia. PSE students were trained to become level 1 and level 2 workers.

SoH also operated two 'Lotus Blanc' (French for 'white lotus') training restaurants and a hotel (which had been expanded from four to eight rooms in 2011) in order to provide real-life experience for the students. One training restaurant and the hotel set in the PSE centre outside Phnom Penh, trained first year students of the SoH; whereas the second training restaurant, near the Independence Monument in downtown Phnom Penh served the final year students. Each of the three was not-for-profit, whereby their incomes covered the operating costs, and if there was any profit, it was channelled into PSE. Banking on this experience and expertise, PSE could start its for-profit hotel and restaurant business in order to generate more funds for PSE.

However, in Phnom Penh competition was intense in the hospitality sector. Two hundred hotels and six hundred restaurants were registered in various tourist guides and websites.[15] Even in the niche market of charitable initiatives, the competition was formidable. For example, a whole section of the Lonely Planet guide, 'dining for a cause',[16] referenced four restaurants that were part of Friends International, including Le Rit's by the NGO NYEMO, Hagar Restaurant by Hagar Catering, the Boddhi Tree Umma Restaurant. In total, about 20 hotels and restaurants were operating in the 'dining for a cause' niche market. PSE would have to differentiate itself to stand out from the crowd.

Catering

PSE already provided catering training to its students. However, after fulfilling the training needs for catering, there was still plenty of business to be obtained. The demand for catering was substantial and PSE could make use of this opportunity by entering the professional catering market. Catering as a business provided many advantages. First, initial outlay on the kitchen equipment was small as it is easy to borrow pre-existing kitchen equipment and facilities from PSE at times when they were not in use. Next, the cost structure comprised largely variable costs such as food and transportation, which made the profits less sensitive to seasonality. Finally,

---

[15]Estimation from the Ministry of Tourism's registry and tripadvisor.com.
[16]*Lonely Planet, Cambodia*, 2012 Ed., p. 74.

PSE could target clients anywhere in Phnom Penh as well as in other nearby cities.

In the near future, the catering business would have to become independent, hiring its own employees, equipment, and facilities. In that regard, the example of Hagar Catering was inspiring. It was a spinoff of Hagar International, an NGO dedicated to the recovery of people subjected to extreme human rights abuse. Hagar and private investors owned Hagar Catering and preferentially hired women and children from the NGO shelters and assistance programmes. In 2012, it had US \$2.2 million in sales revenue and employed 85 (37%) employees from Hagar and partner NGOs, having both good financial health and a durable social impact.[17] PSE could emulate this example and achieve similar numbers.

A new private hospitality school

Demand for skilled employees in the hospitality sector was booming proportionally to the development of tourism in Cambodia. Tourism represented 14% of the GDP of Cambodia, second only to the garment industry. In 2012, 3.6 million tourists visited Cambodia whereas in 2015, it is expected to attract 4.5 million tourists, thereby becoming the topmost sector of the Cambodian economy.[18] Phnom Penh, Siem Reap (Angkor Wat), and Sihanoukville were major tourist destinations in Cambodia. Tourist accommodation like hotels and restaurants were flourishing, with a fair share devoted to luxury resorts and hotels. However, a majority of the 350,000 people employed in the hospitality industry lacked training. As a result, there was an immediate demand of approximately 30,000 skilled workers.

Although the SoH was recognised as the pioneering hospitality school in Cambodia, it graduated fewer than 100 PSE students every year. "If PSE established a private school," Vibol thought, "it would be able to capture a large part of the demand." Moreover, the dean Dave Garrison advocated establishing a full-scale school, projecting a final capacity of 3,000 students enrolled in the private school's programmes. According to Dave, the school would be operating at full capacity in two years and would achieve break-even in just three years. After that the school would channel its profit into PSE. By mirroring the programmes and the pedagogy of the SoH,

---

[17]Hagar International 2012 annual report.
[18]See **Exhibit 4** for an overview of Cambodian economic growth.

the new hospitality school would capitalise on PSE's expertise and fame in the hospitality sector, while generating revenue from the tuition fees. It would create a social impact in its own way by targeting the people in the middle, those who were too rich to enter an NGO (NGOs provided the best vocational training programmes), yet too poor to pay for a good education in a private institute.

The hospitality school would be located near the centre of Phnom Penh in order to attract students from different areas. The project needed significant investments in land, facilities, equipment and human resources to attract seasoned professionals as teachers. Dave estimated an initial investment of US $7 million.

Market research

The SoB's dean, Eléonore Iriart had put together a small market research department as a new training activity for the sales and marketing students. Eléonore wanted to introduce basic and advanced marketing theory and techniques to the SoB students in a practical way. The SoB approached various firms to offer market research at cost price (students were paid US $1 per hour). By 2012, SoB students completed three extensive market research projects.[19] Since then, the exercise had been integrated into the students' curriculum, whereby the students were allowed to use four hours of their study time every week to work on the market research projects under the supervision of their teachers.

Marketing research provided benefits to SoB as well as the client companies. Many foreign companies opening subsidiaries in Phnom Penh were interested in PSE's knowledge of the market to help them set up their operations. On PSE's side, the SoB could build more bridges with the corporate world and participate actively in the students' professional exposure. Overall, the quality of education visibly improved, while PSE's reputation as a reliable partner and a high quality school got a boost. The growth prospects were strong as requests from other companies looking for an affordable but quality service started to pour into Eléonore's inbox.

However, the workload of such projects often put students and teachers under stress. For example in one research project, students started skipping classes in order to finish the research within the deadline. What was meant

---

[19]Interview with Eléonore Iriart, October 31, 2013.

to be an improvement in the students' education threatened to become an impediment. Due to such infractions, the top management and the board members decided to put an end to large-size projects. If the school wanted to go ahead with marketing research, several issues needed to be resolved. First, the workload and the schedules needed to be organised in a way that they wouldn't hinder other activities. Second, although the service was inexpensive, SoB would need additional capabilities in writing professional reports to bring up the standard of the service. Finally, SoB needed to address the concerns that it was not going too far into becoming a commercial business school, while diluting its original goal of providing good education and stable jobs to students from poor families.

Training and assessment centre

Each of the two schools had conducted paid short training sessions in 2012 for companies. For example, a Cambodian subsidiary of a multinational pharmacentical company had contracted business modules with the SoB. It included seminars on Management & Leadership, Marketing & Strategy, and Motivation & Empowerment. PSE billed the company US $10 per hour for course preparation and US $10 per hour for teaching of which 50% went straight to the teachers. For instance, out of US $20 for two hours, US $15 went to PSE, US $5 to the teacher.[20] This supplemented teachers' salaries and put SoB in a better position to retain the teachers. The client company was satisfied, as the cost was much cheaper than market prices and the quality on par with other training programmes. On the SoH side, the teachers regularly conducted training sessions to company staff in more technical subjects like cooking, kitchen management, waiting, or handling the front office. The SoH charged US $50 per participant, and the revenue went to the school's budget.

Typically, in a non-local company, Cambodian employees were hired for their English skills and not for their competencies in any specific jobs. This was a prevalent practice so that the manager, typically a foreigner, could communicate with the local employees.[21] An employee's educational background had little relevance as only 10% of university students found work related to their major. Therefore, companies had the obligation to train their staff in-house, even though they did not have the capabilities

---

[20] Internal documents.
[21] Interview with Philippe Lequeux, November 5, 2013.

and time to provide good quality training. Tapping on this unmet need was a good opportunity for PSE to create a new revenue stream.

The aforementioned ASEAN standards certification was scheduled to come in force by 2015. The certification was not compulsory, but it was highly likely that most high and mid-range hotels would seek standard compliance. In the near future, hotels would need more and more training for their staff to comply with increasingly demanding standards. Assessing a hotel required an assessor who both assessed the facilities and the processes, and trained the personnel to obtain certifications. Training and Assessment provided a good opportunity to design an all-inclusive service: Employees would be trained and certified according to ASEAN standards and at the same time within the PSE curriculum. In Cambodia, PSE would be the first and the only institution to offer such a service and could charge a premium due to its expertise.

The assessment part was a pet project of Dave Garrison. Under the ASEAN Mutual Recognition Agreement that he had signed with the RGC in 2013, he had already accredited SoH teachers to become master trainers in ASEAN hospitality standards. If his project was green-lit by the management, he intended to hire assessors to start a side activity. However, assessment was completely new to PSE and as such it lacked detailed knowledge required to implement it.

Cross-bordering

'Cross-bordering' strategy was two-fold. Extend fund-raising to new countries and simultaneously expand the operations to other locations. The goals were to consolidate the current model, replicate PSE's model in other locations within Cambodia or even abroad, and revitalise fund-raising. Refocusing on its historical activities, PSE would open other 'paillotes', remedial schools, and healthcare centres in other poor cities of Cambodia. Dumpsites were spreading to other parts of Cambodia such as Siem Reap, Sihanoukville, Battambang, and Poipet. The children there were as poor, if not poorer, than the children in Phnom Penh, and were in dire need of healthcare, education, and proper nutrition.

Several entrepreneurs from the Philippines, Vietnam, and Indonesia had approached PSE to export the model to their home countries. PSE's founder was favourable to those projects, as he believed that setting up new operations in other countries would rekindle the enthusiasm throughout PSE, akin to that in the initial years. The initial investment was low, but the social impact was high and immediate. It would also mend the gap between PSE's image as a saviour of children working in the dumpsite and its functional role as a development partner rather than an emergency relief organisation. It was expected to attract more individual donors, enabling PSE to kick-start the new fund-raising campaigns. The objective of generating 25% funds from Asia could be attained by self-generated revenues or donations by a third party, as it would be possible to increase the donor base in Asia. In 2012, PSE had already raised US $200,000[22] of funds through local donations, revenue of the two training restaurants, and an annual PSE charity party. Achieving 25% of funds raised in Asia would be a daunting task, yet not impossible. PSE was already running local fund-raising offices in Singapore and Hong Kong. For the 2014 budget, the Board of Directors had allocated $50,000 for a communication plan in order to run advertising campaigns and to increase the donor base.

Although this strategy could bring new funds and individual donors in the long term, it would not solve PSE's self-reliance problem. Sooner or later, it would reappear and be more pressing than before. Furthermore, replicating the 'paillotes' in other cities would not support PSE's mission. Once out of the remedial school, the children might return to the inefficient education system or to the dumpsite. Its mission would be achieved only when the children could graduate from vocational training (PSEI).

Vibol considered all the options one by one. To him, no solution immediately stood out from the rest. In the next week, he would have to present his views to Sarapich Pin, who would then meet with the Board of Directors with his proposal. As the budget for 2014 was almost finalised, he soon had to allocate the funds for any one or a combination of the above strategies.

---

[22]PSE annual activity report 2011–2012.

Exhibits

Exhibit 1:   Map of Cambodia with Locations of PSE and its Competitors.

Exhibit 2:   Sources of PSE Funding.

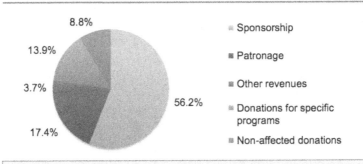

Source: PSE activity report 2011–12.

Exhibit 3: Cost per Child.

- **$75,04** (or €56[1]) – Monthly average cost per children
- Average cost per children in function of the program
    - **$53.6** per month for a child in school, fed, cared for, enjoying extracurricular activities and compensation of rice for his family
    - **$119.3** per month for a youth in vocational training, fed, cared for, enjoying extracurricular activities and compensation of rice for his family
    - **$53.6** per month extra for a child / youth receiving a complementary program such as "Protection / Housing"

Exhibit 4: Cambodian Economy Overview.

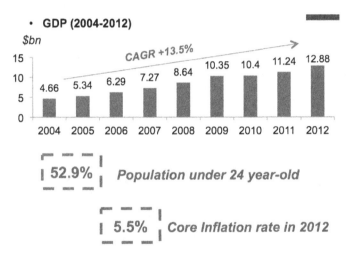

- **GDP (2004-2012)**

$bn

CAGR +13.5%

2004	2005	2006	2007	2008	2009	2010	2011	2012
4.66	5.34	6.29	7.27	8.64	10.35	10.4	11.24	12.88

| 52.9% | *Population under 24 year-old* |

| 5.5% | *Core Inflation rate in 2012* |

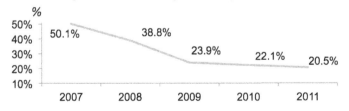

- **Poverty headcount ratio (2007-2011)**

%

2007	2008	2009	2010	2011
50.1%	38.8%	23.9%	22.1%	20.5%

Part E

Introduction

Small Business with Big Ideas

As we have seen so far in this book, there is much to learn from big businesses, given the scale of the impact they have on economies, communities and people's lives in general. But equally, there are valuable lessons to be gleaned from successful small businesses, which have the agility and responsiveness to provide innovative products and services that capture the imagination of consumers. One such company is Kolkata-based Weavers Studio.

The textile company, founded in 1993 by Darshan Shah, has grown over two decades to become successful and well-respected within the industry. Still at the helm, Darshan faces a number of challenges, as her company has outgrown its original structure and she must consider its long term viability without a clear succession plan.

The case offers a fascinating insight into India's history in textiles and the contemporary relevance of a company like Weavers Studio as it continues to use the traditional techniques for dyeing, printing and embroidering, passed down through generations.

It also provides a valuable perspective on the luxury market in India. Weavers Studio products are exclusive and expensive but represent something different from the Western luxury brands that are increasingly popular in emerging markets. With this in mind, is it a good idea for the company to increase revenue by offering prices that give access to a growing middle class? In addition, the case underlines the evolution of a family business model and can be contrasted with that of the traditional family luxury houses of Italy and France.

Chapter 13

Weavers Studio: Use as Many Hands as Possible*

Arijit Chatterjee
Management Department, ESSEC

Weavers Studio: A Critical Stage?

Darshan Shah, founder and CEO of Weavers Studio, a medium sized textile boutique in Kolkata, was reviewing the design of some fabrics for the 2011 spring collection when she received a text message on her phone. The message came from Monoleena Banerjee, a Senior Manager who has been with the company since the beginning: "I would like to leave the company tomorrow." Darshan replied "Go ahead. You better leave today rather than tomorrow."

Some things are created from a need and Weavers Studio was one such thing. A single mother with no background in design and textiles, Darshan developed the company relying mainly on the opportunities and needs of the moment and using her business and negotiation skills. She had initiated a journey of self-development, gaining more and more knowledge from books, from visiting the villages of West Bengal, from exchanging with craft masters and learning from them. She built a team, delegated more and more work, and focused on the development of the business. She had no elaborate plan. In her words, "Whatever came on the table I thought about it at that point of time." But after 20 years, she needed to look at things differently in order to envisage a future for Weavers Studio.

Darshan bridged a gap, connecting the rich heritage of Indian textiles with the global market. According to estimates, the Indian textile industry

---

*This case was prepared with the support of Lamia Berrahma, Marion Logeais, and Florentine Tsayem, and with the collaboration of Capgemini Consulting and the employees and partners of Weavers Studio.

will have a compound annual growth rate (CAGR) of 13% over the next ten years. Exports are expected to grow to US $70 billion.

The stakes are high for Weavers Studio. After Monoleena's resignation, Darshan realised that the team of senior managers she has built over the years might not be there to run the company in the future as they are not committed enough. Weavers Studio was not their priority. As she was getting older, the question of a sustainable succession plan for the company appeared to be a crucial and tricky issue. It had to be tackled as soon as possible.

India, the Cradle of Textiles

India has a rich history in textiles. Cotton-spinning was known to the Indus Valley Civilisation as early as 3000 BC. References to weaving and spinning are found in Hindu hymns written in about 1500 BC. Herodotus, the Greek historian, described Indian cotton as "a wool exceeding in beauty and goodness of sheep". For many centuries, India was the only country known for its cotton fabrics, with the rest of the world being clad in wool. Alexander the Great's invading troops found cotton clothes were more comfortable than their woolen ones. India had a flourishing trade in cotton textiles with Greece, Egypt, Persia, and the Roman Empire. Indian textiles clothed kings, nobles and slaves alike in most parts of the Old World. A robust tradition and the development of several regional techniques gave India an unique expertise in textile production.

Toward the end of the 17th century, the British East India Company had begun exports of Indian silks and various cotton fabrics to other countries. This included the famous Muslin of Bengal, Bihar, and Orissa. By the middle of the 18th century, the spread of British rule over India coincided with the advent of Hargreaves' 'jenny' in 1764 and Arkwright's 'spinning frame' in 1769, both of which mechanised cotton spinning. This was in the heyday of the Industrial Revolution in Britain. The factory system gained ground and what the mighty Roman and Ottoman Empires failed to achieve, the British did. They dealt a deathblow to the ancient Indian cotton industry through massive import of cheaper cotton textiles into India from the United Kingdom.

The Indian monopoly on cotton muslins for more than three millennia ended in less than three decades after the British consolidated their power in India following the defeat of the Marathas in 1818. The growing Lancashire mills needed more and better cotton, and the British Government in India took measures to encourage, and even to undertake, the cultivation in India of more and better cotton and its export to Great Britain. "The territory of India," wrote M. G. Ranade in his essays, "was looked upon by the British colonisers as a plantation, growing raw produce to be shipped by British agents in British ships, to be worked into fabrics by British skill and capital, and to be re-exported to the dependency by British merchants to their corresponding British firms in India and elsewhere." [1]

Today, cotton and textiles are still one of the key drivers of the Indian economy. In 2014, the textile industry contributed about 4% to India's GDP, 14% to India's industrial production, 27% to India's foreign exchange inflows and provides direct employment to more than 45 million people. [2] In a trade-oriented world, textiles are a fierce battle for India, since its historic position has been challenged by China. In 2014, India contributed to 5.2% of worldwide textile exports and ranks in second position beating Italy, Germany, and Bangladesh. [3]

Industry analysts estimate the size of the Indian textiles and apparel industry will reach US $223 billion by 2021. [4] The increase in demand is driven by both foreign and domestic markets. In India, three factors are driving demand: Urban consumers are seeking branded and lifestyle products while the semi-urban and rural population is fast-growing; a young demographic profile and increase in the population of working women; and the retail environment is modernising fast, offering a better buying experience. In terms of exports, retail giants are sourcing in India, looking for the best way to enter the country. Setting a partnership with a local player is one such route. Indian companies, too, are climbing up the value chain and becoming vendor partners of global buyers. In 2013–14, India attracted US $198 million in foreign direct investment in the textile sector. [5]

India and Luxury: A Very Long Love Story

In his *Universal Dictionary of Trade and Commerce* published in 1757, Malachy Postlethwayt, the British expert on commerce, wrote: "Their linen cloth was of such fineness, that very long and broad pieces of it may easily

---

[1] M. G. Ranade. *Essays on Indian Economics*. G. Claridge & Co., Bombay, 1901, Second Edition.
[2] http://www.ibef.org/industry/textiles.aspx.
[3] http://www.dnaindia.com/money/report-india-ranks-second-in-global-textile-exports-1993053.
[4] http://www.ibef.org/industry/textiles.aspx.
[5] http://www.indembkwt.org/India%20Weekly%20Economic%20Bulletin%20-%20August%2012012-18%202014.pdf

be drawn through a small ring." He was referring to the legendary muslin, the superfine variety of cotton fabric from Bengal that was famous the world over. Ptolemy, the second century polymath from Alexandria, mentioned the fabric in his *Periplus of the Erythrean Sea*. In Rome, this delicate fabric was given romantic names such as *ventus textilis* (textile breeze) or *nebula* (cloud). Marco Polo, the 13th century Venetian traveller, wrote about it in his *Travels*. Jean Baptiste Tavernier, the 17th century merchant and traveller, found muslins so fine that "you would scarcely know what you had in your hand". Dhaka muslin that resembled the dew on sand was called *shabnam*. Muslin that could not be seen in water was called *ab rawan*. Muslin used for turbans went by the name of *seerbund*. Tavernier mentions the Persian ambassador Muhammad Ali Beg returning home with a gem-studded coconut that had a 30 yard long *seerbund* (turban) folded inside. Muslins became increasingly popular in 18th Century Britain. And Marie Antoinette enraged the silk weavers of Lyon, when she decided to wear muslin to convey both elegance and simplicity.

For thousands of years, Oriental goods were accorded a certain mystique in Europe. These goods from far away regions in the East included a wide array of products: Spices, silk, cotton, porcelain, jewellery, lacquerware to name a few. Originating from a distant land, the provenance of these products added a certain awe and charm in the minds of Europeans. The superior quality of these products was not only attributed to the exotic ingredients, but also the craftsmanship of the artisans. Writing in 1766, Jeran Rhynier of Basle commented:

> "Our theory and principles are almost the same as those of the Indians, but the latter have the advantages of possessing certain herbs which are more suitable for this method of manufacture [...] Granted all things equal, we could never adopt their methods, for we lack skilled craftsmen and could not keep the maintenance costs so low."

Writing from Pondicherry in 1742, the great Indologist Gaston-Laurent Coeurdoux, observed,

> "It would seem that the Author of Nature, as a set-off against other advantages which Europe enjoys, has granted India ingredients, and, above all, certain waters, whose particular qualities have much to do with the beautiful combination of painting and dyeing represented by Indian cloths."

Indians, however, in return for their exquisite products, did not seek European handicrafts. Instead, India became a dumping ground for precious metals such as silver, mined from Potosi and Iwami Ginzan. Some thought that the mad rush for Eastern luxuries would bring financial ruin to the West. François Bernier described India as the "graveyard of gold and silver".

Europeans used a variety of tactics to compete with Asian products. Some of these methods were import prohibition at home, forcible dismantling of old methods of production in the colonies, and poaching expert artisans. However, the most potent of methods was imitation of technology and design. In Britain, for example, imitation was a national goal. Founded in 1754 in London, the Society for the encouragement of Arts, Manufacture, and Commerce (now known as the Royal Society of Arts) offered premiums to those who could produce better imitations of Oriental goods. The objective was "to improve design, to invent British luxuries and to discover new uses for indigenous and British colonial raw materials". A typical advertisement ran like this:

PREMIUMS OFFERED FOR THE ADVANTAGE OF THE BRITISH SETTLEMENTS IN THE EAST INDIES.

Bhaugulpore Cotton. To the person who shall import into the port of London, in the year 1812, the greatest quantity, not less than one ton, of the Bhaugulpore cotton, from which cloths are made in imitation of nankeen, without dyeing; the gold medal.

Although production processes of exquisite goods or elaborate divisions of labour could not be replicated entirely in Europe, the policy of imitation turned out to be a huge success. As efforts were made to replicate, tinkering with different materials and manufacturing processes resulted in a long list of products that later became sought-after luxury goods. Twenty years later, during the industrial revolution in Britain, David Hume wrote, "Every improvement which we have made [in the last two centuries] has arisen from our imitation of foreigners."[6]

In Asia, on the other hand, there was no urge to retrieve European products. Society turned inward, stagnated, and became self-content. Social institutions that resemble the caste system are not difficult to find elsewhere, but in India these endogamous groups crystallised into a rigid structure. Numerous artisanal castes found themselves at the lower rung of the social order. Expert leatherworkers, blacksmiths, woodcarvers, and

---

[6]Hume, D. (1777) *Of the Jealousy of Trade* in Essays Moral, Political, and Literary.

weavers formed their own tight-knit communities without any hope of social mobility, fame, or recognition in society. Learning from international trade — a key catalyst in fashionable consumption — was almost impossible due to social sanctions that prevented sea voyages.

With the advent of full-fledged colonialism a different but well-known story emerges. From the producer of the world's finest fabric that adorned monarchs, Bangladesh has morphed into a country that provides cheap labour. Weavers of Bangladesh now work in sweatshops that produce run-of-the-mill clothing sold in shopping malls in developed economies. Hundreds, sometimes thousands, die in factory disasters.[7] Garments worth US $18 billion dollars are exported each year. But the revenue from the "blood garments", as one journal puts it, is in lieu of the low wages of the workers.[8] As a consequence, money is made by processing and shipping more orders. The fabled muslin weavers of the past are hard to find. Relentless exploitation of the colonies has not only converted exquisite luxury products into mere handicrafts, colonialism has taken a toll on self-confidence, a key ingredient in the price discovery process. As Sabyasachi Mukherjee, a reputed fashion designer, said, "Luxury is created from a point of arrogance, not subjugation."

Indians were also patrons of luxury products from abroad. Vuitton created famous masterpieces, among them the tea-case of the Maharaja of Baroda. Cartier, the royal jeweller, designed special orders for many Indian rulers, such as the tiara of Jagatjit Singh, the Maharaja of Kapurthala in 1926. Today the Indian market is the new target for international luxury conglomerates like LVMH, Richemont, Kering, and Hermès. The potential is huge. India has numerous festivities all year round, when people buy new clothes and gifts. The wedding is another occasion to spend money on luxury items such as jewels, garments, cars, and new home furnishings. Families, rich and poor, save for decades for their children's wedding.

Demand for luxury items is soaring in the emerging economies. If China has been the main market for a decade, the Indian market is the fastest growing. Its value is estimated at US $15 billion in 2015 supposing an annual constant growth of 20%.[9] According to a 2014 report from Euromonitor International, India's luxury market is likely to grow 86% in constant value terms between 2013 and 2018.

---

[7]Factory Collapse Death Toll Hits 1,021. *The New York Times*. May 9, 2013.
[8]Blood Garments. *Economic and Political Weekly*. Vol. 48, No. 21, May 25, 2013.
[9]http://www.cnbc.com/id/102027722.

While the young generation, (about 60% of the population is under 25), is fond of brands, logos,[10] and is closer to western culture, the older generation is more attached to conventional clothes, tailors and 'no-logo' habits. They are well-aware of Indian textile traditions and techniques. They recognise quality by examining and touching the products. For these people, the key purchase criterion is the quality of the work: The smoothness of the silk fabric, the finesse of the printing, and the details of the embroidery.

The culture of craftsmanship and excellent know-how makes India one of the major producers of luxury. Thus, millions of embroidery workers, mainly from Bengal and Uttar Pradesh, are busy in dirty and poorly lit workshops in the suburbs of big cities to produce wonders at very cheap prices. Their expertise and long hours of precision work answer the orders of prestigious luxury names such as Chanel, Valentino, Givenchy and Stella McCartney. Rarely, though, the artisans are seen as investment. But Jean-Francois Lesage, of the Paris based House of Lesage, and his friends have opened Vastrakala in Chennai with a group of master artisans. Recent orders include the valance for the stage of the Opera de Monte Carlo, and drapes for the royal balconies. Lesage thinks, "It is inconceivable, considering the costs of manufacturing, to produce some models in Paris. Some orders can only be performed here in India."

Re-emergence of world-class luxury brands from Asia is a possibility in the near future, but that is contingent on two factors. The first factor is the supply of entrepreneurs. While organisational forms in the luxury industry have ranged from umbrella companies such as LVMH in France and the more flexible industrial districts of Italy, in India the primary organising form has remained a localised and unorganised community of artisans. Without adequate exposure to the world market, the artisans are not even aware that the products they make are indeed of very high quality and with adequate marketing, could command high prices. The second factor is consumer labour. On the demand side, consumers are the vectors of fashionable brands. Their free promotion, flaunting products and linking brands with status, career advancement or aesthetic value, requires an investment in time and effort. In the world of fashion, consumer labour is not a trivial matter. Selling luxury products is often linked with the art of story-telling; of exquisite craftsmanship, of history and heritage, of

---

[10] *Changing Indian consumer habits*, Brandawazz.biz, accessed on September 8, 2011.

pedigree and lifestyle. When consumers also become storytellers, the process of fasionable consumption enters a virtuous cycle.

From a Personal Business to Promoting the Heritage of Indian Textiles

The Initial Years of Weavers Studio

Weavers Studio was founded in 1993 by Darshan Shah, an alumnus of the Indian Institute of Management, Ahmedabad, and a law student from Mumbai University. The idea of the business arose when Darshan worked as an exhibition organiser for various types of products such as textiles, jewellery, eco-friendly toys, clothes and accessories. Darshan's exhibitions became successful and at the end of the shows, people wanted to know where they could find such products. Exhibitors of textiles asked her if she could sell their products. Textiles were non-bulky, unbreakable and easily transportable. She agreed and it worked.

Weavers Studio began in a little room with just two racks. The office measured about 200 square metres and doubled up as Darshan's brother's office from where he was selling database systems. Eighteen years later, the outlet is at that same place but the entire building in Kolkata's posh Ballygunge area is owned by her. She also owns three other spaces where different business units are located.

From the beginning, Darshan's idea was to "promote and perpetuate the textile heritage of India". The production unit established in 1993, first encompassed a block printing facility. The other fabrics used were bought from exhibitions as well as from villages in West Bengal, where Darshan went to learn weaving techniques and processes. With the production and selling of textile products picking up, over the years Darshan built an institution which would become a vast repository of Indian and global textile techniques.

Weavers Studio was born during a period when there were few such businesses in West Bengal, despite its rich textile heritage. Darshan was determined to "work hard to come out from that mediocrity". Since its founding, Weavers Studio has experienced a steady profit and turnover growth. It has been selected several times to showcase its products in international fairs such as the India Promotion Fair in South Africa, the International Folk Art Market, and the Museum of the City of New York, and has partnered with the textile department of the Victoria and Albert Museum of London.

Value Proposition and Price Positioning
in an Internationally Growing Market

Weavers Studio offers hand-made colourful garments, saris, scarves, stoles and fabrics. It puts its expertise into producing high quality products that are works of creativity and precision. Every piece is original and unique and bears the contribution of a team of weavers, embroiderers, appliqué artists, block printers, and tailors who finish the products. Each product goes through the process of natural dyeing, mud-resist printing, block printing, wax-resist dyeing and various resist techniques from India, Japan, Africa, and Indonesia. An array of textile techniques are used. Some of these are dyeing methods such as Shibiori, and Batik, embroidery techniques such as Chikankari, Kantha, or Badla, and fabrics such as Khadi, Tussar, or Chanderi. The whole gamut of products is distributed through retail channels and wholesale ones, in India and abroad. Weavers Studio also takes special orders for expensive, tailor-made products. Prices range from approximately INR 150 to INR 6,000 per metre.[11]

These products are also environmentally friendly with the use of natural materials and techniques. Natural colours are extracted from flowers, vegetables, leaves, and tree barks. Blue, for example, is obtained from indigo, rust red from madder, brown maroon from catechu, deep gold and grey from eucalyptus leaves, yellow from marigold flowers, gold from henna leaves, beige from tea leaves and gold from onion skins.

Company Organisation

Weavers Studio encompasses two main divisions. The role of the for-profit part of the firm is to produce, sell and export a wide range of hand-made textile products through retail and wholesale channels: Art textiles, scarves, garments, shawls, shirts, fabrics, and saris, characterised by high quality, ethnic and original designs. This segment is mainly organised around two entities: Rangeen and Veda.

Rangeen

In 1995, Weavers Studio had a mall block printing facility. In 2002, the weaving unit was established and consolidated under the name Rangeen, as a privately owned company comprising the two previous units of dyeing

---

[11]In 2012. US $1 was 54 Indian Rupees.

and printing. The weavers at Rangeen came from weaving families in West Bengal villages. The origin of their know-how was Bangladesh. After the partition of India, many weaving families from Bangladesh migrated and settled in Bengal and the neighbouring state of Bihar, relying on their rare knowledge to survive. They learnt weaving from their parents during childhood, as Biren, a weaver working in Rangeen for nine years, explained:

> "Weaving is all about precision, accuracy, a lot of calculations. You need to plan everything before starting the process as it is not possible to go backward. It is fine for us because since we were kids we have been doing this. We started weaving and learning all the processes, because everyone in our families was doing the same thing. So at this stage it is not difficult for us, but definitely very difficult for those who started to learn later."

Due to language barriers and to ensure a constant flow of work throughout the year, the weavers in the villages use an agent to get clients. This system involves four or five intermediaries through which the price of a piece was multiplied by at least four. The weavers were used to having the lowest price. They had to farm as a second source of income and balanced their time between that and their weaving orders. A position at Weavers Studio was, for some, a great opportunity that could enable them to earn 25% higher than they could earn in the villages. Compensation is based on the number of pieces woven and the weekly pay is regular. They could also benefit from a safe and disciplined working environment and from a regular pay policy, escaping the agents who often paid late. The Rangeen unit also ran medical, educational, and vocational training classes for their workforce and management staff. Weavers Studio's core competence was based on tacit knowledge held by poor people who had no idea of the luxurious side of the products they made, as none of them had ever been in the store.

Rangeen is organised around four main activities: Weaving, printing, dyeing, and embroidery. Master craftspeople who specialise in dyeing, block making, block printing, screen printing, and tie and dye techniques, are capable of producing approximately 750 metres of cloth per day. Some orders are sourced from the villages directly. Once or twice a month, a team from Weavers Studio goes to these villages and deals with the agents. They identify original hand-made pieces and bring them to the Rangeen centre, where craftspeople and designers put additional creative work into them before selling them to the final customer.

Veda commercial

Weavers Studio started to export its products in 1993 through its export arm Veda Commercial. Meticulous quality control represented a crucial part of the production process and it was all the more enhanced for exported products. Veda exports to clients in Japan, Italy, USA, UK, Australia, and South Africa, to name a few. To promote its products abroad, Veda regularly participates in exhibitions and trade fairs.

In 2012, Weavers Studio's for-profit activities registered a turnover of INR 37 million for exports, and about the same value for the domestic market. This revenue is almost equally generated by retail sales, wholesale operations to designers and textile retailers, and job work. Raw materials account for about 67% of total costs.

Not-for-profit activities

The main goal of setting up Weavers Studio Resource Centre: The non-profit part of Weavers Studio, was to share the vast collections of Weavers Studio, document them, and bring them to the public domain. The resource centre had two divisions. The *Textile Study Centre* is a collection of textiles and books put in service of textile enthusiasts, scholars, and students for research. The *Weavers Studio Library* brings together a collection of rare and interesting books from around the world. This collection combines the past and present, contemporary and traditional books on design and fabrics representing many cultures. Workshops are held regularly to exchange views and new ideas. This also helps to nurture awareness of textile design. Weavers Studio Resource Centre is registered as a trust and is run professionally as a not-for-profit organisation. The centre also runs charity activities: Vocational training, literacy, healthcare programmes and self help groups.

In 2007, 10 years after the creation of the resource centre, the not-for-profit activities were reinforced with the creation of Weavers Studio Centre for the Arts with the aim of encouraging all kinds of artistic initiatives. It runs numerous programmes to promote all kinds of arts: Visual arts, cinema, theatre, photography, ceramics, sculpture, painting, performing arts, and informal interactions, and has evolved into a space that encourages young talent.

Human Resources in the Textile Industry

The industry structure comprises a few large, diversified players within the textile value chain and thousands of small firms scattered all over the country. The decentralised traditional handloom sector produces about 18% of the total cloth produced in the country (excluding clothes made of wool, silk and spun yarn) and 15% of the total exports of the fabrics. The centralised power loom mill sector is growing faster. Weavers Studio is positioned in the traditional sector since it sources fabrics from handloom weaving villages and all its products are hand-made.

Craftspeople are becoming a rare resource in the industry. The young generation is less interested in the traditional weaves. The pay is little compared to what can be earned working in a hotel or a restaurant in a big city. As Monika, the production supervisor, explained:

> "Skilled labor is going away. The expertise is dying out. As people are becoming more educated, they are less willing to do printing jobs. The problem is less urgent in weaving but the trend is similar. Also, we have fewer craftsmen because when craftsmen go to the academy, they become experts and as master-weavers they begin teaching and writing books and stop commercial production. For example, in weaving, now people are trained on machines with 1,800 lines for the weft. We use from 2,000 to 2,200 because the finesse is much better, but more expensive INR 1,500 compared to about INR 500 for 1,800 lines. Lots of people are also going into mills".

Jean-Francois Lesage has a similar experience. His organisation Vastrakala's challenge today is to meet demand. Lesage says: "We need more artisans, but can't find them. India has the largest variety of crafts in the world, but artisans are seldom celebrated." [12]

The business model of Weavers Studio is complex. Part of the production is in-house in Rangeen and another part is outsourced from the villages. Monika, for example, decides if the production will be done at Rangeen or in the villages depending on the level of exclusivity:

> "We give only basic designs to the villages because copying is very common in India. All the embellishment is done at Rangeen. If we have

---

[12]http://businesstoday.intoday.in/story/vastrakala-turned-a-dying-tradition-embroidery/1/197638.html

an emergency we use Rangeen, because we can control the deadline. In the villages we are not sure of the deadline. We may face a train problem or a strike. Another decision criterion is the requisite expertise. We know the villages and their specific weaving techniques. We send production to many villages in India according to their skills".

Imitation is a problem Weavers Studio complains about. The techniques Weavers Studio uses and promotes are collective techniques, and it is difficult to assign a design or a technique to a particular person since weavers, printers, and other artisans often use their imagination along with community and family knowledge. This oral and exchange-based culture also fuels repetition of work because each artisan knows that if he or she invents something new, tomorrow it will be replicated by his or her neighbours. Designs displayed in trade fairs and exhibitions can be found after a few months at cheaper prices and lower quality production.

The Indian government's role and legal issues

Given the significance of the textile industry in the country, the government of India has taken several steps to modernise it. These efforts include launching Special Economic Zones and textile parks, promoting research centers and allowing 100% foreign direct investment in textiles. India is also one of the few countries (the others are Bangladesh and Pakistan) with a dedicated Ministry of Textiles, responsible for policy formulation, planning, development, export promotion, and trade regulation in the textile sector. Government interventions include welfare schemes for millions of weavers and ancillary workers, creation of marketing platforms, credit linkages and credit guarantee programmes for artisans, and financial packages.

Company Motto: Use as Many Hands as Possible

When Darshan launched her textile business in 1993, she kept her motto simple: "Use as many hands as possible." Indeed, an important consequence of building a successful luxury brand that sells hand-made products is the creation of jobs. This proposition presents an interesting contrast: Democratisation of commerce at the supply side and exclusivity at the demand side. In one of the densely populated states in India with a total population of 90 million people and more than five million unemployed,[13]

---

[13]Socio-Economic Profiles & Inter-State comparison of some Major States of India. Economic Survey 2012−13, Government of India. 2012–2013. p. 276. Retrieved April 21, 2014.

using as many hands as possible makes a lot of sense. Darshan works with over 1,000 weavers from West Bengal, Odisha and Bihar and employs a large number of artisans doing embroidery, tailoring, dyeing, and printing.

The Creation–Production–Distribution Process

Designers are at the heart of the creation process at Weavers Studio. They work hand in hand with weavers, dyers and printers to come up with the most original product possible. They get their inspiration from everywhere: From books, textile samples, visits to exhibitions and fairs, from their earlier work, websites and everyday life. Designers from Veda, the retail outlet, and Rangeen, attend a weekly meeting where they share their latest creations and discuss the main issues they face.

Once a design is agreed upon and approved by Darshan, the designers proceed to the production part. They decide whether to do it in-house at Rangeen or buy a product from the weavers' villages and embellish it at Rangeen, before selling it to the final customer. Designers explain to weavers and printers what exactly they are seeking: The design, colours, and techniques. Every piece goes through weaving, printing, and dyeing, followed by embroidery if need be.

Weaving is a very precise process. Each machine at Rangeen has been set up for a specific kind of weaving, primarily determined by the tightness between two threads. Printing on the original colour of the fabric is the next step after weaving. There are two kinds of printing: Hand printing is about the mixing of textures and playing with colours; block printing, a more traditional process, is about using wooden blocks with special designs and playing with these designs.

Every block is one of a kind. At this stage, often the craftspeople come up with suggestions of their own designs to address the needs of the client or designer. The colours used are natural dyes. An expert is in charge of colour mixing. The printed pieces are put out in the open to dry before being washed and steamed to make sure that there is no colour bleeding. Finally, the dyed, washed and steamed piece goes through a finishing process of embroidery, stitching, or anything else that is needed to complete a certain design. A sample of the designed piece is produced and sent to the client, if the production is a special order; or to Darshan and her managers if it is a bulk order. If everyone agrees on the prototype, then production of the order commences, followed by strict quality control.

Company Culture

At Weavers Studio, each division is responsible for its recruitment with no particular restriction for the number of employees. Newspapers, friends, and family are the main channels to communicate vacant positions and job descriptions. The interviews are mainly conducted by Darshan and the manager of the division. Darshan takes the final decision and the selection is based on the resume, portfolio and personality of the applicant and his or her ability to fit into the company. When new employees arrive in the company, they are trained on the way the company runs.

In the past, senior managers were hired without any background in design or textiles, having degrees in various fields like IT, history or law. Over time, the human resources policy was clearly defined for other employees. The profiles brought into the company were young designers from design and art institutes, and experts specialised in weaving, printing, dyeing and embroidery.

Nevertheless, Weavers Studio is facing a shortage of master craftsmen who can set up new techniques in Indian textiles to create high-end products. Furthermore, Weavers Studio is yet to build a team of fashion designers and people in charge of communication and marketing. Indeed, designers at Weavers Studio are experts on textiles but not in the creation of fashion items.

Darshan had a willingness to help women who wanted to come out of their traditional role in Indian society, by "using work as a way to accomplish themselves". The top managers at Weavers Studio are women, while men do the chores. In India, however, highly skilled and talented women often put a stop to their careers to take care of their families. As a result, Darshan is finding that turnover is very high.

At Weavers Studio, all that is expected from employees is their desire to learn, to be creative and to demonstrate their ability to propose new ideas. Darshan is considered a mentor to everyone. Unlike other design houses where there is a distance between the owner and the employees, Darshan has nurtured the family spirit inside the company. Employees appreciate the freedom and flexible working hours. Overall, Weavers Studio provides opportunities to explore one's creative side. Prerna Saraf, a designer working at Veda Commercial, noted:

> "In other houses, you have to start your career from scratch. You have to work within the production unit for two to three years, and then prove your ability to enter the design unit with the ultimate goal of working

with the owner as a final consecration. At Weavers Studio we have much more freedom."

Weavers Studio Customers

Retail sales

Weavers Studio products are sold in the flagship Kolkata store and in multi-brand stores located in Delhi, Mumbai, Pune, and Chennai. Customers typically belong to the upper middle class and upper class, 35-years-old or older. Ushma Savla, retail and wholesale manager at Weavers Studio, specifies: "Our customers have high-profile jobs and are in the industry; we also see celebrities, movie stars and politicians, and theatre artists coming. They travel a lot in India and abroad."

There is no well-organised database of customers or a system for customer relationship management at Weavers Studio. Even Ushma Savla, the boutique manager, is unable to tell exactly how many customers visited the store or how many sales they made in the last few months. The staff knows the preferences of loyal customers and can recall what kind of product became successful, but nothing is recorded systematically. However, Weavers Studio has very close and personalised relations with its customers. About 200 repeat customers are considered as personal contacts of Darshan, Ushma, and Monika. They know their tastes and measures; they send messages to these special customers to advertise special collections and events. Ushma describes the flagship store as a "mix between tailor-made, custom-made and garment. It is not a store where a customer can pick up any item, ask for another size or another colour. Everything has to be checked in the stock. If you like something, we can arrange to get it done to your satisfaction for a price".

The majority of Weavers Studio's retail customers are Indian women willing to buy an item for a special occasion: A wedding, a cocktail party, a special evening or a ceremony. They are not looking for *saris* or *salwar kameez* for everyday use. The silk and embroidery is not convenient for regular use on Indian streets. Foreign clients require explanation about the specificities of Indian techniques but the main customers are connoisseurs. According to Ushma:

> "Our clients are looking for clothes of very good quality that will last. They want comfortable clothes. That is why we target 30 to 35 years and more. Young people are more interested in changing clothes. They don't want to spend so much money on one piece when they could

afford different clothes. They are more pocket-friendly. We have a unique quality because we have our own production. We only use natural products. We offer something sustainable with no 'bling'."

In the boutique the customers come to admire and look at the newly arrived items. They take time to choose. They are not in a hurry because their purchase is planned for a special day. They also know that they have to wait around one week to have their purchase stitched or embellished. At Weavers Studio customers are involved in the design process. The sales staff talk to the client and suggest personalisation of the item: To add some embroidery or change a pattern according to the client's taste. By taking into account input from their customers, Weavers Studio ensures positive feedback.

Wholesale

About a quarter of Weavers Studio's sales come from wholesale. This includes bulk orders from multi-brand stores and also special orders from artists and textile specialists. The wholesalers can benefit from a discount (up to 20%) if they buy a minimum of INR 200,000. No return is accepted unless there is a defect. Wholesale pieces are limited because Weavers Studio does not have identical pieces. Even if they can replicate the weaving technique, the colour, the stitches, and the size, there is always a difference because the pieces are handmade.

The artistic segment comprises fashion designers and cloth makers who source fabrics, saris, stoles, and scarves to add to their collections after some alterations and embellishment. Most of them are Indians but a few of them are sold abroad. These designers are interested in the high-quality of Weavers Studio products, the heritage of Indian textiles and are also privileged contacts of Darshan. The vast knowledge of the founder of Weavers Studio attracts artists because they need a precise textile or cloth from a precise period. For instance, Weavers Studio created the costumes in the French movie 'Le Parfum' (The Perfume).

Veda Customers

Veda only sells to wholesale customers abroad, mainly in Japan. The Veda team visits their Japanese clients twice a year and these clients come to India as well. Departmental stores such as Isetan and other multi-brand clothes boutiques are among the main purchasers of Veda scarves and stoles. Japanese wholesalers are very demanding of high-quality and natural products that can be sold to the final customer under their own brand name. For instance, Japanese fashionistas are crazy about classic colours such as indigo, red, beige, black and white, and graphic patterns such as stripes and tiles. Japanese customers are careful about every detail. Prerna Saraf remembers,

> "They check everything in the samples, from the weft density of the *khadi* and the dye colour to the wash blending and yarn length. For example, if one scarf has several yarns on the side with one millimetre difference among them, the product is rejected!"

Veda has a few clients in Australia and the USA. Since the Japanese market was weakened by the Fukushima disaster, the export arm of Weavers Studio has been trying to expand globally. Veda's method has been to meet wholesalers at international fairs, show them their samples, and visit them regularly. The management team wonders if this expansion model is applicable to other markets, such as Europe and the Middle East.

A minimum order of 25 pieces for sample orders and 50 pieces for bulk orders is necessary for dispatches. A typical approval process takes about 20 days and, as a rule, customers are given four days to decide if they wish to go ahead with the purchase. After the order is confirmed, 50% is paid right away and 50% just before delivery. The price can be negotiated but Veda has a very strict policy about discounts, as does Weavers Studio. Generally, price depends on the number of colours used, materials used, and design. However the first price proposed to the client is always the best price Veda can offer. Foreign customers often need to be educated about textiles to fully understand the value and quality of Veda products. The Veda team prepares documents and presentations to explain the techniques, the specificities of the textiles, and why the prices are so high and variable.

Competitors

Weavers Studio has an ambiguous positioning and shares its customers with a gamut of actors in the traditional Indian fashion market. Its competitors can be divided into three main categories:

Home-shop tailors

In India, women are used to having their garments tailor-made. While this is a luxury by Western standards, it is quite common in India because of low labour costs. They buy fabrics from weavers and go to small boutiques for made-to-order clothes. Local tailors are a part of Indian clothing culture. They have the ability to produce customised apparel and are very flexible. Some upper middle class customers who could afford and would be willing to buy products from Weavers Studio may prefer to go to these small shops. Their strength in the market is clearly the price. Clients can negotiate and undercut prices to get low-cost imitation of designer creations. Local tailors can also provide services such as measurement and delivery to the doorstep.

Fashion designers

Designers are increasingly making their presence felt in India's fashion industry. Fashion Weeks have become common in the big cities. A majority of Indian fashion designers are expanding in their home country through numerous shows and exhibitions. They also benefit from their links with movie stars and high profile customers. Highly talented designers, Sabyasachi Mukherjee, Manish Malhotra, Ritu Kumar, Anita Dongre, and Tarun Tahiliani, to name a few, are growing their businesses at a fast pace, with turnovers ranging from US $17 million to $60 million. They participate in famous worldwide shows, sell in many countries, and develop their distinct brand images. These designers are both competitors and customers. They have a similar value offer to Weavers Studio: A mix of Indian cultural heritage and contemporary wear from natural handmade and high quality products. But, fashion designers demonstrate higher creativity and can count on very strong brand image, especially for foreign customers. Sometimes they source fabrics from Weavers Studio and embellished them with their designs. Some of these clients and competitors are Sabyasachi, Rohit Bal, and Agnimitra Paul.

Major brands

The third category of competitors comprise brands that have emerged to offer a mix of Indian and Western-style apparel, using traditional techniques and emphasising handmade quality at an affordable price. These companies are larger in size than the fashion designers and they target both local and foreign customers. They work with international partners to secure investment and distribution networks worldwide. Some also do private labelling for apparel and home furnishing wholesalers and retailers. They are often committed to charity and non-lucrative humanitarian projects in India. Even if their offering is not positioned as comparable in luxury to Weavers Studio, the creative aspect of the product gives them some credibility, plus they have stronger brand recognition and are more easily available. FabIndia is one such example with revenue of about US $170 million.

Monika is aware of the competition but asserts that their garments are "handmade and very high quality products from our own production. We have 100% exclusivity. But we always experiment, and we have the burden to sell extra pieces that are not always perfect".

Looking Forward to a New Beginning

Darshan, however, was not that complacent about the future of Weavers Studio. Roles were not assigned clearly among employees, communication between the different divisions was weak, the production process was lagging behind technology advancement, information was hard to gather and classify as little has been recorded and documented over the years, and the non-profit activities were highly dependent of her personal funding.

Looking at all the issues raised, Darshan had no concrete solution in hand to implement. The main concern was uncertainty about where Weavers Studio was heading and what should be done. Having reached a critical size, the current situation was becoming unwieldy. Darshan was mindful that this situation resulted mainly from spending several years without any coherent strategy.

Senior people in the organisation had huge amounts of information in their heads, but it had neither been formalised nor centralised and this was also related to the company structure with different divisions acting independently. Above all, she was the only one in the company who had formal management skills and the only one to take initiative and decisions. She delegated a lot of work, gave responsibility to everyone, encouraged employees to go ahead and even offered to finance management training. Darshan seemed to be the only one bothered by the situation. As Monika said, "We work and get things done, we have guidelines but we also know that Darshan is around and keeps an eye on everything."

The fact that Darshan is at the top of the hierarchy had obviously helped the company grow but there was still a huge gap between Darshan and the other managers. None of them were shareholders, which could have been an incentive to increase their involvement. On the other hand, some managers began to feel uncomfortable as they had to adjust and make compromises according to the situation. With increasing activities, this approach made management difficult. They thought that it would be better to define roles within the company because in spite of the multitasking, "the more people we are, the less work each one wants to do" leading to unnecessary urgencies during rush periods.

At that point, Darshan thought that it might be helpful to get an external point of view and stop running Weavers Studio as the small business she had created two decades ago. She was looking for a long-term perspective. How to develop a sustainable strategy for the for-profit segment that would allow the non-profit part of the business to continue? Darshan was also open to an exit plan. She has received offers from an entrepreneur who worked for Hermes, Isabel Marant and Oscar De la Renta. However, she was keen to retain control over the not-for-profit activities. Would the new entity retain former employees? Would the new entity use as many hands as possible? Alternatively, what could she do on her own?

Exhibits

Exhibit 1: Income Statement of Weavers Studio for the year ended 31.3.2012[1]

(All figures are in Indian Rupees)

Sales		37,023,713
Cost of Goods Sold		27,877,034
Opening stock	4,125,988	
Purchases	27,501,338	
Embroidery Charges	3,242,714	
Dyeing & Printing Charges	29,365	
Less: Closing Stock	7,022,371	
Gross profit		9,146,679
Selling, General, and Administrative Expenses		5,453,069
Operating Profit		3,693,610
Special Items or Extraordinary Expense		
Add : Other income		
Less : Depreciation		393,076
Interest Expense		149,591
Pretax Profit		3,150,943
Sales Tax		59,611
Net profit		3,091,332

[1]Numbers are only for Weavers Studio (retail and wholesale). Veda Commercial's figures are comparable.

Exhibit 2:

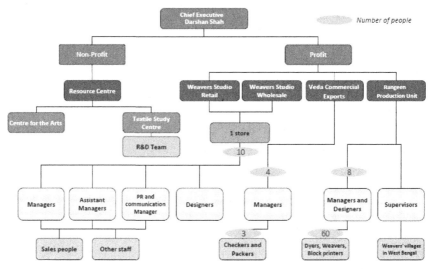

Exhibit 3:

	Art Textile	Scarves	Garments	Shawls	Fabrics	Sari	Shirts
Value Proposition	<ul><li>**Hand-made** : *hand-block printing, handloom, hand embroidery, and tailoring techniques*</li><li>**Traditional and ethnic** : use of natural dyes, mud resist, block printing, wax batik and various resist techniques of India, Japan, Africa and Indonesia</li><li>**High quality**: expertise of 19 years , the contribution of the R&D team and more than 250 skilled crafts persons</li><li>**Original and unique** : role of designers modernizing and reinterpreting traditions</li><li>**Environmental friendly**: use of natural materials</li><li>**Special orders and taylor-made products** : with much higher value and thus much higher price</li></ul>						
Pricing	Depending on the collection and input : from INR 15 000 to INR 25 000	from INR 500 to INR 10 000 - depending on the quality, yarn and value addition	from INR 3 500 to INR 22 500	From INR 5 000 to INR 25 000	from INR 150 per meter to INR 5 500 per meter	from INR 2 500 to INR 35 000	from INR 3 000 to INR 9 000
Channels	<ul><li>**Retail** - Ballygunge store, few other stores in India & export to India, Japan, Australia, USA, Europe , S. Africa</li><li>**Wholesale** - Ballygunge store & export to India, Japan, Australia, USA, Europe , S. Africa</li></ul>						

Exhibit 4:

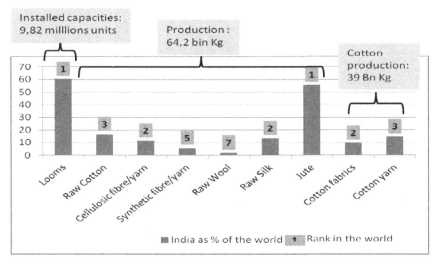

Source: Confederation of Indian Textile Industry.

Exhibit 5: CITI estimates about growth of Textile and cloths industry.

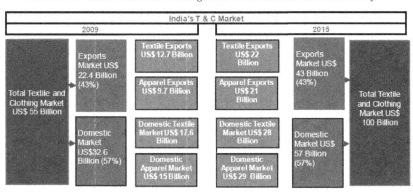

Assumptions about growth:

CAGR of 8% for Textile exports and 12 % for Apparel Exports

CAGR of 10%, for Textiles and Apparel domestic demand

Indian T&C Industry to reach US $ 100 Billion by 2015

Exhibit 6:

Weavers Studio Competitors can be divided into 3 categories: (from the most direct threat to the least)

	Home-Shop Tailors	Fashion Designers	Major Brands
Description	— Craftmen can open-up a small shop inside their home — Highly fragmented category. — Variable skills according to their training. — Quick realisation of models.	— Stylist and creators from various origins — Common vision of modern Indian textile and fashion — Blend of Western and Indian style — Some designers really focus on Indian textile heritage: Manish Malhotra, Ritu Kumar, Abu Jani & Sandeep Khosla.... — Others use their Indian roots to offer innovative collection targeting worldwide customers: Wendell Rodricks, Tarun Tahiliani, Ritu Beri, Rohit Bal....	— International and more institutionalised brands — Blend of traditional Indian and modern style wear — Targeting worldwide customers, retail, wholesale and suppliers for clothes and home furnishing — Diversified offer — Large means of production and promotion thanks to investments — Work with Western funds and partners — Focus on natural products and communicate on some charity works.
Size of this category	— Millions: numerous tailors in every village and city in India	— A dozen are internationnaly recognised — About 50 fashion designers that intend to develop their name in India	— A dozen

Weight	— Unavoidable in India	— Strong worldwide recognition for a few: Manish Arora, Manish Malotra, JJ Valaya, Abu Jani & Sandeep Khosla.... — Others are leading fashion in India especially through the movie industry and bridal wear	— Indian and worldwide recognition by some customer segments — Partnerships with foreign companies
Promotion channels	— Local exhibitions and trade fair — Word to mouth	— Fashion show in NY, Paris, London.... — Partnerships with Western designers — Online websites (multi-designer, own website, Facebook, blog) — Press & magazines — Charity, VIP & movie events	— Online website (own website, Facebook) — Press & magazines — Instore promotions

(Continued)

Exhibit 6: (*Continued*)

	Home-Shop Tailors	Fashion Designers	Major Brands
Sales channels	— Home shop	— Online (online store and multi-designer stores) — Flagships in Indian big cities and some others in the world — Multi-designer outlets	— Online (online store and multi-brand stores) — Flagships in India and other countries — Wholesale worldwide — Foreign retailers
Positioning	Local artisans that work on demand	Unique creator that produces original Indo-Western fusion work of art	Contemporary and affordable Indian wear, from natural and traditional technique based products
Trends	— Part of Indian habits — But long-term tendency to decrease with the restructure of Indian Textile industry towards more organised big actors	— Growing place of designers in India, with the development of fashion school and Fashion Weeks — Strong influence because of the increasing need for movie star clothes along with the rise in Indian people's purchasing power	— Growing demand from export for Indian style textiles — Dynamic urban customer base — Increasing interest from investment funds and foreign partners that contributes to reinforce the brand image and distribution

Exhibit 7:
(All figures are in Indian Rupees)

Silk *sari*[1] with many embroideries and embelishment

	Weavers Studio Cost Mix	Sabyasachi Cost Mix
Cost of goods sold	17,000	34,200
Fabric	10,000	19,200[2,3]
Dyeing	2,000	
Printing	2,000	
Embroidery/Stitching	3,000	15,000
SGA expenses	4,250	8,550
Operating Income	3,750	17,250
Sale price	25,000	60,000

[1] A *sari* is 6 yards or 5.5 meters.
[2] Includes cost of dyeing and printing.
[3] Fabric at 3000-4000 INR/meter.

Silk *sari* with nice colors but no embroidery

	Weavers Studio Cost Mix	Anshu's Rangeen Cost Mix	FabIndia
Cost of goods sold	6,800	3,840	3,920
Fabric	4,000	3,200[1,2]	3,200[1,3]
Dyeing	800	640	480
Printing	800		240
Embroidery/Stitching	1,200		
SGA expenses	1,700	400[4]	1,500[5]
Operating Income	1,700	760	580
Sale price	10,200	5,000	6,000

[1] Fabric at about 600 INR/meter.
[2] No printing or embroidery.
[3] No embroidery; some printing but not much finesse.
[4] No sales people; operating from home; has a website.
[5] Many stores.

Conclusion

The Asian Century is Now

Once a year, after the completion of the consulting assignments that comprise the Asian Strategy Project, we gather together ESSEC students and professors, consultants, and representatives from the participating companies. We sit in a large conference room in the heart of ESSEC's Singapore campus and the students present the results of their work. They speak passionately about the projects they undertook and the people they met. For many of them there were times when they felt very small in the face of the big problems they were expected to tackle, and they wondered if the strategies they recommended would achieve success. However, they also know that by being part of the Asian Strategy Project, they are contributing in a small way to fostering a culture of innovation in Asia.

Thinking about each of the cases described in the preceding chapters is a reminder that we are at the beginning of what has been called the 'Asian Century'. Though the idea has been circulating since the 1980s, it has been reaffirmed since the release of a report by the Asian Development Bank in 2011, which posited that if Asia continues to develop at its current pace, by 2050 the continent will achieve the economic dominance it enjoyed prior to the Industrial Revolution.[1]

We are not short of statistics that point to Asia's increasingly significant role in the world. According to projections from the International Monetary Fund, its developing economies will grow by 6.3% in 2014–2015; for the same period, the United States will grow by 3.4% and the United Kingdom 2.7%.[2]

---

[1] Asia 2050 Report by the Asian Development Bank. (http://www.adb.org/sites/default/files/publication/28608/asia2050-executive-summary.pdf).
[2] IMF World Economic Outlook Update January 2015. (http://www.imf.org/external/pubs/ft/weo/2015/update/01/).

The continent is home to the world's three biggest cities by population: Tokyo, Delhi, and Shanghai; and its urbanisation is continuing apace. By 2050, it is estimated that India will have 404 million more city-dwellers and China will have an additional 292 million.[3] In addition, there are indicators that life for the very poor in the region is improving. In 2010, the proportion of India's population living in poverty was 29.8%; in 2012, it was 21.9%. In Cambodia, the corresponding figures were 22.1% for 2010 and 17.7% for 2012.[4]

Beyond economic growth and urban development, Asia has become an engine of the digital revolution and is shaping the transformation of our societies. China is home to the largest Internet market today with more than 600 million e-consumers, and its Internet giants, Baidu, Alibaba, Renren, Tencent and Sina Weibo, are effectively challenging the dominance of America's four technology behemoths (Google, Apple, Facebook and Amazon). At the same time, leveraging the success of its IT integrated services industry, India has set itself the goal of becoming the global champion of the knowledge economy in the 21st century.

These headline facts make for interesting reading and provide us with a clear sense of the sweeping changes afoot in this region. However, there is value in venturing behind the headlines. We believe the Asian Strategy Project provides just that: A means to better understand what is driving change in Asia at a human level, rather than simply looking at macroeconomic trends. We also believe that the key to sustaining the pace of development in this continent is innovation, because without it, the future will look very different. As the Asian Development Bank's 2011 report says:

"But Asia's rise is by no means preordained. Although this outcome, premised on Asia's major economies sustaining their present growth momentum, is promising, it does not mean that the path ahead is easy or requires just doing more of the same. Indeed, success will require a different pattern of growth and resolution of a broad array of politically difficult issues over a long period."[5]

With this in mind, we hope you enjoyed looking inside the 11 fascinating organisations featured in this book and meeting the many passionate and

---

[3]United Nations, Department of Economic and Social Affairs, Population Division (2014). *World Urbanization Prospects: The 2014 Revision, Highlights.*
[4]http://data.worldbank.org/indicator/SI.POV.NAHC/countries/IN?display=graph.
[5]Asia 2050 Report by the Asian Development Bank.

creative people who run them. What unites them is that they all face the same challenge: To look for 'a different pattern of growth' rather than 'doing more of the same'. The way to achieve this is to put innovation into action. As you have read, the task is not an easy one and perhaps the cases left you with more questions than answers. If that is so, then we have succeeded in our aim, for when it comes to doing business in Asia, there is no place for hackneyed responses or platitudes, something our students learn quickly.

Looking back at the many companies we have worked with over the past five years and continue to work with today, we are proud of what we've achieved, and we look forward to having more stories to tell about innovation in Asia. In the meantime, if you take only one thing away from this book, let it be this: People are not sitting back and letting the Asian Century happen. In countries all around the region they are doing their best to answer big questions by coming up with innovative answers.

About ESSEC Business School

Established in 1907 in Paris, France, ESSEC Business School is an academic institution of excellence which has been characterised by its pioneering spirit throughout its history.

ESSEC offers a wide range of academic and executive programmes to those looking to pursue an extraordinary learning experience that enhances their talent and leadership skills, and allows them to become truly high-level managers.

A research-driven institution committed to an ambitious development of alliances with leading universities, ESSEC constantly strives to expose its students to the latest technologies and cutting-edge knowledge across all disciplines.

Hallmarked by a profound humanistic tradition, ESSEC has succeeded in making the link between business and society a major subject of research. This is also one of the fundamental components of its philosophy in training responsible managers. ESSEC thereby affirms the necessity of placing innovation, knowledge and the creation of value at the service of the wider community.

Strategically headquartered in Singapore since 2005, ESSEC's operations in the Asia-Pacific region present the perfect foothold to be part of the vibrant growth of Asia. ESSEC Asia-Pacific offers innovative academic and executive programmes with Asian insights and perspectives, by leveraging a multicultural faculty based in Singapore and France, and a regional network of high level academic and corporate partnerships.

For more information, visit www.essec.edu/asia.

About Capgemini Consulting

Capgemini Consulting is the global strategy and transformation consulting organisation of the Capgemini Group, specialising in advising and supporting enterprises in significant transformation, from innovative strategy to execution and with an unstinting focus on results.

With the new digital economy creating significant disruptions and opportunities, our global team of over 3,600 talented individuals work with leading companies and governments to master Digital Transformation, drawing on our understanding of the digital economy and our leadership in business transformation and organisational change.

Find out more at www.capgemini-consulting.com.

Printed in the United States
By Bookmasters